Eastern Africa Series

LAND TENURE SECURITY

Eastern Africa Series

Women's Land Rights & Privatization in Eastern Africa
BIRGIT ENGLERT & ELIZABETH DALEY (EDS)

War & the Politics of Identity in Ethiopia
KJETIL TRONVOLL

Moving People in Ethiopia
ALULA PANKHURST & FRANÇOIS PIGUET (EDS)

Living Terraces in Ethiopia
ELIZABETH E. WATSON

Eritrea
GAIM KIBREAB

Borders & Borderlands as Resources in the Horn of Africa
DEREJE FEYISSA & MARKUS VIRGIL HOEHNE (EDS)

After the Comprehensive Peace Agreement in Sudan
ELKE GRAWERT (ED.)

Land, Governance, Conflict & the Nuba of Sudan
GUMA KUNDA KOMEY

Ethiopia
JOHN MARKAKIS

Resurrecting Cannibals
HEIKE BEHREND

Pastoralism & Politics in Northern Kenya & Southern Ethiopia
GŰNTHER SCHLEE & ABDULLAHI A. SHONGOLO

Islam & Ethnicity in Northern Kenya & Southern Ethiopia
GŰNTHER SCHLEE with ABDULLAHI A. SHONGOLO

Foundations of an African Civilisation
DAVID W. PHILLIPSON

Regional Integration, Identity & Citizenship in the Greater Horn of Africa
KIDANE MENGISTEAB & REDIE BEREKETEAB (EDS)

Dealing with Government in South Sudan
CHERRY LEONARDI

The Quest for Socialist Utopia
BAHRU ZEWDE

Disrupting Territories
JÖRG GERTEL, RICHARD ROTTENBURG & SANDRA CALKINS (EDS)

The African Garrison State
KJETIL TRONVOLL & DANIEL R. MEKONNEN

The State of Post-conflict Reconstruction
NASEEM BADIEY

Gender, Home & Identity
KATARZYNA GRABSKA

Remaking Mutirikwi
JOOST FONTEIN

Lost Nationalism
ELENA VEZZADINI

The Oromo & the Christian Kingdom of Ethiopia
MOHAMMED HASSEN

Darfur
CHRIS VAUGHAN

The Eritrean National Service
GAIM KIBREAB

Ploughing New Ground
GETNET BEKELE

Hawks & Doves in Sudan's Armed Conflict
SUAD M. E. MUSA

Ethiopian Warriorhood
TSEHAI BERHANE-SELASSIE

Land, Migration & Belonging
JOSEPH MUJERE

Land Tenure Security
SVEIN EGE (ED.)

Tanzanian Development
DAVID POTTS (ED.)

Land Tenure Security

State-peasant relations in the Amhara Highlands, Ethiopia

EDITED BY SVEIN EGE

JAMES CURREY

James Currey
is an imprint of Boydell & Brewer Ltd
www.jamescurrey.com

and of

Boydell & Brewer Inc.
668 Mt Hope Avenue, Rochester, NY 14620-2731 (US)
www.boydellandbrewer.com

First published in hardback 2019

British Library Cataloguing in Publication Data

A catalogue record for this book is available from the British Library

ISBN 978-1-84701-224-1 (James Currey cloth)

This publication is printed on acid-free paper

Typeset in 10 on 12pt Cordale with Gill Sans MT display
by Avocet Typeset, Somerton, Somerset TA11 6RT

Dedication

In memory of our friend and colleague Yigremew Adal

Contents

List of Illustrations

Note on Transliteration

In the literature, Amharic words are rendered in many different ways, sometimes by a proper transliteration system, and sometimes without much underlying system, influenced partly by what the author 'hears' and partly by how it is has been seen rendered in script. It is often impossible to know the exact Amharic term or place name, unless these are already known. The problem is that for a perfect system, one needs a number of diacritical marks. In this book we have adopted a simplified but rather precise rendering, which should make it possible for somebody literate in Amharic to reconstruct terms and names in Amharic script.[1]

The system as described below is applied to all words and names with the following exceptions:

Ethiopia (Ityop'eya)
Addis Ababa (Adis Abäbä)
birr (ber)
Names of Ethiopian authors and institutions are rendered as by themselves

The system used is the 'Trondheim system', originating in the early days of computerized publishing when fonts were limited and complicated. The advantage of using the same system today is that the characters are easily available and can be used in most software, like databases and GIS programmes.

Each order in the Amharic script is represented by a unique vowel, with minimal use of diacritical marks. Some consonants, mainly fricatives, are rendered by two letters.

Since Amharic is a written language, we transliterate the written symbols, rather than pronunciation. We therefore depart from common practice and do not render gemination (thus 'Gojam', not 'Gojjam'). This feature is an element of speech and is quite variable, and it is also practically impossible to render gemination consistently unless one adopts

[1] The exception is when a number of Amharic symbols represent a single sound, as in the case of 's' and 'h'.

a one-symbol style for all consonants, which would require a number of diacritical marks.

This leads to the following system:

Order		*Pronunciation*[2]	*Comments*
First	ä	ever; *uh*!	Variable
Second	u	r*u*de; b*oo*t	
Third	i	el*i*te; f*ee*t	
Fourth	a	f*a*ther; *ah*!	
Fifth	é	touché	French pronunciation; not diphthong
Sixth	e	f*i*t; ros*e*s	Variable[3]
Seventh	o	hope; n*o*r	Not diphthong

Two-letter consonants:	sh, ch, zh, gn (but j, rather than dj)
Plosives:	t', ch', p', s' and q (rather than k')

We do not use the ' between vowels (but each vowel should be pronounced separately; there is not usually any audible glottal stop):

Mikaél (not Mika'él)

For the sake of legibility and clarity, we deviate from Amharic script by using a hyphen in specific cases (which should then simply be removed when reconstructing the Amharic word):

Genitive-like 'yä':

yä-ekul; yä-märét dälday

In many contexts, such terms may be used without the 'yä' prefix, or with another prefix ('bä-', 'selä-'); the hyphen is intended to make it easier to identify the basic term.

Composite names with a biblical reference:

Wäldä-Maryam Haylä-Selasé

In other publications, such names are often rendered as separate words (Wäldä Maryam Haylä Selasé), and occasionally merged (Wäldämaryam). Our purpose is to make it easy for the reader to identify the correct name, hereunder to distinguish between own name and father's name (unfortunately often used as 'surname' in bibliographies and other registers following Western style).

2 The first examples are taken from Hoben (1973: xi); the second are from Leslau (1976: xiii–xiv).

3 Often aptly rendered as an inverted 'e'. The sixth order also represents the consonant without a vowel; in this case pronunciation varies, e.g. 'gerar' vs. 'grar'.

Other composite names:
We do not use the hyphen for what is technically composite, but non-biblical, names (in any case a rare practice):

Alämayähu (not: Aläm-Ayähu)

Many administrative units have composite names where two units have been merged. To render these, we use '&' rather than 'and':

Mänz & Yefat	One (merged) administrative unit (before the revolution)
Mänz and Yefat	Two separate units (under the Därg)

In some recent Ethiopian publications, such names would be rendered as "Mänzena Yefat", which is technically correct, but confusing to non-Amharic speakers (the suffix '(e)na' translates as 'and').

Dates and Measures

The Ethiopian Calendar starts on 11 September (except in leap years), and the year is seven to eight years behind the Gregorian Calendar; thus 1980 E.C. equals 1987/88 G.C. Since the larger part of the Ethiopian year falls after the Gregorian New Year, in this book, whenever it has no apparent negative impact, we render the year mentioned in our Amharic sources by adding eight years (thus 1980 E.C. is rendered as 1988 G.C). The reader can retranslate this as 1987/88 G.C.

In the text, we use the Gregorian Calendar, as described above, without marking it as 'G.C.'. In quotes and other source material, we may use the Ethiopian Calendar, either marked as 'E.C.', or made clear by the corresponding Gregorian year in parenthesis or by the name of the month (e.g. Mäskäräm 1980 vs. September 1987). Note that in the latter case, we added only seven years, because the exact month is known.

T'emad is officially rendered as 0.25 hectare. What is a *t'emad* is a complicated issue, sometimes touched upon in this book. We therefore mostly report area measures in *t'emad* for the sake of precision. When hectares are used, the figure can be converted back to *t'emad* by multiplying by four, since the hectares referred to in official documents and survey data are not 10,000 square metres, but *t'emad*.

Contributors

Harald Aspen is Associate Professor in Social Anthropology at the Norwegian University of Science and Technology, Trondheim, Norway. He has a Ph.D. in social anthropology (NTNU 1994), and his thesis was published as *Amhara Traditions of Knowledge: Spirit Mediums and their Clients* (Harrassowitz Verlag, 2001). Since the late 1980s, he has done extensive fieldwork in North Shäwa, South and North Wälo. In 1993–2003 he directed a joint research project with Addis Ababa University. He has published several works on livelihoods, religion and development in Ethiopian peasant society. In 2007, he convened the 16th International Conference of Ethiopian Studies (Trondheim) together with Ege.

Svein Ege is Associate Professor in African Studies at the Department of Social Anthropology, Norwegian University of Science and Technology, Trondheim, Norway. He has a Cand.Philol. degree in history (Bergen 1978) specializing in Ethiopia; his thesis was published as *Class, State, and Power in Africa* (Harrassowitz Verlag, 1996). In 1989–2003 he directed several research projects and also did much fieldwork in the Amhara region, with additional regular fieldwork since then. He has published several works on land tenure and peasant society in the Ethiopian highlands. In 2007, he convened the 16th International Conference of Ethiopian Studies (Trondheim) together with Aspen.

Kjell Havnevik is Professor Emeritus in Development Studies at the University of Agder, Norway. For more than four decades, he has been involved in research, education and advisory activities in universities and research institutes in Norway, Sweden and Tanzania. He has published a number of books, major reports and academic articles on agriculture, land tenure and rural development, on the role of development assistance, and on the IMF and the World Bank in Africa. In addition to Tanzania (his primary focus), he has been engaged in analyses of rural development in Ethiopia, Zimbabwe, Vietnam and Sweden. His latest book is *Framing African Development: Challenging Concepts* (Havnevik *et al.*, 2016, Brill Publisher).

Yigremew Adal was Associate Professor at the Institute of Development Research, Addis Ababa University, Ethiopia. His M.A. in Development Administration and Management was from Manchester University (1996). He was Assistant Dean of the Faculty of Business and Economics (AAU) during 1993–95 and Assistant Director of the Institute of Development Research (AAU) during 2001–03. He undertook much fieldwork in the Amhara region and wrote academic and consultancy papers relating to land tenure, poverty and development. He was an active participant in local conferences and workshops. He died of illness in the summer of 2011.

Preface

The densely populated northern highlands are the traditional crisis area of Ethiopia. They have been the scene of famine, civil war and heavy-handed government intervention. Partly due to the hardships that used to be part of fieldwork in rural Ethiopia, not least for the reasons mentioned above, there is a great lack of high quality studies, especially studies seeking to capture the spirit of peasant society, seeing the challenges through peasant eyes. This book brings together a number of empirically grounded accounts, all with a strong ethnographic flavour, located in various parts of the Amhara region. The book has a critical tone, as we seek to contrast the theory that may be constructed from our fieldwork material with the standard accounts.

The land issue dominates peasant life. It also refuses to go away at the national political level despite many attempts to reach a final settlement. There have been periods of reform when it appeared that land tenure might receive the attention it deserves in a society still dominated by its rural economy. Later on the issue has tended to disappear from the national consciousness, only to reappear when it became clear that the cost of current policy was enormous. Due to this on-and-off appearance, the debate on land tenure has often been based more on political ideology than on an understanding of peasant land tenure. There is an urgent need for an informed debate of land tenure issues in Ethiopia – and the current book is our modest contribution. If the new government formed in April 2018 follows up on its promises, this critical development issue may again receive the attention it deserves.

The book started with a workshop to take stock of ongoing research on peasant society and land tenure, 'The Biennial Colloquium in Social Anthropology: Land Tenure and Development in the North Ethiopian Highlands', which took place in Trondheim on 27–28 October 2011. Three of the papers, focusing explicitly on land tenure, were later developed into chapters for this book (Chapters 3, 4 and 7). At the workshop, we also decided to propose a land tenure panel at the 18th International Conference of Ethiopian Studies in Dire Dawa on 29 October–2 November 2012. Two of the chapters in this book (Chapters 5 and 6) originate from papers presented at that conference. We are grateful to the organizers and donors of these two events, and to the Norwegian Research Council which has funded much of the research underlying this book.

Svein Ege
Trondheim

Glossary

This glossary shows how terms are used in the book. Where an English term is underlined, it indicates that particular English term is used in the text as an exact replacement of the Amharic term.

aläqa	headman
aqni abat	founding father (in traditional rest land tenure, notably Gojam)
badma	house site
balabat	landlord (lit.: 'who has a father')
bäräha	distant land (term used in EPRDF land reform; lit.: 'desert')
ch'eqa shum	peasant official (a landowning peasant appointed to collect taxes and pass on orders; before the Därg land reform)
däber	parish
deledel (dälday)	redistribution (lit.: 'levelling down'). The *dälday* are the representatives elected to implement the *deledel*.
gäbäré	farm hand (lit.: 'farmer', but in our context used for male household servants)
geber	the land tax
gebrä-t'el	land for which tax was not paid and so the land is considered to be abandoned
gebut	marriage, where the man serves in the house of his wife's parents, often for several years, before the actual marriage takes place; also known as *qot' aser*
gobäz gäbäré	strong and able farmer
gulma	personal land, or personal property (most common in the form of household land allocated to a son to accumulate the property needed for marriage)
koräfé	local alcoholic beverage; traditional beer
mägazo	sharecropping
mofär zämät	farming land outside the *qäbälé* (lit.: 'campaign with the plough')
motä käda	vacancy (reversion of land rights to the *qäbälé* when

	someone dies; this creates *terf* land)
mulu tämän	full quota (when a household has the amount of land appropriate for its size)
qäbälé	commune (the lowest level of administration, with strong elements of local participation; it may refer to the area, the organization or the administration)
qeyes	border delimitation
semä geber	lit.: 'tax name'; person officially recognized as land-owner by being on the tax (*geber*) registry
shefta	bandit
shegesheg	land redistribution in any form: this term is applied by informants to very different processes
t'äla	local beer
tätäki	successor
t'emad	local land measurement, 0.25 hectare by the standard conversion (in principle the area a team of oxen can plough in one day)
terf	surplus (i.e. more than *mulu tämän*)
t'ilo haj	person who has abandoned the area without leaving any legitimate heir or claimant, as in *yä-t'ilo haj märét*, land of such a person
wäjäd	house-near land (term used in the EPRDF land reform; synonymous with *gwaro*)
wäräda	district; the administrative unit between *qäbälé* and zone
wers	inheritance
yä-qum wers	'standing inheritance': bequeathment in return for maintenance

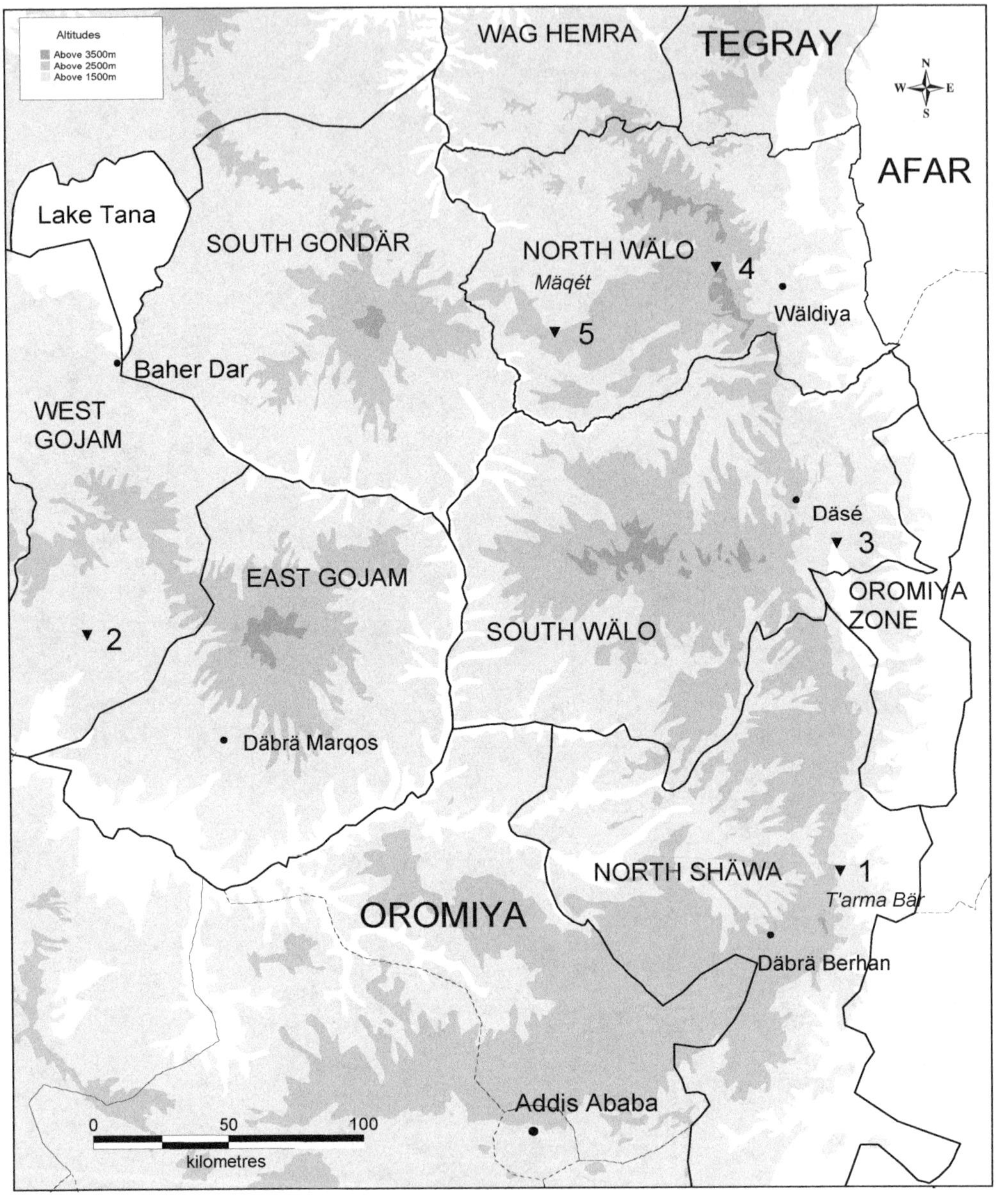

Map of fieldwork sites (Source: Svein Ege)

1 Ayné	4 Baba Säat
2 Dinja S'iyon	5 Jerelé
3 Ch'orisa	

1

Introduction

SVEIN EGE

THE AFRICAN CONTEXT

Africa is still predominantly rural, and Ethiopia is overwhelmingly so.[1] Africans are, more than anything else, smallholders. Despite a rapid process of urbanization across the continent, the total number of smallholders continues to increase due to population growth (Gollin 2014: 6). To be a smallholder in Africa is to be poor, to live at the mercy of forces beyond the farm, to be tossed around by climate, the exactions of the state and conflicts of various kinds, in addition to the constant worries about how to feed the family. Currently, famine strikes occasionally in several parts of Africa, and the choice of many Africans to migrate to other continents, although they know the risks, speaks volumes to the despair they feel.

Smallholder farming usually refers to farms of less than 5 hectares, operated by family labour and producing crops mainly for their own consumption (FAO 2017). In the areas covered in this book, few farms are above 2 hectares, and the average is about half of this.[2] For these peasants, land is of vital importance. One would think that, in view of its significance to the people concerned, there would be a rich and varied literature on the topic, but this is hardly the case. In his introduction to one of the more significant works, Bassett (1993: 3) observed that peasant land tenure was not much discussed in the research literature. Similarly, in his grand review of land tenure and land reform practices in Africa, Bruce (1989: 25) noted that for most countries we simply lack information on peasant land tenure. Even for well-studied topics, such as the Tanzanian *ujamaa* villages, the degree of tenure security for individual farming households (*ibid.*: 21) has been neglected in the research.

By far the most common land tenure regime in Africa is state land ownership, by which I mean the specific combination of formal state

[1] In 2010, the share of rural population was 60% for Africa and 82% for Ethiopia. The agricultural population was 51% and 77%, respectively (FAO 2012: 30–3).

[2] According to official data, the average holding in 2012 was 0.96 hectares (CSA 2012: Table 10).

land ownership with smallholders and pastoralists using the land. This has been, and continues to be, a contradictory situation which leads to tenure insecurity for the smallholders, but not for the reasons usually identified in some strands of the research literature. With very few exceptions, colonial authorities claimed land used by Africans as land of the state, or the Crown. Africans continued to use their land under what was conceived of as customary, traditional or communal tenure, all being rather problematic and potentially misleading labels.[3] The newly independent states inherited this policy, and most of them nationalized such land (Bruce 1989: 24). This created a situation where most of the land was held on rather unclear terms, not necessarily unclear within the community, but with weak rights in the farmers' relationship to the state.

One of the key arguments underlying early reforms was that customary tenure, communal in nature, meant tenure insecurity for the individual farmers who are the operators of the land; consequently, the farmers have little incentive to invest in the land. This argument is strikingly similar to the common view of Ethiopian peasant land tenure under the Därg: the peasants suffered from tenure insecurity due to periodic land redistribution and weak individual rights. In both cases, however, there is a lack of knowledge among researchers about the specific rights, if any, of the peasants. The fact that land is formally owned by the state seems to draw researchers' attention away from the bundle of rights, or in the words of Ribot and Peluso (2003), the bundle of powers by which peasants actually gained access to the land they farm or use. Numerous authors have argued that individual peasants had considerable rights under customary tenure, and land reform could radically upset such rights (e.g. Ranger 1993; Sjaastad and Cousins 2008). Similarly, a key argument in this book is that Ethiopian peasants had rather well-defined and secure rights within the peasant community, and that land redistribution played a much smaller role in their ability to access land than is commonly assumed. However, in the state's view, peasants had no rights and might be evicted without any meaningful compensation for any policy purpose, such as to redraw administrative borders, establish a forest project, or create a producer cooperative. In other words, all too often it seems to be the actions of the state, not customary tenure or periodic land redistribution, which has created insecurity for the peasants.

The available literature on peasant land tenure in Africa has mainly been policy oriented, as indicated above, and is rather weak on convincing ethnographic detail. The programmes to abolish customary tenure in favour of private property or state leasehold regimes[4] drew

[3] For a scathing critique, see Ranger (1993) in Bassett and Crummey's (1993) anthology, which also contains numerous other examples.

[4] This happened at various times in various places: e.g. Uganda from 1908 onwards; Zimbabwe from the 1930s onwards; and Kenya (the key case) from the 1950s onwards. Most of the literature is quite theoretical, arguing economic theories rather than providing good case description (except for Kenya).

heavy criticism, with a flurry of literature in the early 1990s. A number of articles argued that customary tenure was flexible and evolving, and did in fact allow for considerable individual tenure security. Against the generalizing models that had informed previous land reforms in Africa and Asia, there subsequently developed considerable consensus among researchers, centred on the need to recognize complexity and to adapt reforms to the specific context. One key lesson with the positive policy implications was that turning land into marketable private property is not the only way to achieve tenure security.[5]

Recently, there has been a rapidly growing body of literature again promoting the benefits of private property and the market, and Ethiopia has played a pivotal role in this resurgence. In the early 2000s, Ethiopia implemented a massive programme of land titling. The holders did not get the right to sell the land, and there were also some restrictions on rentals and the use of the land. But the stated aim was to give the peasants tenure security. Researchers associated with the World Bank saw this as a potential model for Africa in general (Deininger *et al.* 2007; Deininger 2008). Later research focused very much on the efficiency gains resulting from this reform in Ethiopia. It was clearly not a full-scale privatization; however, it was the market elements which attracted most attention, and it is the standard economic theory of markets that drives this type of research. It is not difficult to see a parallel here with the positions of the 1990s, where proponents of the privatization theory asserted that indigenous land tenure hinders development. The picture is somewhat blurred, however, by the much more nuanced arguments of this new research trend, which places greater emphasis on welfare, equity and women's rights. In addition, some of the sociological literature has also increasingly focused on practical measures to redress the known problems of land reform (e.g. Cotula *et al.* 2004). While the debate is less polarized than it used to be, our knowledge of peasant land tenure, the concrete options peasants have and the strategies they adopt to gain and secure the land they need for their livelihoods, is still little researched.

Ethnography matters, and the call for recognizing context and complexity is as valid today as it was in the 1990s. Bruce (1993: 35) argued that those who recommended privatization reforms presented '[s]tereotypes of indigenous tenure systems that often bear little resemblance to reality'. However, image also matters, not least the stereotypes of peasants, and a lesson from this book may be that these matter more than the actual situation on the ground, because images shape policies, whether the images are correct or not. This is a considerable challenge for ethnography. The role of ethnography is both to provide rich, multi-facetted description and to suggest concepts grounded in this material, and on this basis perhaps to challenge received interpretations (Peters 2009).

[5] For some key contributions, see Haugerud (1989), Barrows and Roth (1990), and Migot-Adholla *et al.* (1991).

THE ETHIOPIAN CONTEXT

Land tenure is shaped both by the agricultural system, closely related to ecology, and by social and political forces. Ethiopia is a huge country with great variation in ecology, ranging from hot deserts to frosty mountains, and a great diversity of cultures. There are many ways to systematize this variation, some being very detailed and complex. One simple approach, suitable for our purpose, is to distinguish between highland agriculture, pastoral or agri-pastoral lowlands, and the specifically Ethiopian *ensät*-based culture of the south-central highlands. The transition between these systems is, where topography and culture allows, often gradual.

Peasant land tenure is about how peasants get access to their most vital resource, land, and the topic is of course relevant for all these different systems, but in different ways. Where *ensät edulis* (false banana) plays an important part, population is very dense and access to land is carefully guarded. At the other extreme are the sparsely populated pastoral lands, as well as the lowland periphery in general. These areas have in recent years received much attention due to the phenomenon of land grabbing, where contractors receive large agricultural concessions from the state, leading to the eviction and marginalization of indigenous people. Highland plough-based cereal farming is, however, by far the dominant system. Here there is considerable pressure on resources, notably in Tegray and much of Amhara. It is when drought strikes in the northern highlands that we see a steep rise in the number of famine-affected people. Such long-term challenges are intimately linked to issues of land tenure.

The typical production units in this northern highlands system have for centuries been the small family-based farms, where the farmers ploughed land that was not necessarily theirs but which they had 'inherited' from their parents. The terms on which the land was held varied between regions, over time, and between individuals, through a mix of feudal and ethno-cultural institutions. We might describe these institutions as ranging from freehold to tenancy, and in extreme cases even serfdom or slavery, although such modern terminology risks violating local realities and should only be taken as very rough approximations.

This book is about the highland system, represented by a few sites located at different places in the Amhara highlands. There is, broadly speaking, much in common between this area and the other highlands of Ethiopia: the northern highlands of Tegray and the southern highlands of Arsi, Balé and the northern parts of Oromiya, both east and west of Addis Ababa. Culturally and historically, however, there are significant differences, and I point out the most relevant of these later in this chapter. Finally, even within the Amhara region, there is much variation, certainly in ecology (see the map of fieldwork sites on p. xx) but also in culture and history, all of which may be expected to have influenced the local land tenure systems. There is, however, limited information on local land tenure practices in the literature, and we have only been able to cover a few scattered sites in our respective fieldwork. It is therefore hazardous to venture any general conclusions, but generalizations are nevertheless needed in order to put local research into the wider context. We also feel an urgent need to do so because some of our findings diverge markedly from standard views in the literature, which are based on equally hazardous generalizations. Knowledge based on research is inherently preliminary, open for criticism and revision, and we acknowledge that many will disagree with our analysis, and that studies from other areas, even within the Amhara region, or using different approaches, may lead to other results. Indeed, we hope that this book will provoke debate and prod researchers to go to the field to gather empirical material to prove or disprove our arguments.

The following brief review of major trends is based on the general research literature. I regard this body of literature to be well known and therefore do not provide specific citations. For those who would like to follow up these issues, however, Crummey (2000), Markakis (1974), Dessalegn (1984), Bruce *et al.* (1994) and Yeraswork (2000) provide good starting points, both for the analysis made and for further references to the literature. I have selected these few works partly for their quality, but also because their coverage ranges from land tenure in the historical empire until the concerns of present times.

In Ethiopia, history and geography are intimately connected. Thus, the common contrast between the north and the south is a historical rather than a geographical divide. This is a story told in numerous publications. I therefore treat it somewhat cursorily. My aim is simply to provide the minimum background needed to understand the following chapters and to put them into context. I do so fully aware that the history in question is a deeply controversial topic, as an expression of future aims as much as of different views of the past. To go into these issues would take us far away from our current project, which is to understand land tenure as practised by local peasants in the Amhara highlands.

The Christian Ethiopian empire was based in the northern highland culture, sometimes referred to as 'Abyssinian' (*habäsha*). Geographically, this referred to highland Eritrea, Tegray, Amhara and Agaw, with considerable ebb and flux throughout its history. The central political structures were weak in the early nineteenth century, but in the second half of that century, there was a rapid process of consolidation. The king of Shäwa finally emerged as the victor in the regional struggle for supremacy and became emperor of Ethiopia in 1889, thus combining hegemony in the north with rapid expansion towards the south. By 1900, the borders were largely as we know them today. This history has inevitably left a bitter legacy.

The Amhara are strongly associated with this history, especially after Tegrayan nationalists during 1975–91 fought against Amhara domination, emphasizing their own peripheral status within the state. Seen from the south, the Amhara tend to look like a conquering people and a dominant ethnic group. It is not difficult to find horrific stories to confirm this view. Seen from within the Amhara community, however, things look different. Traditional 'Abyssinan' society was very much a class-based society, often described as feudal. The key difference from the south was, of course, the features emanating from its conquest: the south was ruled by an alien ethnic group through some crude mechanisms of surplus extraction and political control.

The Amhara paradox (or 'Abyssinian paradox' if you will) is that the old core areas of the empire were dirt poor. The role of the Amhara in the conquest of other peoples is undeniable, but after the Second World War, most of the north appeared ever more as backwaters, suffering from exploitation, environmental degradation and poverty. The history of famine in Ethiopia is to a surprisingly large extent the history of the northern peasantry, and the history of famine is particularly associated with Wälo and Northern Shäwa (the 'Abyssinian' part of Shäwa), in addition to Tegray. It is this impoverished peasantry that is at the core of this book. We think of these peoples not so much as Amhara, but as peasants, engaging with much the same problems as peasants elsewhere.

Land tenure in a feudal context is intimately linked to surplus extraction. The needs of the conquest state structured land tenure in both the south and the north. The south suffered directly from the conquest, while in the north land tenure was geared towards producing soldiers and maintaining the state apparatus. This north-south divide has dominated the image of land tenure before the 1975 land reform. Broadly speaking, the southern peasants are seen as subject tenants without rights to their land, while the northern peasants are presented as members of landowning kinship groups. As a first approximation, this distinction is not without its merits, but the situation was infinitely more complex than suggested by this dichotomy. Social relations in the south varied with ecology, with the way the area was incorporated (conquest or submission) and with the number of settlers from the north. The view of the north has, on the other hand, largely been based on a simplified reading of Hoben's (1973) study of a community in Gojam in the 1960s. In this community, *rest* ('inheritance') land was vested in the kinship group but individually held, and it is this contradiction that structures Hoben's analysis. Many other parts of Amhara deviate from this description. In Mänz the genealogical depth was much narrower (Hoben 1973: 103 n.2). In highland North Wälo the kinship group also seemed to play a much more limited role than what one would expect on the basis of Hoben's description (see Chapter 5), while land tenure in South Wälo was particularly complex due to its history of wars and conquests (Asnake Ali 1988: 264–6). And in many southern and eastern parts of North Shäwa land ownership was close to a freehold system, and land could be legally sold (Ege 1994a: 288).

Several scholars have pointed out the weakness of the north-south distinction. Cohen and Weintraub (1975: 29–30) identified the problem and suggested a classification according to tenure types, which seems sensible, but their typology was so general that much the same mental constructs remained, only with new names. Thus, the southern system was described as freehold, while the basic northern system was described as rights via kinship groups. In the main study of the 1975 land reform, Dessalegn (1984: 23–34) pointed out that the share of tenancy varied considerably between southern provinces, which he believed to be generally low in *ensät*-producing areas.

There were also important changes due to historical processes. Situations that might at one point in time seem rather similar later led to very different results. Thus, the impositions on a *gäbar* (tax-paying farmer) in the south – such as taxes, land rent and labour service – were not fundamentally different from those on a *gäbar* in feudal northern Shäwa, from where the institution originated. But in the south, the farmers often became landless tenants, while in northern Shäwa the *gäbar*, due to a reduction in taxes and services after the Second World War, gradually appeared as landowners.

The lesson to take home here is that although there was an undeniable north-south divide, there was also much variation within each system. The common denominator between both regions, however, was the experience of suffering, with crude exploitation in much of the south and deep poverty and more varied forms of exploitation in the north where society still had a strong feudal flavour. The great Ethiopian novel of Hadis Alämayähu (1958 E.C.), *Love until Death* (*Feqer eskä-mäqaber*), captures well the spirit of Gojam society and should be an obligatory companion to Hoben's 1973 book.

In the 1960s, there was a growing sense of *fin de regime*. The emperor was growing old and the country was stagnating. There was deep social malaise in many rural areas and revolts in a few. Students were taking to the streets, demanding reforms. Their most famous slogan was 'land-to-the-tiller', striking at the very heart of the feudal structure. In early 1974, the emperor gradually lost control of the military, which within a year led to a change of government, the fall of the emperor, and mass execution of the leading figures of the empire. The military government, or Därg,[6] declared itself socialist, and in April 1975 it enacted its land reform (Ethiopian Government 1975), which was much more radical than observers had expected and in fact echoed the slogan of the students mentioned above.[7] This process has been described, from various perspectives, in numerous books.

These were unsettled times, great interests were at stake, the government was weak, and violence was widespread. By and large, the south was soon brought under reasonable control. This had been

[6] 'Committee', or 'junta', the common label for the military, later socialist, government in power during 1974–91.

[7] The official title, 'Public Ownership of Rural Lands Proclamation No. 31/1975', emphasizes state land ownership. However, peasants in the Amhara region refer to the land reform as *Märét lä-arashu*, 'land-to-the-tiller', adopting this from the students and putting the emphasis on what was important for them.

expected because the land reform addressed the immediate problems of the southern tenants. On the other hand, it had been feared that farmers in the north would be less well disposed to any reform that might encroach on their cherished *rest* rights. This was apparently borne out as revolts flared all over the area, in Gojam (Ayele Tariku 2012), North Wälo (see Chapter 5), South Wälo (Dessalegn 2008: 111ff), and North Shäwa (Ahmed Hassan 2002), to mention only those described in the literature. In addition, there were the well-known revolts in Tegray and Eritrea that were eventually to topple the regime.

It seems that the dominant social element in the early revolts, as well as in Tegray, were local notables, with a strong social basis in the upper echelons of the peasantry. They probably also mustered significant support among poorer peasants by appealing to regional sentiments and the defence of local autonomy, and sometimes by the prospects of loot, the traditional reward of soldiers. By 1979, however, most of the major revolts had been defeated, and even the rebels in Eritrea and Tegray had, for the time being, been pushed back to the more inaccessible parts of the provinces. Aster Akalu (1982) visited most provincial capitals in the spring of 1979 and her work provides interesting insights into the atmosphere and administrative concerns of the day. The impression is of a regime gradually hardening, pushing on with its reforms to equalize land holdings and, ever more to the fore, producer cooperatives (see also case studies in Mengistu 1986; Poluha 1989).

This history has implications for the process of land reform. The 1975 proclamation was envisaged in two stages: first, the 'land-to-the-tiller' phase, by which tenants would get 'possessory rights' and cease to pay land rent; and then a second stage which aimed to equalize land holdings. The first stage was in theory operative immediately. In practice, it took some time, depending on the specific local social forces. The second stage required administrative capacity and necessarily took time to implement. In areas of significant local resistance, the process of redistribution may actually have been quite limited. To our knowledge, there is no research describing this stage of the process in any detail about any part of Ethiopia. Instead, the two stages are usually seen as one continuous system of redistribution. In this book (see Chapter 3), I show how the process in Ayné closely matched the provisions in the 1975 proclamation. There is nothing in the literature that makes us believe that this was an exceptional case, although where government control was weak the two phases may have become merged, or the second phase may not have happened at all. As far as the evidence goes, be it in the literature or in our own fieldwork, the drive to equalize holdings soon ebbed out. Comprehensive, equity-driven adjustments were mainly a feature of the late 1970s.

Whether the redistribution of the second phase took place or not, peasants all over Ethiopia received possessory rights of the land they farmed.[8] Our interest is in the peasant practices concerning these

8 '... any tenant or hired labourer shall have possessory right over the land he tills' (Ethiopian Government 1975: Art. 6.1).

rights. We refer to these rights as conditional ownership rights, 'conditional' to emphasize the limits of these rights within the general framework of state landownership, but still strong enough that peasants in most ways thought of their holdings as their own, indicated by the bitter conflicts between peasants over these rights. In fact, within the local community, the struggle for land was at the heart of peasant conflicts. It is this struggle which shapes the local land tenure system. There is reason to believe that this struggle varied according to local culture and social conditions, but here the literature is not very helpful. The land reform had, in principle, established a unitary land tenure system. The degree and forms of variation under this legal superstructure remains largely unstudied. However, rather than periodic redistributions, I believe the general picture was characterized by variants of household land tenure, by which most youngsters would expect to receive land from their parents, or from other persons with whom they entered into specific, culturally relevant relations. All the cases described in this book fit this broad description, and I have not found any convincing evidence in the literature which would fall outside it.

In the early 1980s, government attention changed from the land reform itself to forced development in the form of producer cooperatives, afforestation projects and villagization, to mention only those aspects most relevant for land tenure. These policies had a highly disruptive impact wherever they were implemented. At this time, fieldwork was again becoming possible, and these elements of land tenure under the Därg are relatively well covered in the literature. Now the full impact of state land ownership became clear. State action was governed by higher political concerns and the peasants had no legal protection against the state. The 'possessory right', or conditional private property right, applied to relations between local people but had, as viewed by the state, no relevance in state-peasant relations.

The practical significance of this will have varied, and I believe the literature gives a somewhat exaggerated impression of state intervention, not of its harshness but of its extent. Producer cooperatives, geared towards mechanization and collectivization, were more suitable in fertile areas like Arsi and Gojam and therefore probably more common there. In North Shäwa, producer cooperatives were typically found in the potentially highly productive lowland plains, while the majority of the population lived on rugged ground unsuitable for collectivized farming. Villagization was more widely implemented, but villagization *per se* had limited impact on land ownership. The third main type of intervention, afforestation, meant that land was confiscated from the peasant landowners, with little or no compensation. This could be a disaster for those affected, but in the broader context the amount of land confiscated by the state was limited. What all these policies had in common, however, was to drive home the meaning of state land ownership. This created tenure insecurity, always lurking below the surface and becoming acute for those who might be affected by any of these state policies. While the state had the power to implement the policies, peasants strongly resented them. The cost to the regime was that these policies completely undermined its legitimacy, which had initially been quite strong in many rural areas due to the benefits of the earlier land reform.

Towards the end of the Därg period, when collectivized agriculture had clearly failed and the ideological tide was turning in favour of peasant agriculture, the issue of tenure insecurity came to the fore. The problem of insecurity was commonly attributed to frequent land redistributions. This confused two processes: on the one hand, a general practice of periodic land redistribution in order to accommodate new households (which probably did not happen); and on the other hand, the land confiscation and reallocation resulting from government policy (which did happen), notably the formation and dissolution of producer cooperatives (i.e. state intervention for specific purposes). In this book, we question the theory of periodic land redistribution, and we believe that much of what might be taken as evidence was actually a result of specific-purpose redistributions. This is important because the nature of tenure insecurity differs, and so do the relevant solutions.

The Därg regime came to an end in 1991. In the last year of its existence, the Därg started a process of economic liberalization. The end to forced collectivization and villagization are the most significant elements for our research topic. Producer cooperatives were disbanded and there was, inevitably, a great deal of struggle over how to divide the land, much of which had been confiscated from neighbouring peasants only a few years earlier. In such localities there was again considerable tenure insecurity, but none of our fieldwork sites included producer cooperatives.

The guerrillas in the Tegrayan People's Liberation Front (TPLF) had been implementing land redistribution as they took over new territory in the late 1980s. Ostensibly this was to liberate the peasantry from the oppression of the Därg officials (*birokrasi*), but more realistically it was to tie the peasants to the guerrilla army and to make them join the struggle. There is a considerable literature on these reforms, most of it by supporters of the liberation fronts. The policy of land redistribution was carried over into the united front, the Ethiopian People's Revolutionary Democratic Front (EPRDF), which was formed in 1989. Thus land redistribution went on more or less until the end of the war in May 1991.

The EPRDF then changed from a revolutionary Marxist liberation movement into a somewhat market-friendly government. The transitional government formally suspended its policy of land redistribution and kept the land tenure system which it had inherited from the Därg. The future land tenure system was to be settled by the constitution and the land question was open for debate. Positions were rather polarized. Government politicians argued in favour of state land ownership while much of the opposition favoured full privatization of land. The issue was discussed by government representatives in public meetings all over the country, but these meetings tended to be propaganda for the government position rather than an open discussion of alternatives. The constitution of 1995 ended this phase by reiterating the basic principles of state land ownership, although it gave the peasants 'protection against eviction from their possession' (Ethiopian Government 1995: Art. 40.4). This could be interpreted as a concession to the need for tenure security, but as it later became clear, the constitution did not provide any such guarantees.[9]

The key issue in the mid-1990s was whether the government would reintroduce land redistribution. There was widespread understanding that any new redistribution would lead to tenure insecurity, and government experts were largely opposed to it (Bruce *et al.* 1994: 25, 51–3[10]). Neither was a renewed drive for land redistribution a significant issue in the public debate. As the years passed without anything happening, the peasants seemed increasingly confident that the land belonged to them. Observers tended to agree. It therefore came as a great surprise when the regional council of Amhara state in late 1996 suddenly ordered land redistribution in the areas which had not been covered during the civil war, roughly the southern half of the region. The reform was swiftly implemented and was finished before the 1997 agricultural season. This reform has been widely covered in the literature and there is general agreement that it was a politically motivated and brutal reform aimed to cripple the power of former local leaders. Just as the TPLF reforms before it, this was a very real redistribution of land, although it was limited almost exclusively to the lands of the former local leaders, labelled as *birokrasi*.

Despite the drama of the Amhara land redistribution of 1997 (cf. Ege 1997b) and political statements at the time, this policy now looks like an aberration. No other region followed suit. It could in fact be argued that the re-opening of the question of redistribution instigated legal reform and land certification. The choice was now between generalized tenure insecurity, political turmoil and economic decline on the one hand, or putting an end to the policy of land redistribution and giving the peasants an improved sense of tenure security on the other hand. Tegray, the politically dominant region, started reforms in 1998, giving the peasants individual certificates documenting their land holdings. There was soon a flurry of legal reform and land certification programmes in all the major regions, and by 2010 most of the country had been covered by certification programmes.

We do not directly discuss the land certification programmes since none of us had done fieldwork on this issue by the time of producing this

[9] For an early criticism of the constitution, with some highly pertinent questions, see Yeraswork (2000: 285–7), a published version of his doctoral dissertation from 1995.

[10] This report is an excellent summary of land tenure under the Därg and the situation in the early 1990s, written by three leading experts. We do, however, question some of the analysis, notably the periodic redistribution argument.

manuscript. The topic is much covered in the recent literature and the positions seem clearly defined. The international economists see it as an exceptionally successful exercise in land titling; it gave the peasants secure rights in the land, which they had previously held more tenuously due to the risk of redistribution (e.g. Deininger *et al.* 2007; Holden 2008). Critics like Dessalegn Rahmato (2009) are sceptical and argue that the land may have been registered but the peasants have been granted no new rights. We tend to agree with Dessalegn, but there is clearly a need for more research on this vital issue, specifically empirical fieldwork on peasant attitudes and practices regarding land rights.

This debate on certification bears heavily on our understanding of the current situation. The question is fundamentally whether the land question is a 'dead issue', solved once and for all, as government representatives argue, or whether it remains an unsettled problem that will emerge with renewed force in the future. We touch on various aspects of the post-certification land tenure system in the final chapters of this book – be it the challenges of a near-urban setting (Aspen, Chapters 6 and 7) or contradictions within the system (Ege, Chapter 8) – moving from a description, and sometimes reinterpretation, of the past to current development trends.

Here I have presented a brief review of some of the major shifts in land tenure since the late imperial period. This is a story often told and the literature is voluminous. As mentioned before, since I regard much of this as standard knowledge I have not provided references to the literature, except when I want to draw attention to particular points. I have also sometimes added my own take on this story, in which case the documentation is to be found in the later chapters of this book. It should be emphasized, however, that Ethiopian land tenure is remarkably complex and the evidence is limited and fragmentary. On virtually all issues there is great need for more research, be it on other areas to investigate variation, using other methods to check the robustness of findings, or last but not least, reinterpreting the evidence from other perspectives. Let us now turn from this brief historical review to a presentation of what our book can contribute to the debate.

OUR APPROACH: MULTI-DISCIPLINARY AND EMPIRICAL

The various chapters of this book cover the period from the land reform to the current situation. It could therefore be mistaken for a history of land tenure after the land reform, which was never our intention. Such a book would be very different, as it would have sought to cover all major policies and all major regions, and it would necessarily be largely based on the existing literature. Inevitably, it would have tended to reproduce the views expressed in the literature on which it was built. We are of course deeply indebted to this literature; however, as set out in Chapter 2, this book has to a considerable extent been born out of a feeling of dissonance, that our own experiences do not fit well into key elements of the common interpretation. Our approach has therefore been to focus on the topics we covered in our primary research in order to critically assess peasant land tenure under the Därg, current development trends, and the link between them. The focus is on peasant land rights, rural inequality, and the development tendencies of the land tenure system.

We come from different academic disciplines, and we deal with a broad range of settings and issues. What unifies the contributions in this book is an exploration of peasant agency. All too often, Ethiopian peasants are presented as victims. We do not argue that they are not victims, but this is not our primary perspective. Rather, we seek to understand peasant conditions as they appeared to us in the local communities we studied. This approach underlies the critique of the existing literature and the attempt to sketch out the structure of the peasant farm in Chapter 2 (Ege), the discussion of the land tenure under the Därg in Chapters 3 to 5 (Ege and Yigremew), the investigation of social relations and the strategies of peasant 'urbanites' in Chapters 6 and 7 (Aspen), and the analysis of contradictions in the current land tenure system leading to some proposed principles for a reformed land tenure system in Chapter 8 (Ege).

Our aim has not been to write out and exemplify a peasant agency model, but to present some of the complexities of local conditions and, hopefully, to convey some of the local atmosphere. Thus, there is also a certain empirical bent unifying the chapters, where priority is given to the available empirical evidence rather than to generally accepted interpretation or logical reasoning based on uncertain ethnographic material. While this approach takes us closer to reality, it also introduces a considerable amount of variation, not a model of peasant reality but different peasant realities. It would probably be difficult to make these realities fit into a single model of meaningful precision, and there are certainly also many exceptions to our peasant agency 'model', cases where a standard political economy approach of peasant victimization would be more meaningful.

Apart from the view from below, or peasant agency, the book is held together by a common understanding of the Ethiopian farm, as I outline towards the end of Chapter 2. Whatever the nature of the land tenure system, farms have been operated by individual households – often very small and too small to be stable production units. This creates a peculiar dynamism, closely linked to individual household cycles. Without such an understanding, one may easily misinterpret relations between households as market relations, or one may find evidence of exploitation and class formation, although the inequality observed may be temporary only, resulting from changes in life phases rather than trans-generational inequality.

The interest in peasant land rights is at the centre of the discussion of the *dersha* land tenure system by Ege and Yigremew (Chapters 3 and 4) as it developed after the 1975 land reform. Superficially, land tenure in the two communities analysed, Ayné in North Shäwa and Dinja S'iyon in West Gojam, could be described as periodic land redistribution.

However, land was in practice largely allocated by household processes. All persons present in the household registration following the land reform were in principle equally entitled to a share (*dersha*) of the land in the household where they were registered. This *dersha* principle set in motion a system with well-defined inter-peasant rights, basically a system of inheritance based on household membership rather than kinship. This was not a planned result of the land reform but emerged from the way it was implemented in the local community. Thus, peasant ingenuity created a set of remarkably clear rules and practices. In everyday life and in relation to other local inhabitants, peasants experienced a strong sense of ownership. These ownership rights were also upheld by local courts in struggles between local peasants.

This contrasts with one of the most common generalizations about land tenure under the Därg, namely that there developed a system of periodic redistributions driven by the necessity to maintain equity as children came of age and demanded land for new households. In recent years, this has become a standard part of the economic literature on Ethiopian land tenure. The problem is that there is not much concrete evidence to support such an interpretation. The observations made may just as well be explained by other processes. The *dersha* system is a case in point. The Amhara region has been particularly associated with redistribution (Shifa *et al.* 2015: 26). We show how evidence that is commonly interpreted to indicate high levels of redistribution does not in fact prove the existence of periodic redistribution, and when re-examined more closely, may tell a very different story. For example, in Ayné, at least 60 per cent of households had lost land in the period 1976–89. Detailed analysis shows, however, that this was due partly to household processes and partly to a specific-purpose redistribution following the redrawing of borders, which is something quite different from general, equity-driven land redistributions caused by population growth and a continuous drive for equity. It is precisely in this environment of seemingly rather high levels of 'redistribution' that we found a surprisingly well-defined property system. The methodological point is obvious: we cannot just count the number of 'redistributions'. We need to understand the specific social system in order to make proper sense of these data.

One question of interest is the geographical extent of the *dersha* system. The model was developed from practices observed in Ayné in North Shäwa. Yigremew found it applicable to his site in Gojam, Aspen hints that it was applied to Jerelé in North Wälo, and it is also consistent with descriptions of other areas. We also point out some limitations. The interesting effect of such a model is that it opens up new readings of the literature and one can see that it might fit a number of sites in many parts of the Amhara region, as well as beyond. It can thus serve as a hypothesis and a generator of questions about local land tenure practices.

The 1975 land reform abolished rural class relations and the feudal aspects of Ethiopian society. Here we are in full agreement with the major thrust of the research literature. There is, however, a significant research trend identifying what might be referred to as kulak tendencies. While such analysis is inherently appealing to social scientists, the evidence should be critically assessed. I have indicated above, based on our farm model, that evidence which may seem to indicate inequality and kulaks – processes that can only be described as incipient class formation – may actually be due to household processes. These regularly lead to inequality on measured variables, but these inequalities are often of a temporary nature and do not necessarily prove any class formation. We would agree, however, that social inequality is an important issue, and the current economic transformation may open up new avenues for class formation.

The two chapters on the *dersha* system point towards a remarkably equal society. However, in Baba Säat there was also a marked process of levelling down, starting with the 1975 land reform and continuing with the EPRDF land redistribution in 1991 (Chapter 5). Thus, at the time of the survey in 2002, differentiation within the local community was very limited. The same picture emerges from Aspen's analysis of survey data from Jerelé in Chapter 6, but here we can also see new tendencies. Jerelé is situated on the same highland plain as Baba Säat, but further west, lower down, and above all, on the main road between Wäldiya and Däbrä Tabor. The rural parts of Jerelé are characterized by considerable equality, as is also indicated for other communities in the same district (Aspen and Ege 2010). However, the commune includes a market village, or 'rural town', on the main road. Here inequality is much more pronounced, mainly because there are more opportunities, and some enterprising people have thus become, by local standards, wealthy. However, it appears that differentiation is still quite limited. So far, the major change, as described by Aspen in Chapter 7, appears to be a new attitude to life, a widening of horizons.

While the initial chapters are set within the traditional peasant community, Chapters 7 and 8 look beyond it. One important trend is urbanization, linked to roads, trade, increased production for the market, and even cash crops, as discussed by Aspen in Chapter 7 in the case of a very small 'town' in North Wälo. These are developments observed all over Ethiopia. Ethiopia is still an exceptionally rural society, but these processes point towards a future where Ethiopia is less rural, and, hopefully, where agriculture is for this very reason more productive than today. The chapter gives a glimpse into the rapid change that is taking place, with its challenges and opportunities. In 2003, local authorities still thought of Arbit as a rural community, and urbanization was to be prevented. But in 2010, the mood had changed. The future of these market villages is intimately linked to the commercialization of agriculture, a key ingredient of current development policies. In these settings the value of land increases rapidly, but at the same time the landowner risks expropriation. The scene is thus set for transactions that are, at best, in the legal grey zone, with ensuing tenure insecurity, conflicts and corruption.

The literature has been overwhelmingly critical of government land tenure policy. By contrast, a number of economists, notably Deininger and Holden (see Chapter 2), have recently given very positive assessments of the land certification programmes of the early 2000s. It could, again, appear as if the land question is settled. However, in Chapter 8, I point to contradictions in the current system that makes its future rather uncertain. Finally, I also seek to identify some principles that could form the basis of a stable and more productive land tenure system, and for more constructive state-peasant relations. Both the understanding of the present and suggestions for reforms are informed by the view-from-below permeating this book, based on what peasants do and what it would take to set them free to realize more of their potential.

A NOTE ON TERMINOLOGY

In writing this book, we have tried to keep a simple but precise terminology. Some of this is linked to our theoretical position, some of it are just attempts to reduce the number of Amharic terms. The following outlines our choices and the reasons behind them.

One potentially controversial term may be 'conditional private property' and its related terminology, but this captures well our observation of peasant practices. It has been common to argue that the state owned the land and the peasants had only usufruct rights. Within some approaches this may be enough, but it is singularly unhelpful in the study of local land tenure. In this context, it is clearly necessary to be able to distinguish between the rights of a peasant in his 'own' land, his rights in land he rents, and the rights of a peasant 'landowner' in the land he rents out. There is the additional point that reducing the land rights of peasants to usufruct only tends to diminish these rights and make them less interesting for research. This may have contributed to the lack of interest in peasant land tenure after the land reform. Our findings indicate that for most peasants most of the time, these were the rights that mattered.

This approach also simplifies our terminology. We can consistently, with the reservations implied, speak of landowners and land owned, i.e. the land a peasant holds from the state via the commune (*qäbälé*). This is common practice in the literature, and certainly among the peasants. Those renting land from the landowners by any of the local institutions we refer to as tenants. This is more controversial. Some feel that 'tenant' is so strongly associated with the class relations of the past that it is now inappropriate. Our approach is more generic, considering a tenant as anyone occupying a property that is not his own. Furthermore, the alternatives feel somewhat awkward. In many cases, 'sharecropper' would do, but that covers only one, although the most common, contract type. 'Lessee' would also do, but we find this term too technical and may not capture the atmosphere of the, until recently, mostly informal contracts between landowner and tenant, governed by trust and local tradition and not by stipulations in a written contract.

Of a more practical nature, we have sought to reduce the number of Amharic terms in the text, while also maintaining precision. When we drafted the manuscript we used Amharic terms, but during the final stage of editing, we agreed on certain conventions using English terms that would consistently refer to the Amharic terms, and not be used in any other way. These are specified in the glossary. Often we put the Amharic term in parenthesis the first time the relevant English term is used. The English term can in such cases always be replaced by the Amharic term throughout the text. The reason for this choice is that we are often frustrated by texts where the English terms cannot be reliably translated back to one or more Amharic terms.

Some terms are used frequently. Like many before us, we treat 'Därg' as a term well known enough to not require italics, although we spell it according to our system of transliteration. More of a problem is the ever-present '*qäbälé*', variously conceived of as the lowest administrative level or as the territorial unit of local peasant organization. In the literature *qäbälé*, with varying spelling, is widely used, but sometimes it is also rendered as peasant association, village, and occasionally probably parish. All of these have their own problems. Our solution is to refer to the *qäbälé* as 'commune' and the sub-*qäbälé* (*neus qäbälé*, sometimes *got'*) as 'ward' for the reasons outlined below.

Under the Därg, there was a one-to-one overlap between the *qäbälé* and the peasant association, although the former tended, with variation, to refer to the territory and the latter to the organization. The official terminology of local organization has changed several times under the EPRDF and there is now little pretence that the *qäbälé* is a peasant association. The local leadership is referred to as the *qäbälé* administration, or by the peasants often simply as the *qäbäléwoch* (plural). There have been attempts to organize the inhabitants into mass organizations for youth, women and peasants, but these are basically dead horses and would in any case be different from the old peasant association. We therefore find 'peasant association' inappropriate for our purpose, especially because we will often be referring to the territory. We have chosen to use 'commune' as an exact replacement of '*qäbälé*' as used by our peasant informants, i.e. referring variously to the territory, the organization or its leadership.

Our choice has therefore been to translate *qäbälé* as 'commune'. This is readily understandable to those not familiar with the Ethiopian literature, on the condition that we move away from the image of the commune in socialist China. Our reference is to the French or Scandinavian commune, in which case 'commune' becomes an acceptable term for the lowest level of administration, especially when there is a strong element of local self-government. One specific problem has been how to refer to the sub-divisions within a *qäbälé*. This became problematic after the administrative reforms in the late 1990s when there was a process of merging smaller *qäbälés* into larger units. The old *qäbälé* was initially often referred to as *got'*, but gradually the term of sub-*qäbälé* (*neus qäbälé*) became established and *got'* was used for an even lower organizational level. Here there is considerable regional variation. In this book, we have adopted 'ward' to refer to the sub-*qäbälé*, the territorial division immediately below the commune.

Some researchers seem to use 'village', and perhaps 'parish', to refer to what is probably, but not necessarily, the *qäbälé*. Apart from the lack of clarity, the problem is that the peasants in our study areas do not usually live in villages, which are nucleated settlements of some size, and when they do, these are not usually identical with the *qäbälé*. We thus find this term both imprecise and misleading. We use 'village' when we want to refer to nucleated settlements, be it those created by the Därg villagization campaign, or the rapidly emerging market villages or small rural 'towns'.

2

Peasant Land Tenure: A Critical Review

SVEIN EGE

Much has been written about land tenure in Ethiopia, but there is a scarcity of in-depth research after the land reform of 1975. Land tenure is of vital importance for the peasantry, and this book was born out of dissatisfaction with the current state of knowledge. I have been doing fieldwork in various locations in the Amhara highlands since 1989, and gradually there was a feeling of dissonance, that the standard interpretation in the literature, which has been routinely applied to the Amhara area, could not account for what I heard and saw in the field. In this chapter, therefore, I seek to critically investigate some main tendencies in the literature, and then provide some elements for an alternative understanding, which are further explored in the later chapters.

It should be pointed out that this is a review with a specific purpose, and not a comprehensive review aiming to cover all the literature on land tenure. It is also explicitly critical, seeking to bring out issues where we disagree, to pave the road for our own understandings. Despite this critical purpose, we obviously stand on the shoulders of earlier researchers, not least those whom we criticize on specific issues. Finally, in this book in general and in this chapter in particular, we often refer to our own works, perhaps more frequently than what might appear appropriate, for the simple reason that over the years we often tried to research issues which we hoped could settle our feelings of dissonance, one way or the other. They are therefore particularly relevant for the critical issues discussed here.

THE STATE OF KNOWLEDGE

There is every reason to search for better understanding of peasant land tenure, but this is a surprisingly challenging research topic. Land is a concrete element and may thus seem simple to understand, until one becomes interested in land rights – which are a never-ending story of current rights, latent rights, potential future rights, or should-have-been rights. Much has been written about land tenure in Ethiopia after the 1975 land reform and we may therefore get the impression that it is a well-studied topic. However, a critical reading of the literature shows large knowledge gaps, and even worse, that a number of oft-repeated statements have a weak foundation in evidence, in the sense that they are not backed up by convincing data. There are some survey-based studies that provide some useful empirical data, but interpretation has a strong external flavour, including when done by Ethiopian researchers. These studies therefore appear to be measurements of a system which is not well understood, and which could just as well function according to other principles than those identified.

There is a particular lack of studies trying to capture how peasants have obtained access to land, as well as their current and future strategies, in other words, the land tenure system seen from a peasant perspective. Instead, we are told about periodic redistributions of land, a theory which confuses the issues and ill fits the situation on the ground. We are also told that peasants consequently felt great tenure insecurity but that the situation improved with the more market-friendly policy of the EPRDF government (e.g. Holden *et al.* 2007: 3). In fact, a good case could be made for the opposite, that tenure insecurity was more closely associated with EPRDF land redistributions than with the Därg land reform. Peasant society is also usually analysed as divided into strata, rich and poor, based on the distribution of assets of production, an approach which misreads the evidence. In addition, there are many lower-level problematic statements routinely made in research reports: that land was equally distributed by family size, a statement which is not as clear as the authors of the reports seem to believe; that the leaders of the commune (*qäbälé*) misused their positions and grabbed land for themselves, their friends or whosoever paid them, claims apparently based only on hearsay; or that the EPRDF reforms were innovative in giving women land rights, an argument with weak foundation in both the past and the present.

There will be many reasons for this situation, but here I shall only point towards two main explanations. The first refers to method. Much of the literature is based on the survey method with very limited direct fieldwork by the researchers. Interpretation therefore tends to be based on preconceived theories, with a great amount of recirculation of ideas that are never critically investigated. To go beyond these, researchers need extensive personal fieldwork in order to understand the challenges peasants face, seen from their own standpoint, rather than treating them as agents in a model. The researcher needs time to understand the social environment, the personalities involved and the myriad local conflicts in order to meaningfully evaluate the information. Much of the information will also be sensitive and can only be gathered from informants who trust the researcher, which usually takes time to develop. Finally, a considerable amount of the most interesting information is of a soft nature and cannot easily be recorded by standardized questionnaires.

The second explanation for the lack of good studies of peasant land tenure must be attributed to Ethiopia's dramatic history. By the time the land reform was proclaimed, the 'bloodless revolution' of 1974 had already turned violent – and worse was to come, with tremendous social upheaval and wars. In view of its significance, it may seem remarkable that we have so few studies of the land reform, Dessalegn's (1984) book standing out as the only major study. The unsettled conditions of that time period may go some way in explaining this situation. The dramatic events and the politicized atmosphere must also have made detailed studies of peasant land tenure difficult, and perhaps even seem utterly trivial. Within a few years, the focus of rural studies had changed from land reform to the impact of socialist agricultural policies, notably the grain quotas of the Agricultural Marketing Corporation (AMC), collectivization in the form of state farms, and the ambitious plans to organize the peasantry into producer cooperatives (see Pausewang *et al.* 1990). In the midst of this came the great famine of 1984, mixed in with the wars in the north. The famine itself and the state's plans for massive resettlement naturally seemed more important than studying the everyday life and strategies of peasants, in addition to the obvious difficulties of fieldwork under these conditions. Towards the end of the Därg period came the campaign to move peasants into villages, again an important event which necessarily attracted researchers' attention (Alemayehu 1989; Tesfaye 1995).

The situation improved somewhat after the new government took power in 1991. Därg policies had obviously failed, there was generally more freedom to do research, and there was easier access to the field. From this period emerged several relevant studies, but again it appears that most authors were concerned with policy rather than with understanding peasant land tenure itself (see Dessalegn 1994a; Dessalegn and Taye 2006). In the more recent past, new events and policies again attracted attention, notably the 1997 Amhara land redistribution, followed by the policy of land registration and certification, and finally issues of concessions and land grabbing.

There were good reasons for the choices researchers made. When one experiences state violence, as I did myself in the case of the Amhara land redistribution (see Ege 1997b), there is an urge to write about it. It would even feel unethical not to do so. However, reading through this literature I get a strong impression of missed opportunities. At every point, the 'hot' topic of the day probably seemed more important or urgent than a study of peasant land tenure. Seen from the present, however, detailed and careful basic studies of specific peasant communities, who are of continuous concern, would have been of more lasting importance. Studies of the AMC or of villagization are likely to be consulted by agricultural historians, but not necessarily by those interested in understanding the present. On the other hand, the ethnographic studies of pre-reform communities by Hoben (1973) and Bauer (1973) are still required reading for anyone who wants to understand the peasants of the northern highlands of Ethiopia, and they are valuable for anyone interested in peasant studies. Topical issues tend to be ephemeral, while the trivialities of daily life in peasant hamlets are the stuff that history is made of.

The literature on land tenure is of course broader than what may appear from my critical remarks above. It is not easily summarized, ranging from national surveys to case studies, spanning disciplines from history to economics, and with motivations ranging from academic production of knowledge to policy-oriented papers. There are, however, certain patterns, and many recent studies make arguments along one or more of the following lines:

1. Resource conservation perspectives: tenure insecurity produced by the land tenure system is a key explanation of resource degradation.
2. Microfarms: land tenure policy has resulted in an undifferentiated mass of unviable microfarms.
3. The ox argument: rich ox-owners use their oxen to access the land of the poor.
4. The market approach: agricultural production and peasant wellbeing will be stimulated by strengthening the land market.

In addition, there is the ethnographic literature. I use the term broadly to include studies in the social sciences containing strong elements of fieldwork-based description of local conditions. This is a highly variable body of literature, comprising a few monographs but mostly articles, reports and conference papers, usually with land tenure as just one of many concerns. Consequently, this literature is not easy to use, and those who seek comprehensive analyses of land tenure issues will likely be disappointed. Nevertheless, it does provide essential context for understanding peasant land tenure, and throughout this book, we use this literature to critically discuss current theories relating to land tenure.

RESOURCE CONSERVATION STUDIES

Many studies deal with land tenure as a causal factor behind resource degradation or to explain the failure of land conservation programmes. Some are highly critical of the top-down approach applied in such programmes, be it by the Därg, international donors or the current government (Yeraswork 2000; Hoben 1997; Ståhl 1990). Other studies take a more technical approach (e.g. Bekele 1998; Berhanu Gebremedhin 1998). There seems to be widespread agreement that results have been disappointing in view of the substantial resources spent on these projects. This is attributed to a host of different factors, but land tenure is often identified as a main factor, notably tenure insecurity generated by state land ownership and the policy of frequent land redistributions.

Many of these studies are based on fieldwork in specific localities, often with precise descriptions of farm parameters, like land holdings and land use, supported by locally gathered survey data. The description of the land tenure system, however, tends to be based on general accounts of land policies at the national level. For a critical investigation this is not enough and can easily lead to false conclusions about the mechanisms at work.

The problem becomes serious if the historical account at the national level is incorrect. In Chapters 3 and 4 of this book, we present an alternative interpretation, based on our fieldwork in the Amhara region. While standard accounts, including for the Amhara region, refer to several rounds of land redistribution during the Därg, we argue that there was no system of periodic land redistribution, and by and large there was no land redistribution at all if we apply a definition close to what the reader is likely to understand by the term. The land tenure system under the Därg can best be understood as conditional private property, with strong peasant rights in normal times (see Chapter 3). However, specific policies, such as the drive for cooperatives, villagization and forest projects, created much local insecurity. So if we measure the insecurity resulting from specific policies of the intrusive state and attribute it to a generalized system of periodic land redistribution, we completely misunderstand the land tenure system and its dynamics. The lesson to take home here is that not only the farm parameters, but also the land tenure practices, should be supported by detailed local evidence.

On a policy level, resource conservation studies appear to have a strong preference for private property rights, for obvious reasons. It is easy to make an argument that tenure security is a necessary requirement for peasants to make long-term investments in land, such as terracing, tree planting or simply good land management. Therefore, the coverage of peasant land tenure, their specific rights in specific plots of land as practised locally, and the way this influences land management decisions, are of great interest. Of the many studies consulted, only one study from Tegray goes some way in bringing some nuance to the argument. Atakilte (2003: 107–8, 156–7) argues against the image of uniform tenure insecurity and shows that insecurity varied between plots. Some plots were acquired in a recent round of land redistribution while others were from an earlier redistribution, and some were even inherited. The feeling of tenure security and land management decisions therefore differed systematically.

By and large, the resource conservation studies are disappointing reading for those of us who seek in-depth information on the local land tenure system. More seriously, since there is so much information on other aspects of the farm economy, it is easy to mistake the description of the land tenure system as a locally grounded account. Careful reading will often indicate the opposite. It appears that the authors of the studies believe that the general account of land tenure is well founded and see no need to investigate it critically. The problem with this is not primarily the missed opportunity, but above all that these studies tend to strengthen the periodic redistribution narrative without confirming it locally.[1] One aim of this book is to provide an alternative argument and hopefully stimulate a critical discussion.

TENDENCY TOWARDS MICROFARMS

Another common strand of argument, apparently regarded as self-evident, is that Ethiopia is facing a poverty trap, with farms rapidly declining in size due to the land tenure system. Ethiopian farms are indeed small, and are getting smaller due to population increase. Farmers are deeply concerned with the growing competition for land. These are widely accepted facts, but the specific argument of a tendency towards microfarms goes well beyond this by blaming the land tenure system.

According to Dessalegn (2006), the land reform distributed land rather equally but also established a practice of periodic land redistribution, use rights based on residence in the commune, as well as restrictions on renting out land or using hired labour. The aim was to abolish and prevent the re-emergence of rural differentiation. From this perspective the policy was very successful, but the rather equal distribution of land merely served to make peasants equally poor. Dessalegn contrasts this with the emergence of what he refers to as the 'Ethiopian yeoman' in the 1960s, the enterprising farmer who sought to capture the opportunities created by modernization in general and new agricultural markets in particular.

Dessalegn provides a passionate plea for setting the peasants free from state intervention, in the belief that the dynamism created will lead to development and improvement for all. At the turn of the twenty-first century, this argument resonated well with researchers and donors due to the country's weak economic performance. The implications should not be lost, however. It is difficult to envisage how this differentiation would happen without much pain for many of those affected, since larger farms for some necessarily means that others will be pushed out. In some of the writings arguing along these lines, this problem is somewhat superficially solved by calls for industrialization and the development of modern sectors in general, without much concern for whether these assumptions are realistic. There is a danger that the policy proposed could create more problems than it aims to solve.

In the writings of Dessalegn, for decades the leading analyst of land tenure in Ethiopia, this modernist line of thinking can be identified at least as far back as his original criticism of the land reform (Dessalegn 1984: 61–2, 73, 101). His preference for entrepreneurs is also easily visible in his criticism of the 'rejectionists' who had written unfavourably about agricultural modernization in the late imperial

[1] Yeraswork (2000) is a partial exception. We discuss his information on land redistribution in Chapter 4.

period (Dessalegn 1986: 69–71, 2008b: 87–94). The argument that there is a tendency towards microfarms was much elaborated on in the unpublished paper, 'Manufacturing Poverty' (Dessalegn 1997). It was supported by some evidence from North Wälo, showing very small holdings both of land and oxen.[2] The argument has been very widespread in the literature. It derives its strength from the obvious poverty of Ethiopian peasants coupled with population growth, and the view that this has led or is leading the country into a Malthusian trap (Dessalegn 1997: 6). The challenge of population growth is undeniable. However, historical evidence does not necessarily confirm that peasants have been becoming poorer, and one might suspect that in recent years there has been considerable improvement in rural life, not just in the national economy.[3]

One of the most frequently repeated statements in the literature is that the land tenure system in place has led to the diminution and fragmentation of holdings (Berhanu Nega *et al.* 2003: 107 summarizes the literature). Until the great rural transformation takes place, however, diminution of holdings seems closely linked to population growth and equal inheritance, rather than to the particular land tenure system.[4] It should also be noted that peasants themselves report that fragmentation does not seem to be a major problem (Daniel Kassahun 2006: 117; Deininger *et al.* 2003a: 19). However, while the Därg land reform probably reduced fragmentation through various provisions, the lottery system applied by the TPLF and EPRDF sometimes led to significant problems.[5]

[2] One reason for the very low number of oxen is the use of ploughing by horse in some of the areas (Ege 2002a: 20, 43–6). The data on land holdings in North Wälo also seem strongly influenced by the recent land redistribution which make it rather difficult to accurately record the land holding of a household, as illustrated in Chapter 5.

[3] Contrary to the dominant argument at the time, my impressions from fieldwork in North and South Wälo around the year 2000 indicate that positive developments were taking place, evidenced by many new houses, the quality of clothes and the general physical appearance of people. But there was indeed also considerable famine and hardships, as documented in our publications from this period (Ege and Yigremew 2002: 6–15; Ege and Aspen 2003). For a more recent case showing great improvements in the peasant economy, see Ege (2015).

[4] Equal inheritance contributes to declining holdings, but it has no direct effect on the amount of land held per person. Current inheritance policies and practices are further discussed in Chapter 8.

[5] Two key provisions in the implementation of the Därg reform were: (1) to limit land holdings to the commune of residence, and (2) *amba zur*, allowing people to claim the land around their homestead, usually with a land swap.

For the TPLF reforms in Tegray, Chiari's (2003: 76) descriptions suggest that fragmentation and long distances resulted from the applied rules, notably distribution of parcels of land by commune-wide lottery. I also observed some striking instances in Ayné and Wäyra Amba in North Shäwa after the 1997 land redistribution due to rather similar rules. This created serious challenges for some peasants, but was too limited to have much impact on statistical measures.

The view that Ethiopian peasants are poor and are getting poorer has been pervasive. It is a problem, however, that much the same arguments are advanced whether the average holding in an area is well below 1 hectare or whether it is in the range of 2 to 3 hectares (e.g. Mirgissa 1994: 122). These seem to be quite different situations, and I would expect significant differences in how we understand them. However, the specific data reported have remarkably little impact on the analysis. These are of course complex issues, because the amount of land required to sustain a family on a certain level is closely linked to the nature of the economy. Analysis paying more attention to differences in the evidence could help us to better understand peasant strategies under different ecological, economic and political conditions, and not the least improve our ability to spot positive trends.

There is widespread agreement that smallholders are efficient farmers (Berhanu Nega *et al.* 2003: 104). However, the microfarm argument could imply that there is a threshold in farm size below which this logic breaks down. This is an interesting argument, advanced by several authors but unfortunately so far without much evidence. It may appear that the research literature puts too much emphasis on the land holding – i.e. the land that is officially registered as the land of a household – while too little attention is placed on the operated farm holding and the web of social and economic relations by which peasants lead their lives. Not all peasants or landowners are farmers, and there are systematic differences in people's life situations and strategies. This understanding also underlies our discussion, and ultimately rejection, of the ox argument.

THE OX ARGUMENT

The ox argument is relevant for our discussion of land tenure because it is basically another way of approaching land rentals. Although I tend to reject the ox argument, the literature discussing it is perhaps the best way to approach the peasant economy because it potentially points towards peasant strategies. Its usefulness is thus not so much in the conclusions reached by its proponents, but by the issues raised.

In many reports, peasants are classified as poor, middle and rich by the number of oxen owned. The argument is that a farmer needs a pair of oxen to plough, that there is great inequality in the distribution of oxen, and that those who have fewer than two oxen face handicaps. In its fully developed version, relations between ox-owners and the ox-less are painted as class relations, where those without oxen are either forced to rent oxen in return for labour – which seriously interferes with work on their own farms – or, the more common solution, forced to rent out their land and receive only about half of what they could have harvested (see Ege 2002a: 17–18 and Ege 2002d: 1448–51 for more extended critiques).

The argument has a long and varied history. It can be traced back to the Russian debate, notably Lenin's analysis of rural capitalism in Tsarist Russia and Kritsman's analysis of rural class relations after the land reform (Cox 1979: 77–83). The argument's Marxist background has made many authors treat oxen as capital, which may be problematic in a non-capitalist setting, and dangerous due to the connotations that easily lead to analytical shortcuts. The emphasis on oxen also tends to overlook the real economic value of land ownership, partly because it is in principle acquired for free and thus does not have an official price (see Chapter 8).

In the Ethiopian context, Bauer's (1975) suggestive article 'For Want of an Ox' has usually been the starting point. It also indirectly received a strong impetus from the International Livestock Centre for Africa which, based on its mandate, saw the livestock element as the key to solving the problem of low productivity in highland agriculture (see Gryseels and Anderson 1983). These various strands were masterly brought together in research papers and publications by McCann (e.g. 1995: 72–81) and have since been adopted by a broad range of scholars.

The logic of the argument may be compelling, but it is actually based on weak evidence. The unequal distribution of oxen per household is well documented, but these facts do not necessarily imply class-like relations. The image of class relations based on ox ownership hinges very much on model thinking. Ox-owners are assumed to seek to maximize the benefits from their oxen, while ox-less farmers are caught in relations of dependency due to their lack of plough oxen. However, this is not the way the peasant community in Ethiopia works, partly due to strong elements of a moral economy (see Poluha 1989: 9–10, *passim*), but also because the 'rich' and the 'poor' are often relatives or neighbours who are woven into numerous criss-crossing social relations. Furthermore, although the data look deceptively clear, they are not necessarily robust. This point may be illustrated by my own fieldwork. Sometimes my assistants happened to interview the same household twice, yielding some striking differences in results, which were not due to false answers but to slight variations in how the household was registered and what assets were included. A household that would qualify as 'rich' by one registration might appear as two dirt poor households in the next registration when a parent and a child were split up as heads of separate households (Ege 1999: 52–3). This problem is most probably a feature of the survey method itself. The complex relations within and among households are difficult, perhaps impossible, to capture reliably by this method.[6] The following sketch is a model of a peasant farm which may be

[6] Based on a case study in Sir Lanka, Leach (1967) provided a good example of a critique of the survey method. The points made are specific to the case study but have general application. Our conclusion should not be to abandon the survey method, but to recognize that there are blind spots which must be covered by other, more detailed, methods in order to interpret the survey data more accurately.

useful if it prods researchers to look for evidence that may distinguish between the arguments more carefully.

The underlying process that accounts for much of the observed inequality in ox holdings may be described as 'primary household accumulation', i.e. the process by which youngsters build up their personal property (*gulma*) in order to set up a new household. This type of cyclical household process can be distinguished from the dynamic accumulation that leads to increased differences. In Ethiopian highland agriculture, there is little observable accumulation of oxen beyond the level of the family farm. Few peasant households have more than two oxen, and those who do usually contain embryonic households in the phase of primary household accumulation. For some time, these households appear rich, notably in oxen and labour, and they strive hard to be surplus producing. In fact, social reproduction requires that many of them are reasonably successful. However, when a youngster later establishes his own household, both his household and the parent household may well be at the poorer end of the scale by the standard variables (see also Ege and Aspen 2003: 27–8; Ege 2006: 1039; Atakilte 2003: 66–7). This type of primary household accumulation is obviously very different from the standard accumulation pattern taking place in a business firm.

The household cycle does not preclude social stratification, and the ox argument might still hold true to some degree. I have therefore sought to check the ox argument under conditions most unfavourable to my current views. Ox rentals in return for fixed grain payment have been identified as particularly onerous. However, in a study of ox rentals in the Kombolcha area, I found that the owners of 'capital', the oxen, tended to be poor, while those who rented the oxen were ambitious farmers trying to improve their lots (Ege 2006). While the farmers were poor by any reasonable standard, they were nevertheless typically better off than the ox owners. Furthermore, a study of regional variation in livestock holdings showed that peasants in areas of apparent ox shortage did not necessarily prioritize oxen, as would be expected if the possession of oxen was the most critical resource for their households. Thus, in many parts of North Wälo, ox holdings were very low but holdings of cows were comparatively high. By contrast, in the Yefat area, ox holdings were much better, but cows were scarce (Ege 2002a: 29–34). There is no mystery here; ecology and trade explain the differences, and reduces the explanatory power of the ox argument. To my knowledge, there is so far no documentation that convincingly demonstrates the social relations of dependence specified by the ox argument.

The reason for the popularity of the ox argument is probably because it gives an interesting social twist to somewhat uninspiring survey data, such as a table of ox ownership. Since it appears to provide a satisfactory explanation, it may also impede further questions. But it does not have to be so. The study of ox ownership and management could take us right into the production equation, into the concrete ways by which peasants operate their economy. It is important to understand the impact of the unbalanced farm structure[7] emphasized by Bauer (1975: 242), or the presence of households who cannot plough, notably women and elderly persons (McCann 1987b: 257; *ibid.* 1995: 75). This can help open up for critical investigation of the relations between households, as well as the trajectory of the farming system.

We do not claim that there is no differentiation in the Ethiopian countryside, but that this cannot be directly read from the distribution of oxen. Given the pattern of household formation and resource distribution, oxen will necessarily be unequally distributed (e.g. see Ege and Aspen 2003: 41–2). Coming to terms with social differentiation in the peasant community is not an easy task, but we provide some elements, potentially of wider relevance, in our chapters on peasant communities in North Wälo and in the theoretical discussion of land tenancy.

The ox argument impinges on our understanding of land tenure in at least two ways. Firstly, it states that oxen are the critical resource in plough-based agriculture and that the possession of oxen, not land, accounts for social stratification. This seems somewhat unlikely (Ege 2002d: 1447–51), and the idea can be laid to rest by observing the impact of the land reform. Once land holdings were equalized, the economic rationale for holding multiple teams of oxen also disappeared and ox holdings were rapidly levelled down (Hendrie 1999: 139–41).

The ox argument implies that oxen are a 'mover of land' (Dessalegn 1997: 5); that is, those with oxen are able to rent in land while those without oxen mostly have to rent out their land. This can be easily demonstrated to be empirically true, since active farmers will have more oxen than those who rent out their land, but this does not necessarily establish the claimed causal relationship that lack of oxen forces the landowners to rent out their land. Fundamentally, I would argue that land rentals are tightly linked to the household cycle and to broader livelihood strategies, rather than to a shortage of capital in the form of oxen.[8]

THE MARKET APPROACH

From the mid-1990s onwards, mainstream economists have achieved a dominant role in the study of land tenure. I shall therefore pay special attention to their approach. The dominant position is indicated by the fact that terms like 'transaction costs', 'factor markets' and 'market imperfection' have crept into much of the wider literature. This is partly due to the change from the socialist experiment of the Därg to the 'more market-friendly' economy of the EPRDF (Holden *et al.* 2007: 3), but probably also to the type of research funding available. The researchers tend to be linked to powerful and well-endowed institutions, like the

[7] Land holdings are smaller than what can be ploughed by a team of oxen.

[8] Ege (1994b) showed that possession of oxen was strongly correlated with male labour. In some recent surveys the pattern is less clear, which may be due to measurement problems or to the way the data are presented.

World Bank, IFPRI or national development agencies, and they clearly speak to the concerns of these organizations.[9] From the turn of the twenty-first century, this literature has dominated research on land tenure in the Amhara region, as well as in Ethiopia in general. Anyone who wants to do research on land tenure will have to come to terms with the arguments and the evidence.

The strong side of much of this literature is a very honest and commendably un-ideological presentation of whatever findings the data show, even when these are contrary to the research hypotheses and were perhaps disappointing to the researchers (e.g. Holden and Hailu 2001; Holden *et al.* 2009a). Some reports also contain useful summaries of surveys by other researchers pointing in different directions from their own.

This new crop of professional economists certainly agreed with the preference for a market economy. Their specific contributions take the form of highly empirical studies of the Ethiopian rural economy, investigating such aspects as the effect of different land rental types, the effect of tenure insecurity on investments in land, or the effect of land registration and certification on land markets. Furthermore, while the earlier literature had often presented the policy issue as a choice between equity and efficiency, economists like Deininger and Holden regarded the legacy of equal holdings as an advantage; the latter also expressed research interest in issues of growth with equity, including poverty and women's rights (Holden *et al.* 2007: 4).

Earlier studies of land tenure in Ethiopia often had a strong Ethiopianist flavour, in a tradition going back to the anthropologists of the 1960s, or even to *Zekrä Nägär* of Mahtämä-Selasé. The new economists broke with this tradition and set the issue of land tenure in Ethiopia as a sub-problem of general economic theory on land tenure, citing Cheung, Stiglitz and research done in Asia and other African countries (e.g. Holden *et al.* 2009b: 42; *ibid.* 2013: 383).

This is noticeable in the economists' bibliographies and references to the literature.[10] The authors appear to be very well read on standard economic literature, but the specific literature on Ethiopia, even that produced by many local economists, is rarely referred to, with few exceptions. The impression that this is a somewhat closed group of researchers is strengthened by the fact that many of the key researchers have collaborated with one another, and the writings produced by this network figure heavily in their own references. Furthermore, while there is little use of ethnographic literature in general, a few select works, thought to fit the argument, are frequently cited. This applies above all to a simplified reading of Dessalegn's (1984) study of the land

9 In general, Ethiopian social research is highly influenced by donors, including the consultancy business, but this is an issue well beyond the scope of this book.

10 The most prolific writers in this school are Klaus Deininger and Stein E. Holden. For their main relevant contributions, see this book's Bibliography. My comments are based on the totality of this literature.

reform, especially his description of periodic land redistribution, which is actually a minor, and the least convincing, part of his book. It also applies somewhat to my own study of the Amhara land redistribution (Ege 1997b), although my work describes policies under the EPRDF.

The favoured topic of this school of research is the market economy. Since land sales are illegal and the research is not designed to capture the grey economy, the focus is primarily on various effects of land renting, discussed as the land rental market. This is a major research limitation. It fits the economic theory in question and land rentals are also the most visible part of the land tenure system, but it is certainly not the most significant aspect of land tenure. Of much more importance to the peasants themselves is the way in which they receive rights in land in the first place, with all the different layers of actors and rights, and how land rights are transferred to the next generation; in other words, how land tenure is set within the peasant society. This has, to my knowledge, never been investigated within this literature.

One strong side of the research is its solid empirical basis. However, this is not quite as strong as it might first appear. The method used in these studies is sample surveys, often of impressive size and coverage. Although some reports are locally based, with a sample of only a few hundred households, the ideal aim appears to be to cover all of Ethiopia with a representative sample; anything less appears as an unfortunate compromise due to limited resources. The data are more often than not analysed by sophisticated regression analysis using advanced mathematical models which few of us can claim to fully understand. There are fairly extensive presentations of the sampling method and the mathematical models used. However, coming from another tradition and having used surveys myself and observed surveys by others at close range, I am left with a number of questions regarding the data quality.

The formal sampling procedures are often well described. The actual practice in the field less so. One would like a discussion of the reliability of the data, especially because data on land and production are sensitive. The trust these researchers show in the data is in marked contrast to the all-too-common practice by anthropologists to discard most of their own surveys because they find the data unreliable. The anthropologists seem to do so because they have a fair primary knowledge of local conditions and feel that the survey data would be misleading (e.g. see Poluha 1989: 6; Tronvoll 1998: 11; Hendrie 1999: 300–2). Increasing the distance to the informants and not knowing about the discrepancies between data and reality do not make the problem go away. The issue is most acute in large surveys, especially when a researcher lacks understanding of the local culture or uses an available data set with little knowledge of the ways in which these data were produced. There is therefore good reason to treat these data and the empirical findings based on them with some caution.

Apart from the reliability of these data, the application of the method has some limitations if the purpose is to understand the land tenure practices of Ethiopian peasants. The practical result of the analysis of these data is a set of statistical summaries and correlations between variables. Such data are extremely useful to check out patterns and compare localities or groups, but they do not by themselves tell a story. Statistics are just numbers; interpretation has to come from elsewhere. Here we are probably at the weakest point of this type of research. There are many hard measures of 'what', but when it comes to the more interesting 'why', the authors often become remarkably hesitant, and rightly so.[11] This is in marked contrast to anthropologists who, having been close to the scene, will usually describe local institutions and practices with considerable confidence. The problem is obviously that the methodological choices made have taken the economists in another direction and deprived them of the local knowledge needed to interpret the data.[12] This is not an argument for the superiority of ethnographic methods or against surveys or quantitative data, which are absolutely necessary to check out wider patterns. In fact, significant amounts of quantitative data underlie the research presented in the current book. However, to understand the strategies of the peasants, which is the aim of this book, it is also useful to live with and talk with the actual people outside the limitations imposed by a standardized questionnaire.

Our approach does of course have its own trade-offs. When we seek to go deep into the peasant world, by necessity area coverage becomes narrow. There is, however, good reason to question the drive for all-encompassing samples, which has its own concessions. This approach is necessary if the aim is to generalize to all of Ethiopia, but if we assume, reasonably, that Ethiopian rural society is not one system but a set of different systems, systems we do not yet understand, it is obvious that the large sample approach is not just costly but may also become a hindrance to greater understanding, mainly because it collapses data from different farming systems into a single system. In addition, the researcher lacks the opportunity to get to know first-hand the localities covered, and will typically rely on ethnographical stereotypes when interpreting the data. In the current literature, the discussion of the rather complex issue of female land tenure is a good illustration of this issue.[13]

As mentioned before, the empirical thrust of this literature has also led to the questioning of what has often been taken as self-evident truths. One example is Marshallian inefficiency, the theory that a share-

[11] See Benin and Pender (2009: 225) for an illustration.
[12] There is considerable variation here. See, for instance, Gebrehaweria and Holden (2011) where some of the authors' speculation seems to be based on a good understanding of local conditions.
[13] For example, see Holden (2008: 11, 52, 57, 58); his analysis is based on the assumption that women had weak land rights before the land titling reform of 2004, while the data presented actually shows considerable pre-existing land rights for women. For ethnographic accounts of rural women, see Poluha (1989), Pankhurst (1992), Nässén (2009) and Jåstad (2014).

cropper will invest less in the land than an owner-cultivator, because the former has to balance the cost of investments against his own share of the produce, rather than the total produce. Economists have shown that this may not always hold true and have therefore gradually refined the understanding of sharecropping. The logic of the Marshallian model is strong, but in real life, other forces also come into play, and therefore empirical findings are sometimes exactly the opposite of those predicted by the simple Marshallian model. It has been demonstrated that sharecroppers may have higher productivity on the land they rent than on their own land, arguably due to the threat of eviction (Menale and Holden 2009: 208–9; Holden *et al.* 2009c: 285–6). Another example is that of the effect of tenure insecurity, which is not uniform but varies with the types of investments (Deininger *et al.* 2003a). These examples demonstrate how minor variations in the assumptions made and the method applied can have a large impact on the findings and the resulting policy implications.

Of particular interest are some robust findings which have been confirmed by other studies using a broad set of methods. Such findings can be taken as points of reference in our theory construction. The first is the exceptional degree of equality that is the legacy of the land reform. Surprisingly, inequalities in land holdings are rarely the subject of extensive investigation, but the occasional Gini index reported and the small impact of land holding size on land rentals seem to confirm that differences in land holdings are indeed limited. This is of course old knowledge, central in many of the writings of Dessalegn, but it is always useful to have more proof.[14] Another finding, which seems to have surprised the economists although it had been pointed out by Hoben (1973: 9) even for the imperial period, is what the economists refer to as 'inverse tenancy', the fact that the landowners are poorer than the tenants. The landowner who rents out land is often a woman or an elderly person with limited resources, while the farmer who rents in land is typically an aspiring farmer. A third robust finding, related to both points above, is that the number of oxen tends to correlate with land rentals. Those who rent out land are often ox-less, while those who rent in land have one or more oxen (Hosaena and Holden 2009: 91). This is based on the same empirical observation implied in the ox argument outlined earlier in the chapter, and is also found in our own survey data. The interpretation of these well-established facts does, however, differ, as indicated in my review of the ox argument.

The economists have certainly been very prolific. The body of literature looks impressive from the outside and each article may be an interesting investigation of some specific phenomenon, but taken as a totality it adds surprisingly little to our knowledge of Ethiopian peasant society. This is partly due to the methodological choice of

[14] An interesting exception is Bereket (2008) who explicitly argued against Dessalegn's view. It is difficult to reconcile the high Gini indexes he reports, as high as 0.62, with other reports, both quantitative and qualitative, but the issue certainly merits more research. The data he used are publicly available.

using large samples to cover as many different agricultural systems as possible. This makes the results somewhat unhelpful in the face of any one specific place, which may differ widely from the average pattern established.

Another problem is the weak description of local practices. A good example of this is the central concept of land renting. Sometimes it is not possible to know precisely which local practices are included, although there is more often a helpful distinction between sharecropping and fixed contracts. This can be contrasted with a typical ethnographic description of the institutions involved (e.g. Aspen 1993: 31–59; Teferi 1998: 71–3). The problem is that the more one knows of local practices relating to land renting, the less clear the categories of the economists become. And it does not help that peasants may cover up or under-report unsafe practices they judge to be in a legal grey zone (see Ege 1994a: 293).

An issue of key concern to this literature is tenure security, but the understanding of tenure security remains vague. It is sometimes covered by proxy variables, like the occurrence of land redistributions in the past (without investigating what this meant), or the size of land holdings (large holdings thought to be more vulnerable to redistribution), but occasionally there are specific survey questions regarding peasant expectations about land redistribution. This complex and sensitive issue merits much more serious investigation, preferably with a set of different methods used in one study. I believe it would then have emerged that land redistribution, of any kind, played a much smaller role in the past than usually thought: that there is in fact a feeling of insecurity regarding some plots while others are more secure, that grey zone practices lead to insecurity because they are illegal, and that overlapping inheritance claims are considerable sources of insecurity. Government policy is also a key source of insecurity, but its impact fluctuates with policy statements and specific policies (e.g. the expansion of towns; Chapter 7). Thus, the data may show the expected high level of tenure insecurity, but the common interpretation of the mechanisms at work may very well differ from the underlying reality.

In sum, the recent economic literature suffers from two major weaknesses. Despite its highly empirical approach and willingness to reject any research hypothesis, it is limited by the market paradigm, both in the selection of topics and in the way they are analysed. The superiority of the land market underlies the analysis but is never really tested against local realities. Secondly, there is no proper description or understanding of the local land tenure systems – a precondition for meaningful causal analysis. This takes us to the next section where I shall seek to sketch out some key elements in my understanding of Ethiopian land tenure, elements which are put to use in the later chapters.

LAND TENURE AND PEASANT LIVELIHOODS

Highland peasant agriculture is structured in a way that can be easily misunderstood when analysed by concepts rooted in other realities. We may refer to all rural inhabitants as peasants, but we go systematically wrong if we think of them all as farmers. To approach this issue, we need a clear understanding of the household, the farm, and peasant land rights.

Households are dynamic units, and this applies with force to the Ethiopian highlands where individualism results in rather small and unstable households.[15] The aim of young men is to marry and set up an independent household. They then establish their own farm, often with strong links to the parent household, but these links are to a large extent external links between households. In surveys they may appear as market relations or as relations of dependence between rich and poor, depending on the analytical perspective. The situation is further complicated by equal inheritance. Generational transfer has varied greatly with official policy, and inheritance has always been conditional on official recognition, but the legitimacy of the principle of equal inheritance is strong. This means that the farm is not a stable trans-generational unit; it is intimately linked to the household cycle.

If the farm had been managed by multi-generational extended households, many relations that are now managed by contracts between households could have been solved within the household. Instead, we have the typical trajectory where the young man first undertakes primary household accumulation while living with his parents (as discussed earlier in this chapter). When he marries, the young couple receives some land from their parents. This initial land endowment is rarely enough, and they have to rent in additional land, perhaps from their own parents. If one of the parents is a widow or an elderly man, it is highly likely that most of the land will be farmed by a son or son-in-law on rental terms. When the formal landowner can no longer perform the household chores, he or she merges with one of the inheriting households. In many agricultural systems, these processes take place on the farm, but in the northern highlands of Ethiopia they take the form of transactions and relations between households.

The issue of land rights is quite complex due to the social upheaval of the land reform and frequent policy changes thereafter, changes which are unfortunately ill documented. It is often claimed that peasants had only usufruct rights after the nationalization of land. The problem with this view is not just that it is wrong, but that it also takes the focus away from the practical rights of the peasants.

Under the Därg, a peasant could have only one land holding, or 'tax name' (*semä geber*). In many places, this policy was in principle also

[15] The main study of the household cycle in an Ethiopia peasant community is Bauer (1985). See also Hoben (1973: 63) and the general model of Fortes (1969) on the household cycle.

enforced by the new government. In North Shäwa the principle of only one holding per household was the basis for land rights registered for the 1997 land redistribution; any additional holding was confiscated. However, surprisingly enough, this redistribution under the EPRDF abolished the policy of a single tax name per household. One of the major features of this redistribution was the household approach, or more precisely, the 'virtual household' approach. Every household which received land was to get 4 *t'emad* of land (1 hectare), without regard for household size. Furthermore, all unmarried adults were thought of as half households and entitled to 2 *t'emad*, so that when they married they would have the standard household endowment. Finally, any unmarried woman with a child was considered a full household. While the basic unit of the reform was the household, the link between real households and land holdings was broken (Ege 1997b: 105). My neighbour in Wäyra Amba received only half a household endowment since he married just after the reform, while others were assigned the land of three virtual households for one real household.

In Tegray and the northern half of Amhara, the EPRDF had implemented land redistribution as they conquered territory from the retreating Därg. Here we also find the same type of household approach (see Chapter 5 for a case study). The resulting pattern of land ownership is well represented by tax lists gathered in North Wälo. In three communes investigated, 50–53 per cent of land holdings were 2 *t'emad* or less, and 2 *t'emad* was the standard land holding for a single adult (Aspen and Ege 2010: 25, 55, 82). These small holdings will mainly have been allotted to unmarried youngsters, who might well continue to reside with their parents, although quite a few had left the land with their parents while they sought for better livelihoods elsewhere. The same applies to elderly persons or those who could not or would not live independently. Thus, it was not uncommon to find a farmer who paid tax for two or three landowners, all appearing as separate households in the tax list (e.g. Aspen and Ege 2010: 30). These arrangements are quite complicated and somewhat sensitive, and surveys will often miss much relevant information. When asked, the respondent may well report only his or her own land, not that of a child's or an old mother's or other relative living with the household. When it comes to household size, however, the informant is rather more likely to include everybody as his or her household members.

The EPRDF land redistributions have resulted in micro-holdings, i.e. land holdings which are too small to making a living on. It is less clear whether they have resulted in micro-farms, which takes us from land ownership to operated farms. A farm – the land operated by a farmer – may consist of only his own holding, but it may also include one or more holdings belonging to household members or relatives, resident or not. In many cases the household also depends on renting in additional land. This is a result of economic stress and little more than a survival strategy, but due to 'inverse tenancy', i.e. the fact that tenants are on average better off than landowners, this has often been interpreted as some kind of exploitation and accumulation. Such an understanding is highly problematic, both theoretically and empirically.

Generally, when we talk about tenants, we tend to think of oppressed peasants being dependent on rich, often aristocratic landowners, as was the case in many parts of Ethiopia until the land reform of 1975. However, after the land reform, those who rent out land are mainly individuals who are unable to farm the land themselves (women, elderly, sick). There is thus a class of very poor landowners. However, the land rent is high; in fact, a half share is the most common rent for tenants in Ethiopia, and it is difficult to see how the tenants can be anything but poor – although the landowners themselves might be even poorer. It would also appear strange that tenants are not exploited when a very considerable part of their labour is expropriated by the landowner. The poverty of the landowner does not improve the tenant's situation; rather, the opposite is true. First of all, there is great competition for land even with the harsh conditions of half shares, a well-known complaint by peasants, and measured quite accurately by the economists under the heading 'rationing of tenants' (Hosaena and Holden 2009: 75, 83, 90). Secondly, given the landowners' poverty, they cannot offer support to their tenants in times of distress as they sometimes did in the past (see example in Chapter 5).

The land rent is high, arguably so high that it would not be easy to survive on the basis of income from rented land alone. This is not surprising since many households with a fair land holding struggle to survive even though they can keep all the produce for themselves. It is quite exceptional for a farming household to live from rented land only, and in their presentation of survey data the economists routinely treat the tenants as tenants-cum-owners (e.g. Gebrehaweria and Holden 2011: 47; Deininger *et al.* 2011a).[16] Pure tenants seem to be virtually non-existent, or so few that they are not worthy of any category.[17] This has considerable theoretical implications. If a farmer cannot live from rented land alone, it is problematic to argue that he uses his capital (oxen) to exploit his unfortunate ox-less neighbours, which is the essence both of the ox argument and the common interpretation of tenancy relations in Ethiopia. If the share kept by the farmer is less than what it takes to reproduce the farming household with its resources, we have to rethink how we conceptualize tenancy relations in contemporary Ethiopia.

[16] See also Aspen (1993: 34), which may be the first study of tenancy relations after the land reform, and Aspen and Ege (2010: 56, 82–4). Most probably, a farmer of prime age and good health provided with a pair of oxen and with the right household composition could survive by sharecropping alone. But placing the household in a time perspective shows that this is not sustainable for long. In old age, if not before, the elderly farmer with nothing but his dwindling labour would face certain death. This is simply not the way Ethiopian peasant society works.

[17] In the study by Deininger *et al.* (2011a), the landless comprise only 2% of all households. This figure may very well include persons who in practice have access to land free of charge (e.g. in the form of *gulma*, in this case when a child receives land from its parents). See Chapter 3 on land rights.

Basically, we have a situation where many farmers cannot live from their holding alone; they must seek to rent in land on conditions so harsh that it is, in isolation, a deficit operation. To capture this situation, it is useful to think of the farmer's own holding as a livelihoods platform. The farms of tenants consist of two types of land, own holdings and rented land; the former is a necessary platform in order to rent in land, while the latter is necessary for the survival of the family. Based on the common land rent, we could theorize that farming activities as such are remunerated by half the produce, which has to cover all production costs in addition to 'profit', which is negative. The 50 per cent land rent theoretically paid by the farmer to himself on his own holding then subsidizes this deficit operation and makes the household break even in its total farm operation. Understanding this practice could open up a new type of tenancy studies to shed important light on the production equation of Ethiopian farmers.

The platform argument fits well with the picture of the Chayanovian self-exploiting peasant: the peasant is not a profit-maximizing agent, but a human being who has to provide for his family at any cost (Chayanov 1986). In a strained situation, peasants will invest their labour far beyond the point indicated by the theory of marginal returns. Chayanov confirmed his theory by showing how the area a household farmed varied with household size and consumption needs, in a situation where land was rather abundant but of decreasing fertility. In our case land is scarce, and rented land is available only on very onerous terms, probably with a sharper decline in return for the farmer's labour than in Chayanov's case. But although it is a deficit operation, the few extra sacks of grain the Ethiopian farmer harvests are of vital importance for the wellbeing of his family.

So far, we have investigated tenancy mainly from the point of view of the farmers who are notably healthy and strong males. The same basic picture emerges if we consider the situation of the landowners who rent out land. According to the standard narrative, many households lack the resources, namely oxen, to farm their land. This is accurate but may also be misleading. The preference for independence means that many peasant households are not farming households and not even aspiring farming households. Some of these households will at any time by headed by widows, divorcees, handicapped, ill persons and elderly persons. But rather than being poor just because they lack oxen, we should see these categories of peasants as naturally ox-less, non-farming landowners (Ege and Aspen 2003: 41–2).[18] Seen as part of the total peasant community, they appear as dependents, unable to survive unless they are able to benefit from the labour of the strong and able farmers (*gobäz gäbäré*), who are the typical tenants and the economic backbone of peasant society.

[18] In Ch'orisa commune we estimated the naturally ox-less to comprise 26% of all households.

Given other elements of Ethiopian peasant society, tenancy is an institution of critical importance. Due to household processes, rented land will make up a considerable share of the total farmland. There will be an almost irresistible tendency in this direction even in a situation that starts out with owner-cultivators, as basically happened after the land reform inspired by the 'land-to-the-tiller' slogan. In the early stage, households in principle received land according to their household size, and tenancy was rare and limited to exceptional cases (e.g. female landowners).[19] By the late Därg period, sharecropping was rather widespread; in Yefat we recorded figures indicating that about 10 per cent of the land was sharecropped, ranging from 6 per cent to 20 per cent in the fourteen communes studied (Ege 1994b: 171; Aspen 1993: 36, 42). The land redistributions organized by the TPLF and later the EPRDF had a different design and did not contain any restrictions on renting out land, partly because many beneficiaries were non-farming supporters of the guerrillas. Thus, there was a higher share of land renting from the very beginning. Over time, the two systems tend to converge due to household processes.

The central feature of tenancy in this context is that it provides for those who cannot farm themselves. They are typically very poor in farm assets, but are not much worse off than others in terms of consumption. In fact, the average calorie intake of Ethiopian farmers is so low that it leaves little room for social differentiation within the peasant community. Chiari, who applied a stratification approach, presented data indicating quite small differences in grain production per capita.[20] There are of course differences, but it is not differences between rigid categories that can be meaningfully captured by class-like analysis.

Household processes structure peasant society, but this does not mean that everybody passes through the same stages and that there is no differentiation. When doing empirical investigations, we have to consider three different elements: the household cycle, social differentiation and historical change. Our frustration with the current body of literature is that the same argument has been repeated over and over again and applied to widely different situations, feudal Ethiopia, famine situations, surplus-producing areas, and the present-day, without really being checked or confirmed against what is happening on the ground. We return to issues of household processes, social differentiation and historical change in later chapters.

[19] Land tenancy was allowed for in the proclamation, a point often missed in accounts of the land reform. In those early years there was actually little general need for land rentals, and it would certainly be contrary not only to the letter of the law, but also to the very logic of the 'land-to-the-tiller' principle of the land reform. How could one, in the same law, transfer all land held in tenancy to the tenants (the primary aspect of the land reform), and at the same time permit the new holders to rent out the land to tenants?

[20] If we take the very poor as our starting point, the production of grain per capita for the poor, middle and rich was higher by only 2%, 9% and 36%, respectively (Chiari 2003: 211–12).

We have seen in this chapter that much of the literature has been characterized by a certain external view of rural Ethiopia and dominated by the survey method. By contrast, the next chapter takes us deep into peasant society, specifically the land strategies of peasants and the particular resulting system of land tenure. It offers a reinterpretation of land tenure under the Därg by presenting the *dersha* system of land tenure as an alternative theory, locally grounded in survey data and peasant accounts from Ayné in North Shäwa.

3

The *Dersha*[1] System: Rethinking Land Tenure under the Därg

SVEIN EGE

The dominant understanding of land tenure after the land reform is that there were periodic land redistributions, notably to accommodate youngsters coming of age. This has significant policy implications due to the tenure insecurity such a system would have created. In this chapter, I argue that this is a theory without evidence. Lack of evidence does not by itself falsify the theory, but there is clearly a need for its proponents to provide positive evidence. I also show how one community, which superficially fits the redistribution model, actually worked according to a different principle, the *dersha* ('share') principle. This case is developed into an alternative interpretation. The discussion takes us deep into the issue of peasant land tenure by showing how peasants gained access to and sought to preserve their control over their land, all within the general framework of state land ownership.

The *dersha* theory is developed based on evidence from Ayné in North Shäwa. This is a core Amhara area, although pre-reform land tenure here was individualized inheritance (*rest*), not the more communal variant usually associated with the Amhara, which is based on Hoben's (1973) description of a community in Gojam.[2] There is also positive evidence of the *dersha* system existing in Gojam and other Amhara areas (see Chapter 4). However, the evidence from the other regions of Ethiopia is not precise enough to settle the issue.

There is therefore a strong need to reconsider the received understanding of peasant land tenure in Ethiopia. This does not hinge on the occurrence of the *dersha* system. Future empirical research may identify specific communities where periodic redistribution took place, although the material presented below makes this the least likely outcome. Alternatively, it may show that the *dersha* system represented the standard version of the land reform, which seems counterintuitive in view of Ethiopia's great ecological, cultural and social variation. Finally, there may have developed a number of locally grounded property systems,

[1] *Dersha* translates as 'share'. In this land tenure system, all household members had a claim to a share in the household holding.

[2] I refer to it as 'communal' because *rest* rights were via the kinship group, represented by group officials. In the individual *rest*, land was held directly from the state. In both cases land was hereditary.

probably variants of family-based property, which would seem the most likely outcome. If so, we need to specify the constituent features of these systems. Even if researchers may ultimately confine the *dersha* system to certain communities, cultures or regions, the theory outlined in this chapter will be useful to contrast and precisely identify the elements that shape the various peasant land tenure systems.

REDISTRIBUTION THEORY

Since the early 1980s, periodic land redistribution[3] has figured prominently in descriptions of the land tenure system established by the 1975 land reform. This is repeated in virtually all comprehensive summaries of the land tenure system, and therefore appears as both the most significant and the best-known element of land tenure under the Därg.[4] Any scholar who approaches the issue of land tenure is thus likely to adopt this view and apply it to his study area. The fact that it is so widespread automatically makes the theory appear well founded. A closer look, however, shows that the evidence is weak and the reasoning underpinning this model is rather questionable.

The theory of periodic redistribution works according to a rather simple logic. With the land reform proclamation of 1975, land was nationalized. Peasants were organized into communes (*qäbälé* peasant associations), which became the local administrative units, and peasant households held their land as members of these associations. There was an initial redistribution of land which, despite some venality, did away with the multitude of traditional land tenure systems and generally established uniform land tenure and a remarkably equal pattern of holdings. This system was vulnerable, however. The land of the commune was fixed, while the population was growing. Youngsters came of age, married and clamoured for land for their new households. There was thus a pressure for new rounds of land redistribution, and in most areas of Ethiopia peasants can tell of two to three or even more rounds of redistribution.[5]

3 In this chapter, I use 'redistribution' to refer to a somewhat comprehensive process of land transfers, notably for the purpose of improving equity; I use 'reallocation' for any transfer of land ownership rights, for any purpose and even if small in size.

4 See descriptions in Dessalegn (1984: 42), Clapham (1988: 160) and Bruce *et al.* (1994: xiv, 5). This view was recently restated by Dessalegn (2008: 238) and this account has become a standard part of the writings of economists (see footnote 7 in this chapter).

5 See Dessalegn (1984: 42; 1997: 4). Note that this theory was based on fieldwork conducted in 1981, while the land reform took place mainly in 1975–77. Due to the short time lapse since the reform, which was too short for demography to have had much impact, it could scarcely be a description of existing practices. Rather, it represented a projection of how the system would develop, and I have not found any evidence in the research literature documenting that this is what happened.

The description above, if true, would have serious policy implications. It would have been a strikingly expensive system in terms of administrative efforts and political turmoil.[6] Within such a model, there is no tenure security, since every few years there may be new rounds of redistribution. Mining the soil becomes utterly rational. Investments in soil conservation or good land management, on the other hand, are not likely to pay off. On a theoretical level, this is an open access model. Peasants use the land to achieve maximum short-term gains, since they do not directly reap the long-term benefits or face the penalties of their individual acts. They also have many children, with all the benefits this brings, while the community pays the price of increasing population pressure. There is therefore a race towards the bottom, where every attempt to redress the problems of the new households pushes average holdings downwards, resulting in starvation plots (see, notably, Dessalegn 1997). On the other hand, if there is no redistribution for some time, landlessness will rise to alarming levels. Towards the end of the Därg period, land redistribution reportedly ebbed out and was at last formally stopped. A few years later, there were reports that landlessness had reached a staggering 50 per cent (Bruce *et al.* 1994: 12; Degefa 2003: 7). Such data would point towards an extreme case of trade-off between equity and efficiency, with no obvious solution, although it must create a preference for efficiency – simply because the more palatable emphasis on equity will lead to a Malthusian disaster – within the model, that is.

The popularity of this model must be attributed to at least two factors. First of all, it is highly captivating. It is easy to understand and it appears logical, although it is doubtful whether any peasant community ever operated according to such principles, for the very reasons specified by the model itself: it would tend to lead to disaster, and peasants mostly have too good an understanding of their own situation to engage in such destructive activities. Secondly, the model is highly useful in at least two sets of arguments: the environmentalist narrative and the privatization narrative. Both, quite correctly, emphasize tenure security, and a system based on periodic land redistribution is obviously the opposite. The theory of periodic land redistribution provides an explanation for the problems observed and is therefore a good starting point for proposing reforms.[7] Since the model is so useful, it appears that it has never been empirically tested, or even questioned. In fact, it has not even been described in reasonable detail. Any attempt

[6] Surprisingly enough, the administrative aspect has not been much discussed in the literature. It is highly questionable whether the local administration would have the capacity to monitor land tenure and regularly update the system as implied in the model.

[7] Thus, in the recent studies by economists, periodic redistribution is the prominent aspect of land tenure under the Därg, repeated again and again in standardized historical accounts. For a few examples, see Deininger *et al.* (2003a: 8–9), Berhanu Nega *et al.* (2003: 109), Benin and Pender (2009: 217) and Holden *et al.* (2011: 33).

to do so would probably show that it could scarcely have worked in practice.

The discussion above refers to the rather precise formulation of the theory of periodic land redistribution. There are other strands of the argument. One is the theory of the decreasing land fund: there was an initial period of land redistribution, but as the land fund was depleted, it became ever more difficult to satisfy the new claimants. After some time, the only land available was the holdings of people who died (Yared 1995a: 42–7; *ibid.* 1995b: 7–9; Aklilu and Tadesse 1994: 39–44; Birhanu and Mamo 2010: 105). This is a description much closer to empirical reality, and it can make the basic facts fit into the account, but it is not very clear on peasant land rights and it seems to hinge on the theory of periodic redistribution in its negative state. It is the same underlying elements, with the difference that there was no further redistribution, with obvious problems for equity.[8] Yeraswork (2000: 194–8) takes a somewhat different approach. The many rounds of redistribution are a key element in his study. Superficially, his account might seem to support the image of periodic redistribution, but his emphasis is actually on the many secondary reforms, like villagization and the formation of producer cooperatives; in other words, it fits what I have described as specific-purpose redistribution (see Chapter 4).

Despite their differences, the various strands of the redistribution argument tend to flow together and thus reinforce the dominant view of a system of periodic land redistribution. However, some important questions are left unanswered by these accounts. What precisely is meant by periodic? Does it refer to a regularly occurring pattern, as specified in regulations or driven by population dynamics, or is it simply the occasional occurrence of redistribution (or reallocation) for whatever reason? And what is meant by 'redistribution'? Does it refer to a comprehensive confiscation-distribution process for improved equity, as in my use of the term, or to any confiscation of land or land rights? There is a great disjuncture between the theoretical narrative, with its image of continuous administrative redistribution to accommodate those coming of age, and the empirical accounts of redistribution, which often cast the net wide in their practical definition of redistribution. By doing so, the latter may capture many instances of 'redistribution', but these are practices which can in no way support the theoretical argument of periodic redistribution.

In some locations, large-scale redistributions did happen, but they seem to have been cases of specific-purpose redistribution, typically

[8] Yared's most extended account (1995a: 42–7), one of the best descriptions available, is empirically very similar to my description of Ayné below, but the underlying model is a weak variant of the land redistribution theory. My own first account of the land tenure system (Ege 1990: 228–35) also fits the image of comprehensive redistribution in the early Därg period. The emphasis on pressure for new land redistribution is especially prominent in Aklilu and Tadesse (1994: 43–4).

occasioned by the establishment or dissolution of producer cooperatives (Yeraswork 2000: 201–17; Teferi 1998: 57–60; Poluha 1989: 137; Bekalu 1994: 66). If we treat specific-purpose redistribution as a separate category from general-purpose, equity-driven redistribution, working by a different logic, we will have excluded practically all the empirical material that might otherwise be taken as evidence in support of the theory of periodic redistribution. Furthermore, if we also limit 'redistribution' to the assignment of possessory rights in land the peasants did not formerly own or cultivate, we may also have excluded the standard version of the initial 'land redistribution' following the 1975 land reform. In principle the land reform was accompanied by land redistribution, but the key aspect of the reform was to bestow possessory rights on the farmer who was already cultivating the land. The actual amount of land transferred from one farming household to another may have been very limited (Pausewang 1990: 45; see also the case of Ayné below[9]).

The ethnographic literature provides an instructive contrast to the more general literature on land tenure. If periodic land redistributions were widespread, one would expect to find many case studies in this literature. Access to land is after all of vital concern for peasants and would be highly relevant for any ethnographic account, be it of the local economy or the political system. Locally, a recent or impending land redistribution would be the talk of the day, which researchers doing fieldwork could scarcely fail to notice. A telling example is therefore Poluha who did fieldwork in a peasant community in Gojam in 1980–81 and commented that the land reform was then a thing of the past and not of much concern to the peasants any longer (Poluha 1989: 13). Also other ethnographic descriptions from this period show few traces of land redistribution as an issue for the local community. The ethnographers were busy reporting what they had heard and observed, and this took them in quite different directions, often to the new issues of producer cooperatives or villagization.[10] Sometimes land redistribution creeps into accounts based on fieldwork, but then the picture of land redistribution seems to be more based on references to the general literature than on careful analysis of their own fieldwork material.[11] The emerging pattern is that the more intensive

9 I have not found data on this key aspect of the land reform, but Pausewang's observation seems to be generally accepted.

10 For example, see Poluha (1989; fieldwork in 1980–81), Mengistu (1986; fieldwork in 1981–84), Helen Pankhurst (1992; fieldwork in 1988–89), Aspen (1993; main fieldwork in 1989) and Frehiwot (1998; fieldwork in 1992–94). Partial exceptions are Yared (1995a) and Teferi (1998). It is significant that the latter two based their descriptions of land redistribution on retrospective evidence. Their understanding seems to be heavily coloured by the standard account of periodic land redistribution prevalent in the literature.

11 For example, see Bekalu (1994: 61), Aklilu and Tadesse (1994: 43) and Degefa (2005, compare the summary on p. 133 with the concrete description on pp. 158–9 and p. 164). Some field-based accounts provide material that contradicts redistribution theory, although this does not appear to be clear to the authors

the fieldwork, the less relevant is the theory of periodic land redistribution, in any of its forms. This is rather strong evidence, although circumstantial only.

Notwithstanding its weak empirical basis, the force of redistribution theory is considerable. It does appear to explain many observations relating to tenure insecurity. However, it does so by misreading the evidence, such as counting any kind of land reallocation as evidence of equity-driven redistribution, or taking politically generated high figures of 'landlessness' as evidence of a significant pressure for land redistribution.[12]

In the following, I shall first demonstrate that the data from Ayné seemingly support the redistribution theory better than most locations. Then I shall show that the land tenure system was not in fact characterized by periodic land redistribution, and that elements underpinning such an interpretation can better be explained by the theory of the *dersha* system. Such a reinterpretation may have significant policy implications because it shows that peasant land tenure was well regulated and tended towards tenure security and well-defined rights – unless they were overruled by heavy-handed policy initiatives which might lead to specific-purpose redistribution.

REDISTRIBUTION THEORY APPLIED TO THE AYNÉ DATA

Ayné commune is located in North Shäwa, some eight kilometres north of Däbrä Sina town. Various other sites in northern Ethiopia have been covered by the literature, and the picture emerging from some of these studies is that there were several rounds of land redistribution.[13] My own study from Ayné (Ege 1990) could also easily be taken as empirical proof; it identified at least four stages of land redistribution, notably the land proclamation (*yä-märét awaj*), the land equalizing committee

(contd) themselves; for example, see Ege (1990: 228–32), Aspen (1993: 31–2, 48), Yared (1995a: 42–7) and Yeraswork (2000: 193–207).

12 Figures on the landless are given earlier in the chapter. The view of a locally generated pressure for land redistribution is based on the imagined rights of youngsters to receive land from the commune so that they can establish their households. This was not actually a permanent right, but a right which might apply if redistribution took place. Rumours of redistribution therefore tended to produce many 'landless', individuals positioning themselves as legitimate claimants for land. This happened after the fall of the Därg and the coming of a regime that had built its political constituency on a version of land reform favouring this particular group. The few quality reports we have of these early EPRDF reforms indicate, however, that they were far from popular (Yeraswork 2000: 208–11; Teferi 1998: 64). The atmosphere created by rumours of land redistribution is well captured by Teferi (1997: 4–5).

13 See Markos (1997: 67), Degefa (2005: 133) and Yeraswork (2000: 194). Yeraswork, however, contrasts the high incidence of land redistribution in North Wälo with a much lower incidence in North Shäwa. Such differences may be due to the specific communities selected for the study.

(*yä-märét dälday komité*), border delimitation (*qeyes)*, and 'land redistribution' (*shegesheg*).[14] At this level there is thus nothing setting Ayné apart from the general pattern of periodic land redistribution. As we shall see, if anything, the data might be taken to show more, rather than less, redistribution compared to the average Ethiopian commune. Ayné thus serves well as a critical test case for the theory of periodic redistribution. I shall illustrate this by applying an approach common to land redistribution analysis.[15]

In empirical studies, the occurrence of land redistribution has usually been analysed on the household level, recording whether the household has experienced land redistribution or not. In other words, the loss (and perhaps even the gain) of single parcels of land leads to the same score as would a major change in the household holdings. This is a serious weakness and such data should be interpreted with great care. The problem is even worse in those studies that report the occurrence of land redistribution on the commune level. In this case, a minor reallocation of land affecting a few households, or even a few parcels of land, may be counted as 'redistribution'. By contrast, my land data from Ayné are on the level of individual parcels of land. This makes it possible to compare analysis on the level of households and on the level of individual parcels. The impact on the results is quite surprising.

The following data would indicate more land redistribution in Ayné than what has, to my knowledge, been documented for any community in Ethiopia. For the period 1975–89 (i.e. including the land reform itself), 98 per cent of all households had experienced changes in their land holdings. 'Change' in holding is a commonly used measure of tenure insecurity.[16] More surprisingly, if the analysis period starts in 1976, after the land reform, 90 per cent had experienced change. Finally, even by strictly limiting the data to those who had lost land in

[14] *Shegesheg* has a wide use and is difficult to translate precisely. Since 'redistribution' and 'reallocation' have already been defined for theoretical purposes, I keep the Amharic term to convey both the specific term used in the sources and its vagueness.

[15] For the following exercise, I use the same data as for my 1990 paper on Ayné, i.e. my field survey in 1989 ('GM 1989'). The survey in question was based on a 25% random sample of male-headed households and 50% of female-headed households in Ayné commune. In total, 63 households were interviewed. Weighted for gender, the total number (N) was 50.5 households. The survey registered 390 parcels of land in total, converted to 324 parcels when weighted for gender. This includes land owned and land cultivated by tenancy at the time of the survey or at any time in the past. The data, descriptions and relevant calculations are stored in N6779 in my archive. (See the Bibliography for information on my surveys). For some summary data and ethnographic details, I refer to an unfinished, more detailed draft of the land tenure history of Ayné (Ege 2011).

[16] In the literature, it is all too common to refer to 'change' which could also include gains. It is rarely clear whether that is indeed the intent or if it is use of imprecise language.

the period 1976–89, the figure is as high as 60 per cent of households. By comparison, EFAP (1991: 46), subscribing to the view that there were frequent rounds of land redistribution, cited as evidence data that 37 per cent of farmers had experienced changes in holdings during the period 1976–86, i.e. much less than the 90 per cent in Ayné.[17] However, if the EFAP figure is correct, land reallocation must have been the exception in Ethiopia, not the rule, and is not consistent with the view of periodic or even frequent land redistribution – if the latter is understood as comprehensive processes to achieve or maintain equity, which is the impression one gathers from the EFAP analysis. Similarly, if we counted rounds of 'redistribution' in Ayné, we would probably count all the four mentioned above, and potentially more. Yet the argument presented here is that there was land reform in Ayné but no land redistribution in the stricter sense, i.e. a somewhat comprehensive process of transfer of parcels of land from land-rich farming households to the land-poor.

Land redistribution entails both gains and losses. It is thus fair to include both elements in order to capture the underlying system. From the perspective of tenure security, however, the risk of losing land takes on special importance. If there were periodic redistributions, we would expect peasants to have lost land repeatedly, perhaps receiving other land in return. The data as currently presented, provide some, although weak, support for this. We saw above that 60 per cent of households had lost some land. However, most of them lost land only once. Of all households, 40 per cent had not lost land, 37 per cent had lost land once, 21 per cent had lost land twice, and 3 per cent had lost land on three occasions. This could at most be consistent with two rounds of somewhat comprehensive land redistribution.[18]

What these data do not show, however, is why peasants lost or gained land. Searching for the answer, I shall present the *dersha* theory, a theory about a new local land tenure system. In doing so, I shall use the same data as above, but broken down at the parcel level. The analysis is also heavily influenced by observations made and key informant interviews conducted later in Ayné and other parts of the Yefat escarpment. This analysis will take us from an understanding of peasants captured in an open access system of periodic land redistribution to a system of rather well-defined rights, tenure security, household processes and strategic actors. As this gradually became clear to me, I suddenly understood the way that the peasants were talking about land. The *dersha* theory thus explains the observed behaviour and is confirmed by the peasants themselves.

[17] The period for Ayné ends in 1989 while the EFAP coverage ends in 1986. This is highly unlikely to have much impact on the data because most changes had happened by 1986. The detailed data for Ayné presented below document this well.

[18] The period covered is 1977–89. If we had counted the number of parcels lost, the figures would be higher, with a few farmers having lost as many as five parcels after the land reform.

LAND REFORM IN AYNÉ

The theory of the *dersha* system is formulated on the basis of peasant behaviour as it was observed in Ayné. The land reform process started with the proclamation in April 1975 and may be conveniently divided into two phases: 'land-to-the-tiller', and 'the land equalizing committee' – or the land reform itself and then what is usually thought of as the first land redistribution. This corresponds to the first two phases captured in my 1990 paper.[19] The reform during the first phase meant that the land, as of the date of the proclamation, belonged to the farmer who had been tilling it. This radical reform had a considerable element of self-implementation. There was a period of class struggle and uncertainty, but once the peasants in an area were convinced that this was the policy of a government that was going to stay, the reform could be implemented simply by their ceasing to pay the land rent. This phase did not require elaborate administrative processes. It did not redistribute farming rights to specific parcels, and since the old land tax was replaced by a flat tax on all farming households, it did not even require an inventory of the parcels of each farmer, only a register of the members of the peasant association, which was for all practical purposes the tax list.[20]

This initial stage did, however, have a profound effect on peasant society, which changed from a class-based society to a society of almost-equal farmers. In Ayné, my estimates indicate that roughly half of all parcels were held on sharecropping terms before the land reform, in what had been a deeply feudal society. In my survey, undertaken in 1989, informants reported that 32.6 per cent of lands ever farmed or owned were theirs before the land reform, while 32.8 per cent had been acquired in the year of the land reform (see Figure 3.1). The remaining lands they acquired between 1976 and 1989. In our context, it is the balance between the first two categories that is of interest. The third category refers to changes of ownership status after the land reform, and there is no reason to believe that the balance between owned land and sharecropped land at the time of the land reform for this category would deviate much from the general pattern. The emerging picture of widespread tenancy is consistent with the general historical background of the area. While the northern highlands are usually associated with communities of peasants with land rights via kinship groups, tenancy, on quite harsh terms, was widespread in this part of North Shäwa.[21]

It follows from the 'land-to-the-tiller' principle that active farmers tended to gain the most. Farmers of prime age, with large households and able to farm much land typically ended up with good holdings. Old landowners in the retirement phase who were renting out part of their

[19] This design was clearly modelled on what took place during the Russian Revolution.

[20] I visited a number of communes but never found an independent register of members that was different from the tax list.

[21] For a broader historical account, see Ege (1996: 63–5).

land might suffer considerable loss. Young households typically had good initial land ratios per person, but the total land holding tended to be quite moderate, and they were exposed to considerable strains as the size of the family grew.

There were strict limits to how much land a farming household could farm efficiently by traditional technology. My estimate is that the tipping point was usually about 2.5 hectares for a fully endowed household with two oxen and fair labour supply.[22] After this, extra labour was required. Those who owned significantly more land would usually rent out some of it, even if they were active farmers themselves. This meant that after the first phase of the reform, the maximum limit of holdings set by the land reform proclamation, 10 hectares for a household, tended to become irrelevant. A good illustration is that the largest holding in Ayné after the first stage of the land reform was 3.5 hectares.[23]

About a year after the initial land reform, the peasants were made to elect a land equalizing committee (hereafter LEC), *yä-märét dälday komité*.[24] The task of the LEC was to register all households, including members and land, and to equalize holdings as much as possible. In Ayné this was a slow and careful process, lasting from the summer of 1976 until 1979. Representatives were elected from each locality, which meant that practically everyone had a friend or relative on the committee. The LEC surveyed all the households and their land in the area, and there was a local appeal system to ensure fair results. If the issue could not be solved locally, the district administration might be called in by individual peasants.

It was decided, probably by the district administration after consultations with peasant representatives, that every person would be entitled to 1.5 *t'emad* of land. In Gänät commune south of Däbrä Sina, the standard appears to have been 1 *t'emad* (0.25 hectares).[25] While the standards within areas of the *dersha* system were probably always somewhat above the average amount of land available, this was a remarkably equal goal with a maximum limit set just above the mathematical average. In the case of Ayné, the average amount of land per person, according to the register of the LEC, was 1.36 *t'emad*.[26]

22 The average land size, which includes the old, the ill and female-headed households with weak labour endowment, will necessarily be much lower.

23 These data are from D186, Registers of the Land Equalizing Committee (further discussed in the next paragraph). When converting from *t'emad* to hectares, I have used the standard conversion rate where 4 *t'emad* equals 1 hectare.

24 In some other areas, such as Baba Säat, the settlement of land issues was done by the leadership committee itself. This would often be an indication of a less comprehensive process.

25 On Ayné, D3080: 2, S'ägayé Eshäté (see the Bibliography for details on my interview notations and archives). S'ägayé was the secretary of the commune for much of the Därg period, a much-consulted elder, and an unusually good informant. On Gänät, see Aspen (1993: 32).

26 The LEC registered 281 names (D186) in total. Some are duplicate entries and some are incomplete. My calculations refer to the remaining 274 house

The LEC registered households and members. In view of the literature, which has focused on the formation of new households, it may be worth pointing out that it did not matter, in theory at least, whether a person was registered as a household head or as a member of a household. Formally, land rights were the same for everyone. The LEC started with the tax register for 1976 (1968 E.C.), but adapted the registration of households according to the requests of the concerned parties. If a youngster had married and wanted to be registered as a separate household, the parents were consulted and the young household was registered separately, with members and land. The trade-off was that they would then have to start paying the land tax.[27]

As a result of this registration, some parcels did actually change hands. This initial adjustment has therefore often been referred to as land redistribution, and I myself used to believe that this was *the* major land redistribution. However, this term conjures up a picture that ill fits the process. Very few parcels were actually transferred. According to my survey, only 0.5 per cent of all parcels were specifically reported to have been assigned by the LEC.[28] Even if we add together all parcels that informants reported as becoming theirs, for whatever reason, for the period 1976–79 (1968–71 E.C.), we end up with only 9.9 per cent in total. It would thus seem that the share of parcels transferred by the LEC was somewhere between 0.5 and 9.9 per cent, most probably in the lower half.[29]

It is significant that the figures discussed above include transfers by ordinary household processes, such as inheritance or the formation of new households. In fact the figures are not higher than what one would expect from such processes alone. In some accounts of land redistribution, it appears as if such processes, notably if they involved transfer of land from a defunct household (see vacancy, or *motä käda* below), are included in the concept of land redistribution, but then the concept itself changes meaning and cannot support the implications usually drawn from the theory of periodic or frequent redistributions.[30]

Another way of approaching the data is to check when households became owners of their plots. If there were repeated comprehensive

(contd) holds, registered with 1,097 members (including heads) and 1,490 *t'emad* of land, which yields an average land holding per household of 5.44 *t'emad*. The register is discussed in some detail in Ege (2011: 19–27).

27 D3080: 3, S'ägayé Eshäté.

28 There is considerable scope for misunderstanding here. My data refer only to parcels assigned by the LEC that had previously belonged to someone else. However, in principle all land was assigned by the LEC, even when that meant simply confirming existing ownership (*rest*) rights or the possessory right bestowed on the tenant after the land reform proclamation.

29 The annual figures were: 1976, 3.3%; 1977, 1.7%; 1978, 2.9%; and 1979, 2.0%. The LEC started in late 1976 and it is likely that little or no land was transferred in 1976. The committee was formally dissolved at some point in 1979. In other words, the figure of 9.9% is a high estimate.

30 For examples of such wide application of 'redistribution', see EFAP (1991: 46) and Aklilu and Tadesse (1994: 43). Most accounts and surveys are so imprecise that it is impossible to know exactly what is included under 'redistribution'.

redistributions, most lands would be traced back to the last round of redistribution, i.e. be of rather recent origin. If there were rounds of more limited reallocation, they should show up as marked bumps in the relevant years.

Figure 3.1 shows in detail when the respondents became owners of their lands, including lands no longer held. As shown above, it was reported that 32.6 per cent of these parcels were acquired before the land reform, typically inherited from their parents (during 1916–74). Another 32.8 per cent of land was acquired through the land reform itself (in 1975), having farmed them as tenants until then. By contrast, the year most associated with the work of the LEC, 1977, shows surprisingly low figures. This is wholly incompatible with the view that this was a major land redistribution. It was an event of great social significance because it established a new land tenure system, but it led to minimal transfer of parcels of land.[31]

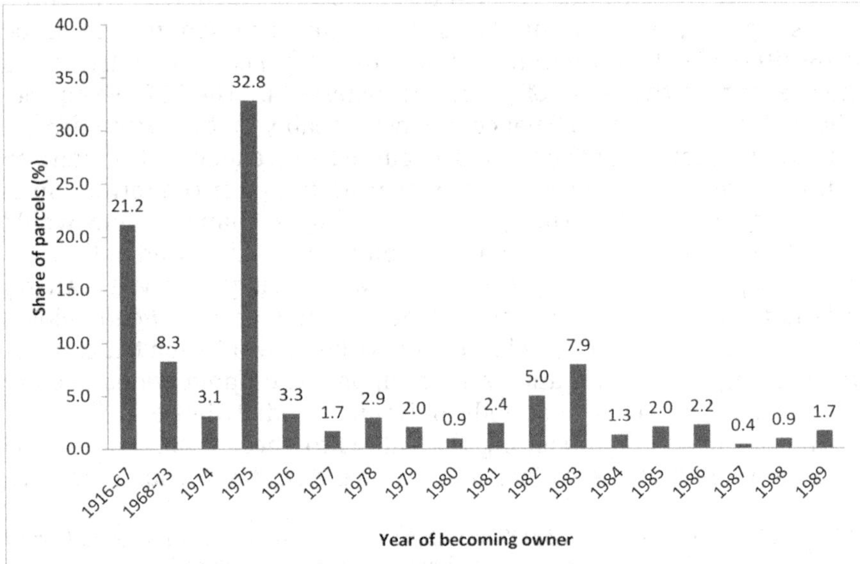

Figure 3.1 Share of current (1989) parcels by year of becoming owner[32]

[31] The very low figure was exceptionally surprising. The time reference of the peasants was often not by year but by episode, notably 'at the time of the LEC', which was coded as 1977 for the year variable. On this basis, one would expect the figure to be exaggerated, also including some lands assigned by the LEC in the neighbouring years.

[32] This is based on my 1989 survey, covering all parcels of land ever farmed or owned by each respondent. The total of 324 weighted parcels was reduced to 271.5, partly due to missing information, and partly because the respondents never became owners, i.e. they held the land by tenancy. The figures in my 1990 paper differ because they refer to a subset of data for which both year of ownership and year of becoming cultivator were known.

In 1979 the district administration terminated the LEC and thus ended the period of land reform. It is the succeeding years that are relevant for testing the theory of periodic land redistribution. I argue below that for the remaining part of the Därg period, the key aspects of land tenure were household processes enacted by the peasants, as well as policy initiatives implemented by the state. The household processes meant that every year some young farmers might increase their holdings, while the parent generation 'lost'. It is this process that could be mistaken for redistribution, but which was in fact ordinary intergenerational transfer taking place within the available institutions.

Elsewhere in Ethiopia, state intervention sometimes disrupted the land tenure system, e.g. when a producer cooperative was established (discussed earlier in this chapter). In the case of Ayné, which seems more representative of highland Ethiopia than the fertile sites usually chosen for producer cooperatives, there was no general redistribution after the work of the LEC. There were some instances of government policy that led to transfer of land between peasants, but the number of parcels involved was rather low and these subsequent reforms also had a specific purpose. There is no evidence of any initiative, be it by the government or the peasant community, to implement a more general land redistribution for equity purposes. By far the most important reallocation of land rights was due to the delimitation of commune borders in 1982–83 (*qeyes*). Traditionally, administrative borders were fuzzy. Ownership rights to the parcels of land were clear, and it was also clear to which commune the owner belonged. But in border areas parcels were interspersed, since ownership was a result of inheritance and transfers over many generations. This created no problems for the peasants, but it was incompatible with the administrative system established, which required each commune to be clearly defined.

The border delimitation meant that any land outside the new borders was confiscated. Those who lost land because of this reform had strong compensation claims to the land confiscated from peasants residing in another commune.[33] We can clearly see the effect of this reform in the data for 1982 and 1983, but it concerned only a minority of households and a small part of the land. The land available for compensating those who had lost land was made available by the same reform and did not involve any reassessment of land holdings in general. According to the survey, only 6 per cent of all parcels were specifically stated to have been acquired due to the border delimitation. The real figure is likely

[33] The peasants who had lost land were given the option of moving their residence, but the problem was that they often had land on both sides of the border, which was no longer permitted. The reform created considerable frustration in some localities. Some households solved the problem through a quick divorce, formally establishing households in both communes. Although this was understood to be a trick, it was probably considered a legitimate move in a difficult situation. I have not found any sanctions against this practice even though the derived households continued to have close relations.

to be somewhere between this low estimate and the higher estimate of 12.9 per cent, the latter referring to all the parcels acquired in the years 1982 and 1983. In this case there was both a specific purpose and a rather limited scope of redistribution. It was numerically significant enough to challenge my definition of reallocation, but the social content fits well with this term as it was concentrated in two limited border areas of the commune.

Another way of investigating how the land tenure system operated is to check the data on when and why peasants *lost* specific parcels of land. These data confirm the account above. We find that of the 324 parcels ever cultivated by the informants, 76.9 per cent were still operated by them in 1989. For a critical test of whether there was land redistribution, we used the approach of high estimates, i.e. counting all cases of land loss in reform years as being caused by the reform. We then find that 4.5 per cent had been lost by the 'land-to-the-tiller' principle, 3.7 per cent by the LEC's activities and 9.0 per cent by border delimitation (*qeyes*).[34] In other words, the picture is one of remarkable stability in land tenure, which is incompatible with the redistribution theory.

The concept of *shegesheg* is often taken to mean land redistribution, and the reference to *shegesheg* during the Därg period may thus be mistakenly interpreted as evidence of a persistent practice of land redistribution. *Shegesheg* was frequently referred to in Ayné and one would expect it to show up quite prominently in the data. However, only 2.6 per cent of all parcels were reported as lost by processes that could be attributed to *shegesheg*, while only 1.2 per cent were explicitly attributed to *shegesheg*.[35] The commune was clearly not implementing rounds of periodic land redistribution. We must therefore turn to the local meaning of *shegesheg*.[36]

The discussion above indicates that there was no land redistribution in Ayné, neither during the land reform nor later, with the partial exception of the disturbances created by the border delimitation. An indication of the local meaning of *shegesheg* can be found in the remaining reasons reported for 'loss' of parcels. Only 0.3 per cent of all parcels were recorded as having been given to a child.[37] This figure covers a

[34] The total figure for loss of land includes transfer by ordinary household processes. We also saw above that about half of all parcels may have been under tenancy arrangements before the land reform and were transferred to the tenants. However, the farmers who responded to the survey in 1989 had lost only 4.5% of their parcels to tenants at the time of the land reform. This indicates that the landowners who lost land were often non-resident, while some were elderly and had died in the intervening period.

[35] In Figure 3.1, I included land reported as lost when someone had died (*motä käda*), as surplus land (*terf*), or for unspecified reasons. This again tends to lead to an estimate that is slightly too high, a bias that is unfavourable to my argument.

[36] Note that in other contexts *shegesheg* may refer to full-scale land redistribution.

[37] Note that most parcels were owned or used by the respective informant

period of fourteen years (1976–89) and it seems clear that it must represent a quite serious under-reporting of real household processes. It is likely that most cases of land transfer between generations were actually subsumed under the other headings, and especially under that of *shegesheg*.[38] In Ayné, *shegesheg* meant only the reallocation of land between households according to the rules of the *dersha* system, a system that worked by a logic very different from a system of periodic redistribution. It was much closer to a system based on inheritance rights, although with its own twists and turns.

THE *DERSHA* PRINCIPLE

The new system of land tenure was the logical result of the work of the LEC. Land holdings were organized by households, and the official recognition of household status was expressed in membership in the peasant association, which was identical to paying the land tax, or having a 'tax name' (*semä geber*). When land holdings were equalized, all household members were enumerated and given the same weight. Any surplus (*terf*) above the local standard was in principle confiscated and allocated to those falling short of the standard. The aim was thus that all households should have the full quota (*mulu tämän*); in Ayné this was 1.5 *t'emad* multiplied by the number of household members. All persons living in the household were counted as households members. In this way the vacancy principle (*motä käda*, vacancy when someone died) was implied in the principle of full quota.[39] It is the later adjustments between households as the number of members changed that were referred to as *shegesheg*. These were continuous micro-adjustments rather than comprehensive rounds of land redistribution. Gradually, the *shegesheg* elements also tended to disappear, for reasons explained below.

This understanding provides the entry point to exploring the new land tenure system. The design of the initial land equalization process

(contd) throughout the period. In addition to the reforms covered here, a few parcels lacked data, a few were exchanged with other farmers, and a few were sharecropping land returned to the owner, each category comprising less than 1% of all parcels.

38 Other reasons for the low figure of 0.3% are: (1) the particular household structure created by the land reform, with its exceptional opportunities for establishing new households; (2) the probable reporting of parcels as one's own from the time when the informant took possession of it within the household in the form of personal land (*gulma*); and (3) the fact that the survey covered informants in 1989, while a major source of land gained by young households would arguably be by way of inheritance from persons who had died and thus were not included in the survey.

39 Note that *motä käda* also has a wider reference, such as when a landowner (taxpayer) dies without an accepted successor. This is practised well beyond the *dersha* system. Only in the *dersha* system did the death of a household member create a vacancy.

was based on an ideal balance between household size and land. Within a few years, this balance would be upset and new inequalities, resulting from demographic changes, would emerge. The rules of the land equalizing reform logically implied certain reversionary rights of the community to counteract these tendencies. This was therefore not a fully developed private property system, even if we disregard the limitations set by state intervention.

The land tenure system established what might, however, be described as conditional private property. Peasants had weak formal rights and they could at any time be exposed to the whims of government policy. They might also lose land by *shegesheg* locally, but as they learnt the risks, they developed defensive strategies. The rules that might lead to land confiscation were there, but they rarely came into action. This explains the paradox that qualitative information may tell about the vacancy rules (*motä käda*), but the statistics show that cases of confiscation by this principle were rare, for the following reasons.

Any reasonably informed peasant could tell what might happen to their land if a household member died. They had to know the risks in order to manage them. A household that had received its full quota of land had one share (*dersha*) per member. Thus, whenever someone died, there was in principle surplus land. The same applied in principle (but less regularly in practice) if someone left the area or married outside the commune. Those entitled to more land were partly households which had not initially received the full quota, but more systematically they were young households in the phase of rapid expansion. Somewhat accidentally, but sometimes rather numerous, they were households which had initially received the full quota but had suffered land confiscation due to some government programme. In Ayné, this was mainly the border delimitation described above.

The key element in this system was the concept of *dersha*, where everyone was entitled to a share of land. It should be obvious from the description above, and even more so from the available empirical evidence, that legitimate claims for a full share outstripped the supply of land released by people who died or left the area. This strain on the system would grow as time went by. The driving force in this model is, as in the redistribution theory, population increase, but the system operated quite differently. Throughout the Därg period, the concept of *dersha* remained the key principle of local land tenure, and land was not confiscated unless the holding exceeded the full quota. The standard for assessing this was not adjusted downwards as population increased, which would have required a round of full-scale registration and equalizing adjustments along the lines implied by the periodic redistribution argument.

Quite significantly, *dersha* was the principle that people referred to when they litigated over the land.[40] It is often assumed, be it with regard to landlessness in general or women's land rights in particular,

40 For a sample court case described in some detail, see Ege (1997a). This case took place in the late Därg period and the early EPRDF period when land tenure rules were in a state of flux.

that land was owned by the household head, the person in whose name the land was registered on the tax list. However, in the *dersha* system, everyone present in the household at the time of the LEC established a claim to his or her *dersha* of land. When a young man left the parent household after marriage, he would demand his share of the land. If the parents refused, he could appeal, and the local court would allocate him a relevant share of their land.[41] The same applied when a woman married. Even someone who had lived as a servant at the time of the LEC could demand his or her share of the land and move to another household or establish a separate household. This principle soon became so strong that, after the initial years, it was rarely contested in court, although the specific amount of land or the underlying facts of household membership might be contested.

In sum, the key element in the *dersha* system was that everyone present at the time of the LEC had a right to land. However, well-behaved sons (and daughters even more so) do not take their parents to court, and good parents are kind to their children. Thus, the normal form of land transfers between generations was not litigation over *dersha* rights, but *dersha* rights wrapped up in the customary practices of the locality, especially personal land grants by parents to their children (*gulma*).[42] Property rights expressed in traditional peasant institutions were immediately visible, while the underlying *dersha* principle tended to be hidden. However, those who breached this principle risked being exposed to *shegesheg*.

We can gain further insights into the workings of the *dersha* system, and its limitations, by considering the household cycle. According to the model, although less neatly in real life, a young household would have two shares. As children were born, they were entitled to one share per child, but in practice there would be more overall claims than available land, leading to sub-standard land allocations in order to satisfy as many as possible. On the other hand, old households also lose members. As children married they would take their share to their own new households. In the end, the old couple would be left with only their own two shares, and a widow would in theory (but again less so in practice) be entitled to only one share. Thus, what was once a large holding would be scattered across several successor households.[43]

41 There is solid documentation of this practice in Ayné, and it also confirmed by evidence from Gojam (see Chapter 4). The description given is based on the assumption that the young man was initially a member of the household of his parents, but the same principle applied to any other household type.

42 In Ayné, personal land grants (*gulma*), sharecropping (*mägazo*) and pensions (*t'uräta*) were all important local institutions. *Gulma* was especially associated with sons, but it could also apply to daughters. See Aspen (1993: 42–51) for institutional descriptions in nearby Gänät commune. The same institutions were found in Ayné.

43 On a rather abstract level, this was similar to the pre-reform ambilineal inheritance system of the Amhara (see Hoben 1973). However, in the *dersha* system, household membership, not kinship, was the critical variable, and all the relevant household members had, in theory at least, equal rights in the land.

The model above captures the tendencies in the system, but these tendencies were experienced as problematic and the peasants soon learnt how to play the system. According to the *dersha* principle, there was surplus land if the number of household members decreased. But there was no surplus if the household had also added a successor (*tätäki*), someone who had not previously received a share.[44] Whenever a child was born, there was a candidate to serve as successor somewhere, directly or indirectly. In its simplest form, the child would succeed another household member who left or died. In a slightly more complex move, a child would be transferred to the household of grandparents who needed a successor to compensate for someone who had left or died. In even more complicated moves, it would be an older, shareholding child who moved, and this older child would again be replaced by a younger child to serve as successor. The last scenario came into play at a very early stage when a household lost a member and there were no newly born children, but a son married and brought in a woman to fill the vacancy in the *dersha* system. If her parent household had received the full quota, they in turn would need to add another 'landless' member to fend off the risk of *shegesheg* after their daughter moved out, unless her *dersha* could be transferred to her new household.

It should be emphasized that the *dersha* system was not a system specified by precise statutory law. It was basically a modern customary legal system, with legal practices evolving from the land reform and the way it was implemented, but shaped by local concepts, traditions and the political situation. The work of the LEC came to serve as the constitution of this system, but it was not a planned legal system. The relevant law, the land reform proclamation itself, dealt with the land reform process. It was extremely vague on the land tenure system to be established. The ideal for the young radicals drafting the law was probably cooperatives, which would make many issues of peasant land tenure irrelevant.[45] Furthermore, the principles of the *dersha* system could hardly be specified in this law, not just because the principles were not yet known, but above all because if these principles had been formalized, the peasants would have been granted such strong ownership rights that it would tend to annul the claim of state ownership. As we shall see in the last section of this chapter, the *dersha* system had a natural tendency towards private property if not overruled by state policies.[46]

The local people did not think of this as a new system; they just created it by their acts. The LEC was concerned with equalizing land

44 Note that 'successor' may refer to household members, not just the headship. Here, I use 'successor' as a direct translation of *tätäki*.

45 Producer cooperatives were typically located on rather flat and fertile land. In Ayné and surrounding areas, as in most of Ethiopia, the ecology is harsher and no attempts were made to establish producer cooperatives.

46 I refer to the *dersha* system as customary law rather than common law due to its contradiction with formal law. It was, however, routinely, but probably not consistently, applied by local courts.

holdings, or more precisely, obeying orders to do so. Individual peasants were concerned with protecting their own interests. The earliest cases where one can see the *dersha* principle were in decisions by the LEC to register adult children, already married but living together with their parents, as separate households with the relevant land. Every case might create precedence, and gradually it became what we can conceive of as a customary legal system – a system that was not formulated in law, that few locals could fully describe, and that could be adjusted according to the specific situation, but also a system with precise enough rules to be culled from the arguments used in struggles over land.

REGIONAL VARIATION

The *dersha* system has been described based on the land reform experience in Ayné. This takes us to the geographical extension of the *dersha* system. Having re-read the literature looking for precise information, I have not yet found any case where it cannot have existed, but the absence of such negative evidence may simply be because the literature is not precise enough. In the following section, I shall only point out the existence of some positive evidence in specific locations.

In the next chapter, we show that the *dersha* model is useful to understand the Gojam case investigated by Yigremew. Teferi's (1998: 56) description of the first land reform in Täwa in South Wälo would make this site a strong candidate for the *dersha* system, since it was based on equal shares of land for all household members. However, due to the establishment of a large producer cooperative, there was a second reform a few years later by which children obtained significantly less land than their parents (*ibid.*: 58). Under such conditions, the *dersha* principle would tend to be curtailed so much so that the system operated by a different logic.[47] I am more hesitant about Ch'orisa in South Wälo (Ege and Aspen 2003: 60–3) as well as the two locations in North Wälo presented later in this book. All these are very localized studies, but they are scattered over a huge area. This suggests that the *dersha* system may have existed in much, although probably not all, of the Amhara area, and perhaps beyond. Based on these cases, it is also possible to indicate some factors which may have influenced whether the *dersha* system developed in any specific locality.

In many parts of Ethiopia, the first years of the Därg period were tumultuous, and administrative capacity was quite limited.[48] Once the

[47] It should be emphasized that peasants in some areas may refer to their *dersha* of land, without implying the *dersha* land tenure system as outlined here. The significant aspect of my description of *dersha* is the individual latent rights of all household members and the possibility for these members to enforce this right by taking the household head to court.

[48] There was an extensive but short-lived revolt in the lower parts of Yefat. See Chapter 1 for an overview of the literature on the various revolts.

political situation was under control and the peasants had been organized into communes, the next step was to equalize holdings and solve problems arising from the first phase.[49] The second phase was probably heavily influenced by local culture, the specific conflicts in the area, and the political situation. In some areas, notably in the south, the two phases seem to have overlapped, while in some areas of the north, somewhat outside government control, the second phase may not have happened at all, or was implemented in a minimal way later on, as in Baba Säat in North Wälo (see Chapter 5). The following account is based on the process in Ayné, where the reform very closely followed the main pattern envisaged by the 1975 proclamation.

Differences in the implementation of the land reform seems to have shaped the later system of land rights. If dependents were not enumerated and entitled to specific amounts of land, they also did not have precise rights that could be enforced by law. For instance, in Baba Säat (see Chapter 5), I found no indication that youngsters had ever taken parents to court to demand their rightful share (*dersha mäbet*), and it appears that parents had a much stronger position. Such a land tenure system can best be understood as standard family-based systems, which usually have a certain patriarchal flavour. While relations within the family would differ, this could also generate a fair degree of within-the-community tenure security – that is, security for the registered landowner and for his spouse.

One effect of the *dersha* theory is to open up, even prod, empirical investigations of peasant land tenure systems. General theory has to be generated from numerous empirical observations, searching for the rules as well as the limits to these rules. The standard account of land redistribution has worked the other way around. The redistribution model was initially a fair hypothesis for the observations made, but it then turned into a model that tended to replace descriptions of local realities. This chapter has deliberately focused on a model description, although one close to a specific reality. The purpose has been to bring out core system features, but the really interesting questions arise in the confrontation with the multitude of empirical realities. This opens up exploration both of recent land tenure history, providing a much more vivid picture, and of understanding regional variations. The point is not that the *dersha* model should be applied everywhere, but by presenting a rather precise model, it is possible to test it, modify it wherever needed, or propose system descriptions working on other principles.

In such an exercise, particular attention should be paid to inheritance systems. The *dersha* rules fit very well with ambilineal Amhara inheritance, which in principle assigns equal rights to all children. Therefore,

49 This is clearly illustrated by Aster (1982) who sought to explore the degree to which land holdings had been equalized. She visited most of the provinces in 1976 and 1979. Security issues had held back implementation of the land reform, but in 1979, the ambitions of the administration were on the increase.

it would be interesting to know how land tenure worked in communities that traditionally had patrilineal descent and inheritance rules, e.g. the Oromos. Although there was a considerable drive for gender equality under the Därg, we certainly cannot assume that traditional inheritance rules had no influence. However, even if the *dersha* model may not have been applicable, it does not mean that there was periodic redistribution. Here one needs to understand the particular property system of peasant smallholders under state land ownership and the specific ways in which peasants accessed land.

WIDER IMPLICATIONS

In the first part of this chapter, I argued that the image of periodic land redistribution is not supported by evidence. I then went on to show that the typical evidence used to underpin this interpretation is exceptionally strong in the case of Ayné. Finally, I showed that the underlying system in Ayné actually worked according to a different principle, following strong individual property rights as long as these were respected by the state. In the absence of positive evidence supporting the theory of periodic land redistribution, this should make us reconsider land tenure under the Därg. Certainly, there is likely to have been regional variation, but there is too little information of sufficient detail to outline any alternative system. It is unlikely that the *dersha* system operated throughout Ethiopia, and I return to this issue towards the end of this chapter. This is, however, a minor point. The *dersha* model may be useful in presenting an alternative, making it clear that the post-reform land tenure system could function without land redistribution. From this starting point, one can search for regional variation.

The problem with the redistribution model is that it has been applied to all of Ethiopia although there is, to my knowledge, not a single convincing case described in the literature. If it turns out that land redistribution was much less common than the received interpretation would indicate, it will change our understanding of current land tenure issues.

According to the currently dominant understanding of post-reform land tenure, the key problem was tenure insecurity due to periodic land redistribution. Therefore, the recent land registration and certification programmes may have solved the problems, as argued by some international economists (e.g. Deininger 2008; Deininger *et al.* 2007; Holden 2008). However, if their basic assumption is unfounded and there was actually a fair degree of local tenure security – although with insecurity created by the developmental state – it is far from obvious that increased state control, another side of the land registration, is the appropriate way to go. I have argued elsewhere that the initial evidence for increased tenure security after land certification is weak; it might even seem that in the early stages the reform created considerable tenure insecurity (Ege 2017).

The *dersha* theory may also be used as a heuristic device to sharpen analysis. An issue separate from, but linked to, the *dersha* system is the common understanding of the commune. The point here is that redistribution theory tends to imply considerable administrative capacity, while the *dersha* system is much lighter in its demands on the administration. Although Ayné was a well-organized commune with a competent leadership, the peasant association consisted mainly of two things: the tax list, as the nexus between the peasant households and the state; and various committees made up of elected peasants. Whenever there was an order from above, the leadership committee had to meet to discuss the problem, and problem it usually was. There was little or no initiative nor an attempt by the commune to act as a local, self-governing organization. The various stages of the land reform and policy initiatives – like the initial land adjustment by the LEC, or prohibiting farming land outside the commune, or the border delimitation – were all ordered by the state, and not based on local initiatives. Neither did the commune monitor land tenure and undertake *shegesheg* on its own initiative. This process was driven by individual households who observed that some neighbour had surplus land after a household member had died or left, which prompted them to appeal for the land. In fact, several neighbours were likely to file competing applications. Typical arguments would be kinship, that the land was close to their own, or that they had been members of the same household for some time. Such cases might well go beyond the local court, and the local leaders risked being rebuked and even fined if they were found to have made errors.

As the peasants gradually adapted to the new rules, the commune administration became more and more like a secretariat, simply recording decisions that were in practice taken by peasant households. The head of a household informed the leadership committee that a grandchild had joined the household, this was noted, and it was concluded that there was no surplus land in the household. The new member might even be thought of as the inheritor of the tax name, although only informally and with some extra moves required to complete the transfer. I do not go into these rather complicated issues here. The point is simply to emphasize that the commune administration had an essentially passive role and generally did as little as they could get away with, partly because they saw themselves as kinsmen and neighbours rather than as administrators. Taking too much action could create not only friends, but also foes.

Another issue is the rights of the various household members. In this case, the *dersha* theory impacts both our understanding of the rights of women and the issue of landlessness. The *dersha* theory specifies certain rights, which were often upheld, but I have also indicated that these rights would probably be attenuated over time. Such changes do not happen lightly, and the specific rights of individual members in a household were probably a highly contested field. There is a fair amount of evidence indicating intergenerational conflict in Ayné,[50] and one would also expect conflict between siblings, notably siblings who might claim different rights according to the formal rules, varying from full share to no share – a distinction with dubious legitimacy within a family.

There are also important questions to be raised about the rights of women. These cannot be deduced from the model, but the model can be used to generate hypotheses and questions. According to the model, a woman who married received a share of land in the new household. There were indeed such cases, but the common practice was more likely for the woman to bring in some land from her parents' household. In both these cases, we would expect her to keep the land if she later divorced. But if this was a cross-border marriage, the formal rules indicate that she could not bring in land from her parents' household. And if she had been given land in the household of her husband, she stood to lose it if she divorced and returned to her parents in another commune. It should be pointed out, however, that women did have equal rights as men. The question is whether there was any discrimination despite this equality in rules, or whether the system, even in the absence of formal discrimination, worked to the disadvantage of women. On this question I am so far agnostic, and could cite cases going either way.[51]

The *dersha* theory may also shed light on the issue of landlessness. Land rights in the *dersha* system were highly individual and can be conceived of as consisting of three levels:

1. *Dersha* rights, of all household members
2. Personal land (*gulma*), typically of maturing sons
3. Tax status (*semä geber*), of the head, usually the man.

The fundamental level was the *dersha* right; this was a latent right of all present at the original land registration and anyone officially recorded later.[52] Whether such rights actually translate into allocation of an actual parcel corresponding to the right would depend on decisions made by both the right-holder and other household members and by external factors we may refer to as luck. By custom, boys would receive some personal land (*gulma*) while they lived with their parents, in order to start building up the property needed to establish their own household. This was also a process of converting the *dersha* right into

50 See also Teferi (1994: 101–3) for intergenerational conflict in a commune in Baso & Wäräna district, near Ankobär.

51 The precise timing of events is important because local practices changed significantly during the Därg period.

52 I have borrowed the term 'latent rights' from Helen Pankhurst (1992: 24) who used it to refer to the rights married women had in the land officially registered in the name of their husbands. At least in the Yefat area, children had similar rights, as did the household head. The standard practice upon divorce was to split the holding equally and assign custody of children to both parties.

an actual parcel of land. When youngsters married, the man would get, or demand, his full share of the land, and the woman would, if possible, bring in her own share from her parent household. In the early period, notably under the LEC, when such a household might be fortunate enough to obtain the holding topped up by an allocation from the commune (i.e. surplus land reallocated from another household), the new household was registered and started to pay tax. However, by the time of my fieldwork in 1989, it appears that the common practice was for such young households to live under the umbrella of their parent households. We may refer to them as *gulma* households, since their land was held as a personal land grant from their parents and was covered by the parents' land tax. If tax status is taken as being identical with land ownership, these households were considered landless, but why then would my young neighbour in Ayné, Lägäsä Täshomä, complain that he was paying land tax while his age mates did not.[53] They were 'taxless', but not landless. His age mates did not necessarily have less access to land, but they were covered by their parents' land tax. Locally, the personal land grants of independent households were thought of as the property of these households, and one day in the future this was likely to be formalized, i.e. when the land tax was transferred to the new household. My impression is that the households tried, and largely succeeded, to not increase the number of taxpayers.

Approaching recent history with the *dersha* theory and the critique of redistribution theory may also lead to reinterpretation of the mixed economy reform of 1990. The standard view is that this put an end to periodic redistribution, but, as argued above, this practice never really existed, at least in the Yefat area.[54] The reform was not very precise. To my knowledge, confiscation by vacancy (when a family member had died) was not explicitly abolished, but *shegesheg* was ended and landowners kept their holding unchanged. Thereafter, confiscation by vacancy happened only if the registered landowner died without a legitimate heir, rather than if a household member died or left. In our context, the main innovation brought by the mixed economy reform was that inheritance (*wers*) of land became permitted.

In fact, inheritance as we usually understand it, i.e. including what is here described as succession (discussed below), was practised throughout the Därg period. Inheritance (*wers*) had been prohibited by the land reform proclamation, but this applied to formal inheritance rights and especially to bequeathment, typically in the form of 'standing inheritance (*yä-qum wers*), by which an elderly person bequeathed the land in return for maintenance or a 'pension' (*t'urätä*). This could actually convert the land of old people into property with a price, and was a traditional method for better-off farmers to accumulate land. The more common aspects of inheritance, a wife or a child succeeding as the formal landowner, were routine events throughout the Därg period

53 Survey 1994 (GMS: Hh 347: L946 Däläl) Lägäsä Täshomä, 24.02.87 EC.

54 I did fieldwork in 12 communes in total, from the highlands around Däbrä Sina down to the Rasa plain bordering on the Afar.

and was formally allowed. According to the land reform proclamation, no one could claim land in the capacity of inheritors (*wärash*), but they could do so as successors (*tätäki*).

It is ironic that the 1990 reform aimed to abolish what the peasants had in practice already abolished, *shegesheg*, and to give tenure security by respecting inheritance, probably thinking of inheritance mainly as what has been described above as succession. It seems that the policy measures were based on a weak understanding of the peasant land tenure system, reforming what did not need to be reformed (but which only needed to be respected). On the other hand, within the peasant community, these reforms had quite different effects. In the 1990s, the value of land held by elderly people increased dramatically; bequeathment in the form of 'standing inheritance' became much more common; old people moved between households according to who would provide the best care; there was much litigation over contracts; and there were bitter conflicts between close relatives, persons who would under other circumstances be good friends.[55]

Another effect of the reforms was to freeze the system. In the short run this created tenure security, but in the medium term it contributed to the 1997 Amhara land redistribution and thus to greater tenure insecurity. After the mixed economy reform, land holdings were no longer decreased when someone died, which was a Janus-faced reform, especially when coupled with the prohibition against selling and buying land. It did mean that some elderly people, notably widows, might end up with very good land holdings, while many young households suffered acute land shortage with no way out. Sharecropping became the norm for young households or for established households with adolescents, especially those in the phase of primary household accumulation. There were strains on the system, and many a youngster might envy the privileged endowment belonging to an old neighbour. Young people might even have supported the idea of new land redistribution to re-establish the basic fairness of the early Därg period.[56] What they got instead was the 1997 land redistribution, something quite different and a shocking experience to the peasant community (Ege 1997b: 44–5, 51). This redistribution created considerable tenure insecurity, not only in the areas where it was implemented, but throughout Ethiopia. However, the Amhara land redistribution was not driven by population growth, although the cadres exploited the youngsters' eagerness for land. It was a cruel policy to wipe out the perceived social basis for political opposition to the regime.

The *dersha* system was curtailed by the mixed economy reforms of 1990 and in principle abolished by the Amhara land redistribution of 1997, although the right to a *dersha* continued to influence peasant

55 See Ege (1997a) for an example of a tragic conflict between a farmer and his niece, both incredibly poor and very nice individuals.

56 For the atmosphere in the mid-1990s, see Teferi (1994: 112) and Aspen (1995: 27).

thinking about legitimate claims.[57] There is also every reason to believe that even if it had been permitted to continue to function, it would have gradually changed into a standard family-based system, with parents taking a strong position as the representatives of all household members, simply because fewer and fewer children would have full *dersha* rights.

The land tenure system described here, born of the land reform, if left alone would also have likely developed into a system of private property, i.e. the opposite of periodic redistribution and insecure individual rights. Land tenure was vested in three social layers: the *dersha* rights of individuals, the reversionary rights of the commune, and the rights reserved by the government as the representative of the nation. Government policy could destroy any farmer, but this element is outside our current discussion (see the discussion of 'specific-purpose redistribution' in this chapter and in Chapter 4). The main impact of the *dersha* system was to limit the practical effects of the reversionary rights of the commune, strong in theory but weak in practice. It appears that towards the end of the Därg period, it rarely came into play. The data from Ayné even suggest that it may have had little direct impact throughout the period, with some exceptions during the early years.

In the 1990s, this developed one step further. The initial prohibition against renting out land had lost most of its force by the late Därg period. Land sales, on the other hand, were strictly prohibited and not common during the Därg period. However, after the mixed economy reform of 1990, the land tenure system was in limbo, with unclear rules. This continued with the EPRDF regime. Although land sales were still formally illegal, the district administration took no action against landowners as long as the land tax was paid. Due to the combination of this inaction and the new inheritance rights, many landowners started to treat land as full private property. Land sales and closely related practices became widespread – and the talk of the day (Ege 1994a: 293).

To summarize, we have seen that the redistribution theory is at odds with the data from Ayné. The *dersha* theory was developed to explain my observations there. It is of course closely linked to the specific trajectory of the land reform in Ayné, but there are at least three reasons to believe that it has a much broader application. The first is that the empirical evidence underlying the theory of periodic redistribution is rather weak when critically assessed. The second is that the Ayné case fits so well into the stages envisaged in the land reform proclamation that it is fair to assume this may indeed have been a standard approach, widespread wherever the Därg was in firm control. The third is scattered evidence from various localities, discussed above.

Against this background, the next chapter about land tenure in Gojam is of particular interest, especially as this is an area of the Amhara highlands associated with the more communal variant of the

57 Even as late as 2013, I came across a case where one person invoked a variant of the *dersha* principle (D10988: 4, Däbäbä Bétä).

rest system, in marked contrast with the individualized *rest* of Ayné and much of North Shäwa. Based in traditional culture, Gojam would seem to be one of the least likely areas for the development of the *dersha* system with its highly individualized rights. If the *dersha* system operated there, it could basically operate anywhere, or more specifically wherever the early stages of the land reform took forms which made it a logical outcome.

4

Land Tenure in Gojam under the Därg[1]

YIGREMEW ADAL and SVEIN EGE

The 1975 land reform was a revolution in land tenure and social relations. The literature on this reform is mainly either a restatement of the proclamation of 1975 (Ethiopian Government 1975) or it presents the image of frequent land redistributions upsetting peasant tenure security – in both cases without much information about what happened on the ground. In the previous chapter, Ege outlined the *dersha* theory of peasant land tenure based on the process in Ayné. In this chapter, we show how this also fits a community with a rather different pre-reform land tenure system, Dinja S'iyon in Gojam. We also build on the contribution of Yeraswork, who distinguished between land reallocations aimed to improve equity in landholdings and those which sought to transform peasant society by policies such as producer cooperatives or villagization.

EVIDENCE OF REDISTRIBUTION

'Redistribution' is a frustratingly imprecise term. It may cover various local terms, such as *kefefel* (division), *deledel* (levelling down) or *shegesheg*, and sometimes it is also used for household processes such as giving land to a son (*gulma*). Furthermore, the causes of redistributions were varied. A study by the Ministry of Agriculture (MoA 1989) shows that causes of reallocation included the formation of producer cooperatives, villagization, afforestation projects, state farms, estab-

1 Yigremew died in 2011, soon after he had submitted a draft paper to our workshop on land tenure, at the Biennial Trondheim Colloquium in Social Anthropology. The original paper was first drafted in October 2000, following up on an outline of the *dersha* system in rather general terms (Ege 2000). Yigremew's paper remained dormant until 2011. It contained much ethnographic detail that fits the *dersha* theory but which was not part of Ege's original sketch of the system; it thus provides a rather strong case for the existence of the *dersha* system in the Gojam community studied. All the fieldwork was conducted by Yigremew, and the ethnographic account is based on his draft. His paper did, however, contain considerable overlaps with Chapter 3 and did not integrate well with this book's focus. So it was rewritten, shortened, reorganized and edited by Ege to bring out the salient points regarding the issue of land redistribution and the *dersha* system.

lishment of different institutions and projects, expansion of towns and sites for schools – as well as accommodating emerging households. The handling of the last element, in the form of periodic land redistribution, has dominated our understanding of the land tenure system under the Därg. However, closer examination shows that accommodating new households was only one of the causes of land reallocation. In addition, it was mainly a corollary of other important concerns.

In Chapter 3, Ege distinguished between comprehensive redistributions for improved equity and various kinds of specific-purpose redistribution, which he referred to as reallocations. A similar distinction can be culled from Yeraswork's (2000) study of sites in Wälo and North Shäwa, in which he classified redistributions as minor or major. 'All land redistribution drives affecting a sizable number of member households were presumed major redistributions, whereas those affecting only a small number of people were considered minor ones' (Yeraswork 2000: 194). In the following discussion, we shall use his data to shed light on the issue of periodic redistribution under the Därg, which is of course much narrower than Yeraswork's concern on the impact of land redistribution, of any kind, on peasant incentives for resource conservation.

The distinction between major and minor redistributions corresponded largely to differences in primary objectives. Yeraswork (2000: 201) categorized the factors causing redistribution into two groups: those which resulted from a conscious attempt to reform landholdings (such as implementing the land reform and equalizing holdings)[2]; and, on the other hand, all the programmes that sought to transform peasant economy and society (such as villagization, cooperatives and land conservation projects). The latter did not primarily aim at changing holdings, although they unavoidably resulted in such effects.

Whatever the causes, the frequency of land reallocations is an important issue. Counting only the incidences, this varied widely. Yeraswork found that in 1975–92, there were about seven rounds of reallocations, major and minor, in both Ambasäl and Yäju and five in Däsé Zuriya (all in Wälo), but only two in Tägulät (North Shäwa). Following the same approach, there were seven redistributions in Dinja S'iyon. However, in Ankobär (North Shäwa), there were no important land reallocations after the initial land reform (Yigremew 2000a). While the national law and the pressure to find land for youngsters applied everywhere, this kind of regional variation suggests that local factors played a prominent part. The analysis in this chapter points strongly towards policies to transform the peasant economy, in addition to land confiscation for public purposes like schools and offices, as critical factors in land reallocation.

In many cases, the instances of reallocation counted were apparently quite limited in scope. The data of Yeraswork on the number of reallocations (up to seven) might seem to indicate a rapid turnover of hold-

[2] This corresponds to the first two phases of the land reform identified in the previous chapter.

ings, but other data moderate this. He found that after the land reform, 39 per cent of respondents had changed some parcel once, 44 per cent had changed twice, 14 per cent had changed three times, and only 4 per cent more often than that (Yeraswork 2000: 195). He also found that 54 per cent of holdings were acquired before 1975, 23 per cent during 1975–88, and 23 per cent during 1989–93. While these figures are high, they are per holding, not per parcel, and this may lead to a highly exaggerated impression.[3] Furthermore, the period covered includes two major events that have little bearing on the issue of periodic land redistribution under the Därg. This first event includes the adjustment of holdings by household size which followed soon after the land reform, i.e. the process corresponding to the LEC (land equalizing committee) in Ayné. This seems to have taken place in all the eleven communes covered.[4] Secondly, the period also includes the EPRDF land redistribution that took place in the last phases of the civil war in several of the communes.[5] If we deduct these two processes (which do not bear on the issue of periodic land redistribution under the Därg), there was no major land redistribution in Tägulät, Mänz and Däsé Zuriya, one in Ambasäl, and on average 2.7 rounds in Yäju (*ibid.*: 194).

Yeraswork's study may seem to provide empirical evidence for the theory of periodic land redistribution, although the data presented actually tell another story. It is clear from his account that equity-driven redistribution was not common in the years after the land reform had been fully implemented. Thereafter, only four of the eleven communes experienced a major redistribution aimed to equalize land holdings. Most instances of redistribution captured by Yeraswork were the corollary of specific policy initiatives, notably the establishment or dissolution of producer cooperatives (Yeraswork 2000: 201). It is also important that the topic of Yeraswork's study was afforestation and terracing projects. This meant that the selected communes were far from representative. They were chosen precisely because they were subject to a type of government intervention that required confiscation of land. A high rate of 'redistribution' is therefore to be expected.[6] This was not a demographically driven redistribution for the purpose of equity. It is better understood as a specific-purpose redistribution, or mostly more moderate reallocations, resulting from the interventions

3 For the questionnaire used in the survey, see Yeraswork (2000: 323). See also the discussion in Chapter 3 of the difference between household and parcel data.

4 Table 9 in Yeraswork's (2000: 201) study shows that there were eleven instances of this type of redistribution, presumably one in each of the eleven communes.

5 This seems to have had a large impact on the data for Yäju, Ambasäl, and Mänz. For instance, in Yäju, 49% of the holdings had been acquired after 1989, compared with 7% in Däsé Zuriya and 1% in Tägulät (Yeraswork 2000: 196).

6 For a critical assessment of an afforestation project and its impact on peasant land holdings, see Melasuo and Amare (1990: 41) who reported an average land loss of a staggering 30% in the Gärado area just west of Däsé, reaching 49% in the commune of Asgädo.

of the developmental state. This distinction is empirically and theoretically important.

In Ankobär, reallocation was of even less importance (Yigremew 2000a). 10 per cent of respondents had acquired their land before the land reform, 76 per cent at the time of the land reform, and only 14 per cent acquired their land after the land reform. Furthermore, 19 per cent of the respondents indicated that they had acquired all of their land through inheritance. Concerning frequency of changes in holdings after the land reform, 89 per cent reported that there were no changes, while 6 per cent had gained some land and another 6 per cent lost some land. This indicates a very high incidence of tenancy before the land reform, and that the land reform had great impact in terms of equity. However, the area was densely populated, and the absence of major reallocations suggests that inequalities in operational holdings was not a major problem. Above all, in this rugged and inaccessible landscape, there was little government intervention in the production system.

LAND REALLOCATION IN DINJA S'IYON

The role of specific government policies is brought out rather clearly in the data from Dinja S'iyon in West Gojam, gathered by Yigremew in July 2000. According to former leaders of the commune as well as other knowledgeable peasants, there were seven rounds of land redistribution, including the land reform itself:

1976 The land reform. Three individuals were elected to allot land and three to serve as judges. This reform led to the abolition of tenancy and confiscation of land held outside the commune. The latter feature was probably rather common in this community, due to its communal *rest* tenure, a feature it shared with Baba Säat (see Chapter 5).

1978 Distribution of land according to family size. Unmarried women also received land. This was implemented by the commune administration under the supervision of the district administration and district peasant association.

1980 A minor reallocation to give land to new households and to others with little land. Unmarried women also received land. The source of land was vacancies (those who had died or left[7]).

1982 A minor reallocation, mainly to provide land to new households. Some of them received 0.75 hectares.

1985 A minor reallocation to redistribute the land of the producer cooperative when it was moved to another area, outside the commune. Most new households were given two parcels of land, while many others who already had small holdings were given one parcel.

1986 Reallocation due to villagization. Land was given both to those

[7] *Motä käda* and *t'ilo haj*, respectively.

who were villagized (house sites of 40 metres by 25 metres) and to those who lost their land for this purpose. Land was allocated both for farming and for grazing.

1988 Reallocation to enforce villagization, which was obligatory. In order to prevent people from going back to their previous villages, their former grazing fields were allocated as farmland to other households.

Of the seven rounds of land reallocation, the three from 1985 onwards were clearly specific-purpose reallocations, and most probably affected only a small fraction of the land. From the descriptions given above, the first four appear to be equity-driven, of which two were clearly minor readjustments. The data on the first two make them appear as major events, but the discussion of the peasant land tenure system in this chapter, as well as the breakdown of similar data from Ayné (Chapter 3), may suggest that rather few parcels of land actually changed hands.

Table 4.1 Allocation of land for different purposes[8]

	Purpose	*Ha*	*Source of land*
1	School construction	2.25*	Peasant holdings
2	Office construction	1.50	Peasant holdings
3	Adult training centre	7.25*	Därg opponents
4	Church construction	2.75*	Communal grazing land
5	Office for Women's Association	0.50	Vacant land
6	Office for Youth Association	1.00	Vacant land
7	Afforestation sites	56.80*	Peasant holdings
8	Nursery for seedlings	0.50	Peasant holdings
9	Store of Service Cooperative	1.50	Peasant holdings
10	Store and office for AMC	2.00	Peasant holdings
11	Store and office for Service Cooperative	2.00	Peasant holdings
12	Producer cooperative, 85 households	-	Peasant holdings
13	Villagization	64.00*	Peasant holdings and grazing land
14	Revenue for the commune	8.00	Därg opponents
15	Revenue for maintenance of church	3.00	Vacant land
16	Priest (*märigéta*)	2.00	Vacant land

Note: Figures with an * are from the records of the district agricultural office. The remaining figures are from estimates by the commune leadership.

8 This table is based on a field survey by Yigremew Adal in 2000. 'Vacant land' refers to land without any recognized legitimate claimant. 'Därg opponents' refers to the land of those who had waged armed resistance against the Därg regime in 1978. Many of these holdings belonged to former district officials or individuals with government positions.

Dinja S'iyon is adjacent to the district capital, Gäbäzä Maryam, which was a threat to the rural commune in terms of land confiscation. According to the former leaders of the commune, lands of the commune were confiscated for various purposes. Table 4.1 summarizes the information.

Those who were involved in decisions about land reallocation included the district administration, the district peasant association, the commune, political cadres, and the district villagization task force. In some cases, like allocating land for church revenue, some elected elders were also involved, and the issue had to be approved by the community at large. The leaders of the commune complained that the district capital, a small town, had been undergoing constant expansion. There was no consultation with the commune leadership when land was needed for urban-related purposes. The district administration simply informed them about its decisions and instructed them to compensate the peasants who lost land by giving them land elsewhere. Since there was not enough land available, many of the peasants were not compensated.

Land was also assigned to provide revenue for institutions, whether for the church or the peasant association. Leaders of the commune reported that under the Därg, priests and the local church committee asked for land to be used for the maintenance of the church and for buying needed articles. The church was given half a hectare of land that belonged to someone who had left (*t'ilo haj*). The priests cultivated the land for two years and submitted the produce to the church. Since then it had been rented out to sharecroppers. They also said that the church had retained the land in the 1997 Amhara land redistribution.

The commune had no budget from the government even though many of its tasks belonged to the sphere of formal administration. The commune needed to cover operational expenses, like paying *per diem* for travel, buying office furniture, constructing office, buying stationery, etc. The decision to allocate land for such purposes in every commune came from the district peasant association. The local committee identified land that belonged to people who had been killed during and after the 1978 resistance against the Därg. The people of the commune cultivated the land and the commune was then able to accumulate about 6,000 birr. Later on, the land was suddenly snatched from the commune and allocated to the adult training centre. The local leaders appealed to the district administration, but were told that this decision had come from higher authorities and could not be changed by the district.

The villagization campaign, which started in 1986 in Dinja S'iyon, was one of the major causes of land confiscation. Houses were dismantled and moved to the new sites. People from other communes were made to participate in this work. Houses with roofs of corrugated iron were located in one site, while those with thatched roofs were located in two other sites. There was strong vigilance and control by the district authorities (as representatives of the state) over the campaign until

1988. The local leaders said that they had tried to resist. The people had elected representatives who appealed to the party at Finotä Sälam and had even gone to the zone administration at Bahir Dar. But their application was turned down. When these representatives came back from Bahir Dar, some of them were imprisoned at the district administration. When the peasants tried to resist villagization and returned to their previous locations, their former grazing lands were allocated to others for farming. After the fall of the Därg, some of those grazing fields were returned to their previous users. During the political turbulence in 1990, people recognized that the government was weak, and the majority of those villagized took the opportunity to return to their original house sites.

The other principal disturbance in peasant land tenure was the creation of the producer cooperative. The area to be used for the producer cooperative was demarcated by a committee composed of representatives from the district administration, political cadres, mass organizations and others. Eighty-five households were recruited and were given a lot of land. Those who had land in the area were given the choice to join the cooperative or to abandon the area (see also Poluha 1989: 137; Yeraswork 2000: 205–7). Those who refused to join were meant to receive land in compensation, but this did not actually happen. Some of these peasants later joined the cooperative. If someone allowed livestock to graze in the cooperative's area, they were fined or even imprisoned. Fortunately, the cooperative was soon closed and moved to another district with an excellent site for irrigation.

Dislocated peasants were always theoretically entitled to receive other land as compensation. However, in practice very few obtained full compensation. First of all, not all received new land, and those who received compensation might find that their new parcels were far away, on poor land, or exposed to attacks by animals.

In the late Därg period, all types of land transfer through committees were banned by a directive. Land sales intensified due the decline of the government's control over the area. It was especially common for people to sell the land they had been assigned in the villagization sites. In the beginning, each parcel of 40 metres by 25 metres was sold for 40–60 birr. Later on the price went up, fetching 100 birr as an annual rent and more than 300 birr if sold.

Land exchange among peasants was practised both during and after the Därg period. During the Därg period, exchanging land within the commune was allowed. The reasons for such exchanges mentioned by the leaders of the commune included distance to the land, to produce different crops on different soils or altitude, to consolidate holdings, to escape quarrelling with an unfriendly neighbour, to get a good house site, or to avoid problems due to the encroachment of another farmer's livestock. Agreements concerning exchange of land were made in front of witnesses. If disagreement later arose, each party would get back his former land.

PEASANT LAND TENURE IN DINJA S'IYON

Pre-reform land tenure in Dinja S'iyon corresponds closely to the communal *rest* land tenure system described by Hoben (1973). In 2000, the commune consisted of three parishes. Before the 1974 revolution, each parish was administered separately as a fief (estate of *gult*). Peasants held their land from the lineage group, represented by the 'father of the land' (*rest abat*). Everyone who belonged to a lineage of *rest*-holders was a landlord (*balabat*), while outsiders had no rights to the land of the lineage. Farming was undertaken by individual households, and there was considerable tension between the rights of individuals and those vested in the lineage. Other farmers might mobilize latent inheritance claims based on rights traced as far back as the 'father of the land'. Land disputes were therefore common.

The principal way of accessing land was *rest* via the kinship system. In some areas, with uncultivated land that had not yet been divided, farmers could ask the representatives of the kinship group who controlled the area to be granted land as newcomers. They had to clear and farm the land in order to gain possession. There was also sharecropping, but in Gojam this was much less common than in North Shäwa. The common share for the landowner was one-fourth of the produce, but it varied between one-sixth and one-third. Land could also sometimes be borrowed for free on the condition of paying the annual tax.

Inheritance was mostly awarded to sons, daughters, wives (if they had children with the husband) and other close relatives. Sons received personal land grants (*gulma*) from their parents when they decided to establish their own households. Daughters usually moved to the residence of their husband, but in principle they had equal land rights. If determined enough, daughters could possess some land and rent it out even if they did not live in the area.

The land reform abolished the rights of landowners, including the *rest* rights. Within the peasant community, the reform negatively affected mainly older farmers. It should be pointed out that these were most likely to lose land anyway, mainly as a normal part of the household cycle, but also perhaps in defeats in a land case within the *rest* system.

Eleven elderly farmers (with an average age of fifty-seven years) who had established their households well before the land reform were asked about their lands. Four of them said that they had lost some land located in other communes during the land reform. Ironically, later on the communes were merged, making it permissible for them to farm the land. They had also lost some land which had been farmed by sharecroppers at the time. Both these elements were aspects of the early phase of the land reform. Another six informants reported that the commune had taken some of their land after the first reform. Ten of them reported that they had married off some sons (on average 2.3 sons each). Ten of the eleven said that they had given a good deal of personal land to their married sons. Some of them indicated that as a result, they currently did not have enough land and were farming some additional land on sharecropping terms. They underlined, however, that it is a moral obligation to give land to sons. In the group discussion it was also noted that sons, of course, have the right to ask for their *dersha* through the commune if the parents refused. However, they considered such cases to be embarrassing.

Eight of these eleven elderly farmers reported that all their current parcels were theirs before the land reform, and three reported that about half had been theirs the whole time. In total, however, it was found that all had experienced some change in their holdings since the land reform, be it positive, negative, or in both directions.[9] Of these changes, three were both additions and reductions, two were additions only, and six reductions only. Rather than periodic land redistribution shifting parcels of land around, the impression is of a process of levelling down, whereby land considered as excess (*terf*) is confiscated, in addition to the effect of specific-purpose reforms.

We expect elderly farmers to be net losers, within the *dersha* system as well as within a redistribution system. However, if there were periodic redistributions, we would also expect those who established households after the land reform to report losses as well as gains of land. In other words, the distinction is between a quite normal process, certainly within Amhara society, of transferring land from the parent generation to the new generation, which creates 'tenure insecurity' for the older generation – and a system of redistribution and turmoil, which creates tenure insecurity for all. The following analysis is based on discussions with forty-two male household heads, all of whom established households after the 1975 reform.

According to local custom, young males married while living with their parents. This was quite an extended phase, lasting on average 3.5 years. During this period, the household accumulated the animals and land needed for sustenance, while the young wife learnt how to run a household. The young man would usually farm some of his parents' land (perhaps also that of his wife's parents). Eighty-one per cent of the sample had lived like this. The arrangement with the parents varied, but 70 per cent of those who went through this phase had been paying one-third of their produce to their parents (*siso*). Six per cent had been farming the land on *ekul* (50 per cent) terms, while 21 per cent paid one-fourth, and 6 per cent worked and ate together with their parents. The last category was especially common if only the mother was alive.

During this phase, the son did not own the land he farmed nor did he pay the land tax. Traditionally, after living some years like this, the son would expect to receive land from his parents as his personal land (*gulma*) and become the head of an independent household. After the land reform, the household was in principle entitled to land via the commune. However, the main source of this land was also the parent

[9] Four during and seven after the reform.

household. During the land reform, land had been allocated based on household size, and so the youngsters had a claim to a share (*dersha*) in the household of their parents. This fitted well with the customary *gulma* practice; it was a moral obligation for parents to provide a fair land endowment for their children. Finally, there was little other land available, although some was released when a person died or left the area without recognized successors. All the elements here seem to fit closely with the *dersha* system described for Ayné (see Chapter 3).[10] Usually parents assigned land to their children more or less voluntarily. When they established own households, 79 per cent of the sampled young males had received land only from their parents, which had been given willingly. However, 19 per cent reported that although the source of land was their parents, they had had to force them by appealing to the commune. This was a quite serious and rather embarrassing measure, usually applied only after mediation by elders had failed.

Only 57 per cent of the sample had received any land from the commune, up until the end of the Därg period. The data are not very precise, but on average 2.5 parcels had been transferred from the parents, while 1.9 parcels had been allocated by the commune. By comparison, at the time of the fieldwork in 2000, 2.3 parcels were held in tenancy. There is no information available on any land loss by these young households, rather strongly indicating that this was not a major concern.

One case may illustrate the most common, and certainly the most culturally appropriate practice. A 35-year-old farmer with three children told how he received land from his mother:

> I was living with my mother. She was divorced. I had one older brother, but he was living elsewhere. All my sisters were married and had gone to their husbands' places. My mother and I were working and eating together for four years. When I established my own household in 1987, we arranged to share the produce equally. The whole land was in her name. In 1997, when there was land registration, we divided the land in such a way that one parcel belonged to her and three to me. The registration committee endorsed our arrangement. Now she has one ox and I have one ox. I plough her land for free.

Note that he established his household rather late in the Därg period, and he did not pay the land tax before the fall of the Därg. When he finally started to pay the tax, and thus formally became a landowner, it was simply an official recognition of what he and his mother had practised for years.

However, the intergenerational transfer was inherently problematic, partly because of the different interests of parents and children, and partly because the number of children usually exceeded the amount of land available for allocation. This situation is illustrated in the case of a 37-year-old farmer with five children:

[10] The main difference is the extended period of co-residence, which in Ayné was usually very brief. It appears that in Dinja S'iyon, primary household accumulation took place to a large extent after marriage, which would place the parent generation in a stronger position than in Ayné.

> In 1981, I established my household. I had one ox and worked with my parents for one year, paying them one-third of the produce. In 1982, I wanted to get my own farmland. I asked my father for land. He gave me a parcel just for a house and refused to give me more, using the pretext that the rest of the land belongs to the younger children. I tried to resolve the issue through elders, but I failed. Then I appealed to the committee. The committee took 0.75 hectares of land from my father and gave it to me. They also wrote a letter stating that thereafter those parcels belonged to me, and instructed my father not to cultivate those parcels again. My parents got irritated and they complained to relatives about such a letter. Later on, my grandfather mediated to prevent hostility. My father learnt a lesson; when my younger brother established his household, my father gave him enough land willingly and there was no problem.

This conflict happened rather early in the Därg period, just after the first two phases of the land reform. According to key informants, there was also a minor allocation of land by the commune in 1982 (see timeline given above). Most probably, at this time, the rules of the *dersha* system were not well established and the father may have expected his son to receive land which had been confiscated by the commune from others. For all we know, the case reported above may have been one of the first in which the *dersha* principle was enforced. Such cases served as examples not only for those directly involved. They were widely discussed and showed to everyone that the rules had changed.

The pre-reform *rest* system was based on kinship. This certainly continued to exert influence via the expectations it created, but in the *dersha* system, the decisive element was household membership at the time of the land adjustment reform (LEC in Ayné). The next example illustrates the tension between claims based on household membership rather than kinship, as well as the intergenerational conflict. A 35-year-old farmer with six children told how his wife's parents had refused to give him land:

> After I married, I lived in the house of my wife's parents for one year as *yä-wäskämbiya lej* [a married son living in the same house as his parents or the parents of his wife]. I established my own household in 1986 in the village of my wife's parents. I worked for two years with my wife's parents, getting one-fourth of the produce. When I started my own farming in 1987, I asked them to give me land. They gave me only 0.25 hectares. I complained saying that I have already children from your daughter, I am a member of your family and hence I deserve more land, but they refused to give any additional land. I asked them through elders, but they still refused. However, the fact is that when the committee had redistributed land, I had been counted as a member of their household. Therefore I appealed to the committee for my share of land [*dershayén t'äyäqhu*]. The committee ruled that I am entitled to a third of the land and they took two parcels from my wife's parents and gave them to me. Her parents got angry. They tried to end our marriage and expressed regret that they had brought me to their residence, but they could not do anything. They had not even given me a homestead, and therefore I moved to another location and constructed my house there. Later I noted that they allotted enough land to their son when he established his household.

CONCLUSION

This chapter is based on a brief fieldwork in Gojam. By its nature, it is explorative rather than conclusive. It is, however, supplemented by previous work in Ankobär and a reading of Yeraswork's study of government policy in Wälo and North Shäwa.

Local informants told about seven rounds of land reallocation in Gojam. Similarly, Yeraswork found up to seven rounds in Wälo. This may be compared to the four rounds identified by a similar method in Ayné (Ege 1990: 229, and Chapter 3). However, only the first two rounds seem like major cases of land redistribution, and even in these cases, we suspect that rather little land was transferred from one farmer to another (see Chapter 3). It seems that the reforms referred to were first when farmers took possession of all the land they had farmed, including rented land, followed by a second phase when holdings were adjusted according to household size.

The tenure histories of old and young household heads suggest that most of the transfers were by household processes, even when they happened via the commune. After the initial reform phase, the main alternative source of land was, apparently, from people who had died or left. The accounts focus on household processes rather than the rounds of land redistribution by the commune.

Several of the rounds of redistribution mentioned were due to specific government programmes, notably producer cooperatives and villagization. Although these were not very extensive in terms of the land covered, they sent clear messages to the peasants that the land ultimately belonged to the state. The eminent power of the state does imply the potential for arbitrary eviction. This aspect of the land tenure system should be further studied in the context of the nature of the political regime.

The differences between the land tenure system in Dinja S'iyon and that of Baba Säat in North Wälo (in the next chapter) are interesting. Both had communal *rest* land tenure before the 1975 land reform, so we might thus expect the reform to follow the same trajectory. In Dinja S'iyon, there was a process of adjusting holdings around 1978, and as in Ayné, this seems to have served as some kind of land tenure constitution, the point of reference for later claims. Baba Säat, however, did not see a single comprehensive reform to readjust the holdings, only a series of minor reforms. In terms of equity, they may have achieved much the same result, but, as described in the next chapter, it would appear that the *dersha* system did not develop there.

5

Land Tenure in Baba Säat, North Wälo

SVEIN EGE

The previous chapters dealt with land tenure in the more central parts of the Amhara region. In this chapter, we turn to the extreme highlands of North Wälo, which is less accessible and of less interest to the government due to its low agricultural potential. Here land tenure followed a different path from the southern part of the Amhara region, both under the Därg and afterwards. There was no initial complete registration of households and their lands. Consequently, the *dersha* system did not develop. Neither does the redistribution theory provide a good fit. Instead, this is a case of standard family-based land tenure with a typical patriarchal flavour. However, a series of reforms led to a step-wise reduction in inequality during the Därg period. This was taken one step further by the EPRDF land redistribution in 1991. From the available descriptions of this reform, this appears to have been a very real redistribution that established exceptional equality; but it also seems to have created much uncertainty about government land policy, evidenced in the way peasants talked about their land holdings. For them, new rounds of land redistribution in the future were probably not off the table.

There are only a few studies of land tenure in northern Ethiopia after the land reform. For the Därg period, the only major exception I can think of is the study from South Wälo by Teferi Abate (1998). There are some unpublished M.A. theses at Addis Ababa University, and a number of published studies touch on the subject but do not make it their focus. The TPLF-EPRDF period is apparently much better covered, although here the literature tends to fall into one of two camps: the pro-TPLF studies from Tegray (Young 1997; Hendrie 1999; Chiari 2003), and the rather critical studies of the 1997 land redistribution in the Amhara Region.[1]

There is reason to question what we know, or rather believe we know, about land tenure in northern Ethiopia. This specifically applies to such key elements as the widespread understanding of *rest* as the general

[1] There are quite a few relevant studies here, with a fine spread throughout the Amhara region affected: Askebir (2012) on South Gondar; Ege (1997b, 2002c) on North Shäwa; Getie (1999) on East Gojam; Teferi (1997, 2000) on South Wälo; and Yigremew (1997, 2000b, 2001) on West Gojam.

land tenure system in the north; of *rest* as communal land tenure; that the Därg period was characterized by periodic land redistribution; that the peasants were eagerly awaiting the EPRDF land reform; or that women lacked land rights until they were liberated by the EPRDF.

Fieldwork for this study took place in 2002 and 2003 using survey methods, qualitative notes related to the surveys, and independent key informant interviews. There were eighty interviews of the last type. Although all these form the basis of this chapter, I have sought to keep references to a minimum. Local informants are referred to by their names, but if the information is deemed in any way sensitive, I have used pseudonyms, marked by an asterisk (e.g. Alämu*). A list of such pseudonyms is found in my archive, document number 10839. I do not provide the date of the interviews since they were made over a short period of time.[2]

The study area was Baba Säat commune, in Guba Lafto district (Wäldiya). It is divided into Lambäch'ama, Säat and Baba wards, from north to south.[3] The fieldwork focused on the hamlets of Wäf Kätäma, Shemageloy and Dubaw Tärara, all in southern Säat. Baba Säat is an extreme highland area, about 3,500 metres above sea level, producing barley and livestock. The typical highland crop, horse beans (*vicia fava*), is not cultivated here due to frost. Before the road from Wäldiya to Däbrä Tabor was built in the early 1980s, this area was somewhat remote. Now it is rather close to the road but still has a markedly rural atmosphere, underlined by the harsh climate. We are near the upper limits of human settlement in this part of Ethiopia.

THE LATE IMPERIAL PERIOD

Baba Säat was a land of *rest* ('inheritance'). Informants liked to contrast the highlands stretching from Baba Säat to Gondär, the land of Emperor Fasil, with the service-dependent tenure in the conquered Yäju lowlands. In Baba Säat land belonged to the peasants, while in the lowlands it belonged to the government.[4] Reality was of course a bit more complex, and in the highlands there also existed tracts of government land, where tenure depended on specific services rendered. And in the lowlands, locals would presumably in many cases consider themselves as landowners, adopting a somewhat different view of ownership than the highlanders.

In the Säat area, all peasants were landlords (*balabat*), holding land by *rest*, unless they were newcomers who had married into the area. There appears to have been very few such exceptions. The main reason for any

[2] See the Bibliography for information on my interviews, including the dates.

[3] For a map of Baba Säat, see Ege and Yigremew (2002: 18).

[4] This is mentioned in several interviews (e.g. D9656: 1–3, Yaläw Kälkay). The pre-reform tenure in Yäju was *alänga märét* (lit. 'whip land'), by which tenure was dependent on military service. This seems rather similar to the *gendäbäl* tenure of the Yefat area.

'newcomer' to settle in Baba Säat was usually to protect *rest* rights, as in the case of Täfära Ejegu, whose parents lived in the Wäldiya area and had most of their land there. Täfära moved to Baba Säat with the specific intention of taking over the 6 *t'emad* of land belonging to his father.[5] His five siblings preferred to stay in the lowlands, where their mother had much land.[6] Thus Täfära, born in Zobel and raised in Wäldiya, was considered a newcomer – albeit one with deep roots in Baba Säat, able to trace his lineage back to Eno, one of the three founding fathers (*aqni abat*) of Säat. There are a number of similar cases, and it appears to have been a common strategy for children, male or female, to marry where one of their parents had land. The other type of newcomer could be a landless person who married someone with land in Baba Säat; in this case, their children would become landlords when they inherited whatever land the local parent had.

Rest rights in Baba Säat can best be understood as private property. The role of the headman (*aläqa*) – one for the land of each founding father – was to collect contributions for the church and taxes for the government. In case of land disputes, he and other elders would also seek to reach a compromise, and he would represent the estate of the founding father in the case of an external attack, when an outsider sought to insert himself into the genealogy, as happened in a famous case in 1945.[7] In fact, it appears that all the known elements of the *rest* system were present, but land ownership was much more secure and more individualized than commonly thought (cf. Hoben 1973). Informants seemed to think of the inheritance of their parents' land as a routine matter, although there may very well have been some squabbling within the family. Exceptions were mentioned, but the fact that they had to be picked from a rather large area and over a long time span indicates that this was a very small part of all the land transfers, although it might be quite traumatic when it happened.[8]

Although practically everyone was a landlord, this was not a society of equals. In the past, it had supported a feudal structure, and there were still strong remnants of this social system in the late imperial period. While one landlord might have only a few *t'emad* of land, there were cases of local persons holding more than 100 *t'emad*,[9] and one informant even counted his father's holding in *gasha* ('shield'), a land unit that was both much larger and, above all, associated with the state rather than peasant farming.[10] In all the cases I know of, the larger holdings were

5 D9658: 1, Täfära Ejegu.
6 D9659: 4–5, Täfära Ejegu.
7 D9659: 5, Täfära Ejegu.
8 For sample cases: see D9658: 3, Täfära Ejegu, about a case from neighbouring Baba; and D9659: 3, Täfära Ejegu, about a case from Chebena. Both cases were experienced as extremely unjust, which is probably why they were remembered.
9 By standard conversion, 1 hectare equals 4 *t'emad*. For a brief discussion of *t'emad* complexities, see Ege (1997b: 13–15).
10 The standard conversion of a *gasha* is 40 hectares, which equals 160 *t'emad*. In northern Ethiopia the *gasha* was often much smaller.

scattered, with land inherited through different lineages in different localities. It also appears that in the case of really large holdings, most of the land was in the lowlands, sometimes in rather distant locations.

From the source material, it might appear that most established farming households at this time were quite solid. A number of case histories tell of possession of 20 to 40 *t'emad* of land, two to four oxen and many other animals. We might easily get the impression that everyone was rather well off in those days. However, the same case histories also point towards groups of near-invisible persons, the farm-hand (*gäbäré*) employed to till the land, the poor woman grinding the grain by the handmill, or the poor who had to ask for loans of grain or money.[11] Famine was also a frequent experience, as far back as informants could tell, and there is every reason to believe that hardships and famine particularly affected the lower echelons of society.[12]

Thus, the information points to a society bound together by 'big men', although quite small big men.[13] Täfära Ejegu is a rather typical example. Before the land reform, he had 18 *t'emad* of *rest* land in total. In addition, he farmed 10 *t'emad* through sharecropping. He had four oxen and hired a farm hand. At one point he had a fifth ox that he rented out to a peasant in Koso Amba, ten to fifteen kilometres away. He also had five cows and two horses. He used to harvest at least 40 quintals a year, more than the household needed, and all his stores were full.[14] Grain was occasionally spoilt by being stored too long, but he also lent grain and money, not just to his relatives, but also to neighbours and poor people in the area. He used to give away some 10 quintals a year in the name of loans. There was no interest paid, not even in the customary way of working a certain number of days. Often the loans were not even paid back.[15] The elements described here are rather typical, not least the social aspect of lending. In fact, in all my material for the whole period spanning my study, I found only two counter-cases: a better-off peasant who used to give loans in return for interest; and another who lent in return for labour.[16] To lend to the poor, persons with whom one associated regularly, was a social, even a religious, obligation.[17]

11 D9693: 23, Käbädä*; D9648: 2–3, Mola Agazhu.
12 D9650: 3-6, Amarä Yazäw; D9651: 3, Ayälä Mola; D9652: 5–7, Wärqé Mälaku; D9654: 14–15, 19, 21, Sheshegu Aqatä.
13 This concept has been used perceptively by Hendrie (1999: 254–5) to describe society in Enda Maryam (Tegray) before the revolution. It captures well the post-feudal inequality of the late imperial period.
14 I have translated *kuntal* as quintal, and *ch'enät* (donkey-load) as 0.5 quintals, all common conversions used by the peasants. These are, however, variable units.
15 D9658: 4–5, Täfära Ejegu.
16 D9658: 5, Täfära Ejegu and D9693: 3, Käbädä*. Both these practices are well known in rural Ethiopia, but both in Baba Säat and in the Yefat area they are much less common than what is usually assumed in the literature.
17 See D9681: 1, Wärqu Kasaw, for a very telling example, where the informant refused to name his debtors because this concerned only God.

The society described here was very different from Ayné in Yefat, where I had previously done extensive fieldwork.[18] In pre-reform Ayné, very many of the peasants were tenants, and the rich were a class above the working farmers. In Baba Säat, most of the land was cultivated by owner-cultivators, and much of the sharecropped land may have been cultivated by peasants topping up their own holdings. Furthermore, in the source material from Säat, sharecropping barely figures, and so far I have not come across a single farmer who mainly depended on rented land for the upkeep of his family. There may have been considerable local variation, however. For instance, the governor of the sub-district had acquired a tract of land in Baba, which was presumably cultivated by tenants.[19] There is fair reason to believe that there were similar pockets of land belonging to large landowners scattered all over the highlands, but in Säat itself the impression is of a quite tightly knit community where the rich were better off, but not very different from their neighbours. Much of their surplus was spent on supporting the less fortunate, investing in social relations rather than in property. For Täfära, these were happy days: 'There was always milk, meat, local beer, and we lent as we wanted'.[20]

Land rights did not discriminate between men and women, adhering to the principle of ambilineal descent.[21] This was much more than abstract theory. Without going into detail here, it may be pointed out that females figured as frequently as males in the genealogies tracing land claims.[22] The obvious implication is that at one time in the past, a woman held these land rights, while her husband normally held other rights. Furthermore, the composition of household land in the late imperial regime replicated this pattern in modern times; the land holding consisted of the wife's land as well as that of the husband's, with the latter not necessarily any larger than the former. Although the land was actually worked by the husband or other males, *rest* rights were not empty facts. In case of divorce, the woman would routinely take her *rest* land to her next household.

THE DÄRG PERIOD

The fall of the emperor in 1974 came as a shock and the highlands were soon in revolt.[23] Initially the Därg, by means of the student

[18] I use the historic term 'Yefat' to refer to the eastern escarpment formerly covered by Mafud and Qäwät district.
[19] About the land of the governor, *Fitawrari* Gétahun Kasa of Sanqa, see D9658: 3, Täfära Ejegu.
[20] D9658: 5, Täfära Ejegu.
[21] This part of Hoben's (1973) study fits Baba Säat well.
[22] D9659: 1, 4, Täfära Ejegu. For instance, Eno was a woman and thus, in the language of modern feminism, a founding mother rather than founding father (*aqni enat* rather than *aqni abat*).
[23] Dessalegn (2008: Chapter 3) provides an extensive account of revolts in South Wälo, in areas bordering on Baba Säat.

campaigners, was able to establish a rudimentary commune administration, but due to the revolt, the first chairman, Ayälä Mola, had to flee the area. The rebel army took control and was able to fend off several attacks by the Därg administration; they even thought of attacking Därg positions at Muja town in the valleys of Gedan. It all ended, however, on 22 November 1975 (12 Hedar 1968), when a large force of the Därg army, supported by militia from the Yäju lowlands, invaded Baba Säat, burnt houses and slaughtered or drove away the livestock. People saved whatever they could by taking refuge in the inaccessible Zhet'a valley, starting a little west of Baba Säat. This was a most traumatic experience. The area suffered famine for the next few years, mitigated by government aid and by sharing whatever was available.[24] After this event, the Därg was in complete control and apparently also quite successful in winning over the peasants, although this was later undermined by forced recruitment: for the army, for resettlement and for cotton picking in the Humera lowlands.[25] In Baba Säat itself, the typical development efforts of the Därg in the form of afforestation or producer cooperatives had little impact, and this left peasant land tenure less disturbed than in more accessible areas.

Informants emphasized that there was no proper land redistribution under the Därg. There may be several explanations for this situation. First of all, it may have represented a standard application of the land reform proclamation, which treated the northern *rest* areas as a special case.[26] Secondly, it may be that the political situation made it prudent to limit intervention in this particular area. Thirdly, by the time Baba Säat was controlled well enough to implement careful land redistribution, the time for this type of reform had already passed, and the official policy was leaning more towards replacing peasant agriculture with 'modern' collective farming. Fourthly, I am quite sure that no official wanted to stay long in the bleak highlands of Baba Säat, perhaps preferring to concentrate their efforts in more comfortable and rewarding areas. Finally, it may even be that there was no strong need for any large-scale redistribution of land, a point which finds considerable indirect support in the evidence, as outlined below.

After the 1975 proclamation, land rights had completely changed, and there were very significant equalizing processes taking place. Firstly, the land-to-the tiller principle meant that tenants became owners of the land they cultivated, unless the owner was a very poor person. Secondly, in 1979, after the new commune administration was well established and the administrative borders were defined, no one

24 This episode is covered in several interviews, most extensively in D9651: 3–7, Ayälä Mola; and D9654, 15–21, Sheshegu Aqatä.

25 The loss of state legitimacy was expressed not only by those who suffered from this policy, but also by the local leaders. For interviews with some prominent former leaders, see D9661: 7–8, Sisay Adisu; D9663: 3, *Qés* Ert'eban Negusé; and D9662: 1, Mulugéta*.

26 The account of Gojam in Chapter 4 suggests, however, that there was no special treatment of the *rest* areas in general.

could hold land in another commune. As described above, larger holdings consisted of lands from different areas; any land located outside Baba Säat was now lost. Those who lost land might be compensated by land made available in Baba Säat by the same principle, but large landowners systematically lost out against the priority claims of poor people.[27] Although this reform seems to have aimed primarily at administrative rationalization, the equalizing effect should not be underestimated. From the case histories it appears that it was this reform which most effectively levelled out inequalities in land ownership.

A few years later, in 1983, there was a reform with the specific aim of equalizing holdings. There were no precise guidelines, however, and the process was handled by the leadership committee itself, rather than by a separate committee. Everyone, including the chairman in charge at the time, as well as the richer peasants, seemed to agree that the effect was rather limited. A few *t'emad* were transferred from those with good holdings to those with little land. Further adjustments followed the 1984–85 famine and the succeeding resettlement, both of which had less impact here than in many other areas of the north due to the highland climate of Baba Säat.[28] All these events are mentioned in key informant interviews about land reforms, but they do not appear to have significantly changed the social structure, and they do not usually pop up in case histories. Neither do they fit well into the standard image of periodic land redistribution. Superficially, we might count them as some four rounds of land redistribution, but the social content and the implications for tenure security were rather different than those of the periodic land redistribution model.

The levelling down that took place during the Därg should not be underestimated, however. Gone were the holdings of 100 *t'emad* or more. One informant, who served on the land committee for the EPRDF reform, listed the following as large landowners in 1990, on the eve of that reform: Adanä Läma, 20 *t'emad*; Kasa Negaté, Mola Agazhu and Däjän Achänäf, 16 *t'emad* each; Bärihun Däsalägn, 14 *t'emad*; and finally Täfära Ejegu, 12 *t'emad*; in other words, they ranged from 3 to 5 hectares using standard conversion.[29] Despite the fact that there was no major redistribution of land, there had been a quite dramatic levelling down.

Land tenure is more than the size of holdings. Peasants no longer held land in various *rest* estates where they could claim inheritance. Formally, the household, not the individual, now held land from the commune. Within these limits, however, peasants appear to have

27 See D9661: 1–2, Sisay Adisu for a general description and his own case; see D9644: 1, Ayänäw Gäbré, who was a comparatively large landowner at the time. In the EPRDF reform in 1990, he was officially classified as feudal even though by then he had lost most of his land.
28 D9663: 2–5, Ert'eban Negusé; D9654: 22–3, Sheshegu Aqatä.
29 D9662: 4, Mulugéta*. By international standards, such holdings would usually be considered to be well within the smallholder category, but they were mentioned as examples of the upper level of land holdings in Baba Säat.

thought of their *rest* land as just that, *their rest*. For the peasant who only had *rest* land within Baba Säat, the change may not even have been very apparent. After all, this was for most of them land they had worked on since childhood, land which their parents and near relatives had worked before.

The new situation will, however, have had considerable impact on marriage practices. Obviously, the incentive to marry outside the commune, wherever the family had land, disappeared. In theory, new households were landless until they obtained land from the commune. In practice, new households mainly received land from the parents on both sides. This did not preclude cross-border marriage, but there were risks, and it was certainly easier to marry within the locality.

From the description of marriage customs, it appears that the specific arrangements did not change. There was a quite elaborate exchange of gifts, and the young couple would initially live together with the groom's parents and work the family holding jointly. When they finally established their own household, they would receive a share of the grain harvested, some farm animals, and most importantly, some land, later to be increased by inheritance. Animals and land were contributed by both sides, according to the marriage contract.

Marriage practices can tell much about the social system, notably the transfer of property rights from one generation to the next. Of particular interest is the degree to which parents could control their children's access rights and how rights differed between males and females. The impression from the life histories gathered so far is that there was surprisingly little change from the previous period. As has been pointed out, although the *rest* system as such had been annulled, the micro-elements of *rest* continued to operate within the community. Apart from the major adjustments in holdings resulting from the various reforms – as well as the fundamental fact that all land was now held from the state via the commune and could be taken away by any political whim – within this framework, transactions in land went on much as before, notably in the form of gifts at marriage as well as inheritance from parents or other appropriate relatives. It is these practices that pop up again and again in the life histories, but sadly enough, these practices are under-explored in the literature.

The behaviour of young people continued much as before. They typically had to serve the parents with whom they lived: the man's parents in what was thought of as the standard type of marriage; or the woman's parents if the young couple lived with them.[30] Service by the young couple involved a considerable transfer of labour, although what is of interest here is not so much the amount as the type of dependency relations established. The system contrasts strongly with the practice in Yefat, where youngsters had a much more independent position and typically accumulated own property and held personal land (*gulma*)

30 The latter was referred to as *gebut* marriage. Service to the woman's parents could start years before the actual marriage. This equals the *qot' aser* of Yefat.

before they married. In Yefat, a young man could even take his parents to court if they refused to give him his share of the land. So far I have not found any evidence of this practice, the key element in the *dersha* system, in Baba Säat. The impression is rather strongly of the parent generation being in control, not usually in any negative sense; and the formation of new households was regulated by age-old customs and a sense of proper relations between parents and children, rather than by new laws and a more individualistic spirit.

I do not have good information on divorce practices under the Därg, a key indicator of women's rights. In theory, land was allocated to the household, usually represented by the male. This may be thought to have weakened women's rights compared to the pre-reform *rest* system, but it is not necessarily so. First of all, there is reason to believe that divorce usually led to a division of land according to the local notion of justice.[31] The fact that women had equal rights in both the *rest* system and after the EPRDF reform, combined with the fact that the informants did not point towards any difference in this respect during the Därg period, provides rather strong circumstantial evidence. It may even be that in many cases, each spouse just took their own *rest* land, especially if this seemed fair. Finally, in the case of divorce of young households who had received land from their parents, the standard practice would be for each spouse to keep their own land, and perhaps to return to the parent household.

THE EPRDF REFORM

From 1989 onwards, the EPRDF marched from victory to victory, until the Därg was finally toppled in May 1991. The liberation of an area was soon followed by land reform in order to consolidate their hold on the peasantry. The process in Tegray and the northern Amhara provinces seems to have followed the same basic pattern.[32] In Baba Säat, land reform started only a couple of months after the area was conquered, and the process lasted from November 1990 until February 1991. At the time of my fieldwork, this was just about a decade ago and one would expect it to be easy to establish a detailed and reliable image of this process. Not quite so.

The land reforms implemented in Tegray and the northern Amhara provinces just before the collapse of the Därg have been covered in several studies, but they are not well understood. The studies are often rich on interpretation but very brief on how the reforms were actually implemented in the locality, notably the specific rules – often hiding

31 My tentative interpretation of this is influenced by my fieldwork in Yefat; it is consistent with my evidence, but this topic has not been critically investigated.

32 The EPRDF land reforms were suspended after the fall of the Därg and thus not carried out in the southern Amhara provinces, until they unexpectedly restarted in 1997.

behind general statements about local variation without providing any specific evidence, or even giving any hint indicating the author actually investigated the claimed variation. This applies specifically to the main studies from Tegray, which seem to shy away from any critical issues and are content with describing this as a very just reform, as it was officially claimed, in contrast with the Därg reform (Young 1997; Chiari 2003; Hendrie 1999). The studies from the Amhara region show much greater scholarly independence, but also here it is somewhat difficult to understand how the reform actually worked (Mekonnen 1999: 180; Teferi 1998: 64). In general, the reform itself is treated very briefly, and the concern is more with the effects of the reform than with its content.

The problem is that we still do not have any clear understanding of the reform. For instance, it is generally claimed to have had a great equalizing effect, but so far, I have not seen any study even attempting to document this, again with the partial exception of the study by Teferi (1998). In the case of Baba Säat, there is good evidence that this reform further levelled down inequalities.[33] In Baba Säat, I undertook a complete census (the Indicator Survey).[34] As part of this, my assistants were instructed to record their estimation of the economic status of the households on a score ranging from one to ten, with 'poor' recorded as three, middle as five and 'rich' as seven. These are the standard values, while the other scores may be used as necessary. The categories have a local flavour, as even the 'rich' may suffer occasional food shortage. We have used this method in many locations, and it is common to find a fair spread across this variable. In Baba Säat there was an exceptional concentration around the middle value, with only 18 per cent classified as poor, 10 per cent as rich, and a few households beyond these values. Of particular interest was that many were classified by the intermediate values of four and six, which are not normally much used. Apparently, my assistants found it too extreme to classify somebody as poor, although the household was perhaps a little below the average. Thus, 63 per cent of all households clustered into the narrow range of four to six.

There are also some apparent misunderstandings about the EPRDF reform. These are somewhat complicated issues and it may therefore be useful to outline the argument in simplified model terms. In the common accounts, it is usually stated that husband and wife were entitled to one share of land each (sometimes half a share each), and this share is then described as something approximating a *t'emad*. Such a holding would thus equal 2 *t'emad* (half a hectare). By contrast, I

33 Most, but not all, informants agreed on this. Perhaps the most telling piece of evidence is a summary statement by Ert'eban Negusé (D9663: 6), who was sometimes vice-chairman and sometimes chairman of the commune for most of the Därg period: 'What makes me sad is the time of the Därg, not the current one'.

34 For a further description of the method, see Aspen in Chapter 6 of this book, and Ege and Aspen (2003: 19–20).

believe that the underlying model was that husband and wife got half a share each, and – this is the significant difference – each of these shares consisted of one house-near land and one distant land, each of 1 *t'emad*. Thus the standard household holding would be 4 *t'emad*. The flaw in the standard account is mixing the shares of husband and wife with the unit of measurement, rendered as *t'emad* in my model.

In this simplified version, I have disregarded ecological or regional variation in the basic design of the reform, which I believe was less than claimed in the literature. The size of the land might vary with ecology, but the underlying model seems to have been widespread, perhaps even universal in the late years of the civil war. I have also disregarded children, who added only a little land (see the following discussion below). Finally, there are the rules to compensate for variation in land fertility, which have also been misunderstood. The standard account makes the error of claiming that a peasant received the lands of all three fertility classes (i.e. fertile, medium fertility and infertile). In my view they received whatever land was available, but there were conversion rules to equalize the values of the land. This meant that what was allocated as 1 *t'emad* could actually be much more in terms of area, but not in its supposed value.

My reinterpretation is partly based on the information from Baba Säat, although the information there is somewhat opaque, as discussed below. I am also strongly influenced by the rules underlying the 1997 Amhara land redistribution, which was arguably an extension of the earlier EPRDF reforms.[35] However, due to the lack of detailed descriptions of the reform in various locations, this reinterpretation should be regarded as a hypothesis, rather than a well-documented theory. It does, however, bring some order to the evidence from Baba Säat.

Let us review what we know, with some critical remarks pointing out the problematic elements. The following is based on the totality of the literature, coloured by my own understanding of the process in Baba Säat:

1. The basic unit was the *geber* ('tax'), the amount of land thought to be appropriate for a household, or more specifically for husband and wife. The actual household holding could vary in both directions, depending on the composition of the household.[36]

[35] The EPRDF model, with all its concepts, was very much a TPLF design. Teferi Abate (1997: 63–4) has some brief but very telling comments about the perplexity of peasants in 1991 when they heard of the strange new terms, like *wäjäd* for the house-near land, and the distinction between *birokratoch* and *ch'equn*, between Därg officials and the oppressed. See also Yeraswork (2000: 209) for the EPRDF class analysis. This may be compared with accounts of the 1997 Amhara redistribution (e.g. Yigremew 1997: 67).

[36] The Amharic term *geber* is less commonly used as a landholding unit than the corresponding Tegregna term, *gebri*. It is, however, clearly visible in the common reference to half *geber* and in the rules underlying the reform.

2. Single adults, like widows, received half a *geber* (and thus they had the status of *gemash geber*).
3. Unmarried youngsters above specific age limits, lower for women than for men, were treated as single adults, and thus in practice as half households, even if they lived with their parents.
4. There is, however, quite some confusion as to what a *geber* is, and only in Teferi's study is there a serious attempt to break it down into its constituent parts. In some studies, this household unit is confused with the operational unit of land measurement, in Baba Säat referred to as the *lek* ('measurement'), which was the standardized *t'emad* of 50 metres by 50 metres.[37] Thus Chiari claims that the *geber* in his study area was 50 metres by 50 metres, that entitlements ranged from a half *geber* to two *geber* for single adults and large households, respectively. This would make holdings range from 0.13 to 0.5 hectares, but his survey data showed a much more reasonable average of 1.02 hectares (Chiari 2003: 79, 123; see also Bruce *et al.* 1994: 23; Asmelash 2006: 48). This is important for us because some of the sources from Baba Säat could easily be read in the same way.
5. Land was divided into different categories, notably house-near land (*wäjäd* or *gwaro*) and distant land (*bäräha*, lit.: 'desert'). Some land would additionally usually be set aside for communal purposes, and in Baba Säat the peasants also received private grazing land.[38] The latter resources can easily be left out in survey reports, but they may be of considerable economic importance in some areas.[39]
6. The land was measured with the rope (*gämäd*), often presented as a TPLF innovation but was actually an old custom in Ethiopia. Land was also distributed by lottery. This may create the somewhat misleading impression of a full-scale process of land measuring and the assigning of all land by lottery. Indications, however, are that the rope was used to assess the size of the house-near land, while lottery might be used here and there when actual land redistribution was undertaken elsewhere.
7. Land was classified into different fertility classes. This did not mean, as is sometimes claimed in the literature, that everyone should have land from all classes. It was instead a complicated system of standardization. Thus, by rules widely reported, 50 metres by 50 metres of fertile land could be replaced by 50 metres

[37] It is also often referred to as *gämäd* (rope), by the instrument of measurement. It may also be referred to as *t'emad* or *tsimdi*, which by standard conversion equals 50 metres by 50 metres. However, the size of the unit might vary with ecology.

[38] D9333: 1, Berhanu Bétä.

[39] It also makes it problematic to compare land estimates from different areas. In Wäyra Amba (Yefat) grazing land was part and parcel of the holding. In Baba Säat a question about the household holding would normally only record the farmland, while the grazing land would often add 1–2 *t'emad*, that is, increase the holding by roughly a third.

by 75 metres of medium quality land or 50 metres by 100 metres of poor land.

8. It is frequently claimed that all entitled adults received land. This is incorrect, although it will probably be a routine claim by officials. A problem with the standard accounts is that they seem to be based on quick interviews with key informants, often officials, and the formal rules are mistaken for what actually happened. There were certainly people who did not receive any land, or received much less than their formal entitlement. If there was less land than assumed by the rules, youngsters were especially likely to lose out, as happened on a massive scale in the 1997 reform in the southern Amhara zones. Due to differences in design, the problem was probably smaller in the reforms around 1990; at that time land was confiscated from everyone, not just from the Därg officials, and thus there was more land available for distribution.
9. Similarly, it is a widespread view that women received land independently, thus marking a 'milestone' in the liberation of women (e.g. Young 1997: 185). The statement is true in the sense that the basic household entitled to one *geber* can be thought of as two adults, who would each be entitled to half a *geber*. However, the basic unit was still the *geber*, and in the later tax lists such holdings were usually registered in the name of the husband, just as under the Därg.[40] The obvious difference could potentially be in the case of divorce, when the woman would take her half *geber* with her. However, this is not fundamentally different from the *rest* system previously described, and it may also have been common practice under the Därg, as it clearly was in Yefat. It might also be added that widows, a common type of female-headed households, should in principle lose by this reform and would actually risk destitution.
10. Children counted little, and this was a major difference from the Därg land reform, at least as implemented in Yefat (see Chapter 3). In what appears as a standardized practice in Tegray, a household with five or more children would be entitled to one additional *geber*, that is a child would count as less than half an adult, and in the case of large households even less than that (Chiari 2003: 80; Asmelash 2006: 48). As reported from Wälo by Teferi (1998: 64), the discrimination against large households could be quite dramatic. The basic household holding amounted to 5,275 square metres (just above 2 *t'emad*), while eight additional children would only lead to an increase of 625 square metres.[41] The information from Baba Säat is highly variable in the precise rules, but otherwise it fits into the same basic pattern.
11. Finally, in all the cases reported, this major reform appears as a very speedy process, finished in just a few months, often in a situation of

[40] For the Baba Säat tax list, see D9221.

[41] Teferi may have misunderstood some elements, but even the most optimistic correction (adding the children's share to each of the parent's parcels) leads to serious discrimination, requiring eight children to double the farmland of a couple.

> war. In some studies, and in all the official information as well as in local information tailored to be politically correct, the emphasis is on the democratic process, with meetings and elections, and not the least measures taken to prevent corruption and favouritism. But this was actually a top-down approach where all the basic parameters were set outside the commune. It was democratic as defined from above, with forced popular participation and probably demonstration of support, but not democratic as experienced from below.

It should be pointed out that the discussion above has focused only on the official rules. These rules were not always followed, perhaps for very good reasons.[42] Favouritism and small-scale corruption was widespread. Claims to the contrary in some studies are almost certainly reflections of political preferences rather than based on careful investigation. In Baba Säat we were also initially told the official version, but as soon as we gained the confidence of the peasants – by living close to them this did not take long to happen – we were flooded with stories about manipulation and favouritism. Such stories even tended to cloud the main issue of the official rules. These rules are, after all, by far the most important element for understanding the reform, and the point of departure for local adaptation and tricks. Such tricks were ubiquitous, but they typically led to only minor adjustments.

It is not easy to make sense of the empirical material from Baba Säat due to numerous contradictions and half-truths. Either informants were not able to describe the reform in a comprehensive and logical way, or they did not want to. There are indications pointing to the latter, at least as a partial explanation. It also seems to be much the same situation as faced by scholars studying the process in Tegray.[43] This is very different from my studies of land tenure under the Därg, both in Yefat and especially in Ch'orisa (Qalu). In both those cases I was surprised by the quality of the information originally provided when I later checked it using more in-depth methods. In Baba Säat, however, from the very first day there was a certain smoke-screen over the information. Such differences tell much about the underlying history of land tenure and state-peasant relations.

Our first informant may serve as an example. We met Alämu* during a brief visit in October 2000 (Ege and Yigremew 2002). He told us that he had only two parcels of land, one house-near land and one distant land, each amounting to 1 *t'emad*.[44] This seemed very little, but he insisted

[42] It is easier for peasants to bend the rules than to make officials change problematic rules.

[43] See especially Hendrie (1999: 300–1) for a description of the problems of obtaining reliable information. Such problems may also help to explain some of the misconceptions about the reform.

[44] This fits the standard account of the EPRDF reform outlined earlier in this chapter.

it was correct. We had to leave the topic for the time being.[45] Later, during the Indicator Survey, he reported having 3.5 *t'emad* plough land and what might amount to about 1 *t'emad* of grassland. If we had been sipping local beer and chatting in a friendly atmosphere, I would not have been surprised if the holding increased considerably, especially since Alämu* turned out to be one of the better-off farmers.

This pattern also emerged from another case. Käbädä* told us in an interview that he had 4 *t'emad* of farmland and 2 *t'emad* of grassland – what we might consider the official version.[46] In another setting, he repeated this, but added that the farmland actually amounted to 6–7 *t'emad*.[47] In the Indicator Survey, the amount of farmland decreased to only 2.5 *t'emad*, a figure good enough for outsiders, whether they would report it to the administration or were drawing up plans for some kind of aid. Furthermore, although most peasants registered 4 *t'emad* or less in the Indicator Survey, some reported up to 10 *t'emad*, plus grazing land, figures well above what would be permitted by the official rules. These peasants did not necessarily have more land than others. It is rather that some peasants reported the real holding, some reported the official version, and many, perhaps the majority, reported a somewhat downscaled version: 3 *t'emad* when they had actually been assigned 4, which they would happily think of as amounting to 6–7 *t'emad*. Or as one peasant replied with a big smile when I asked how he could possibly live from just 2 *t'emad*: 'The land here can be very productive'.[48]

It is really very difficult to establish a clear picture of the specific rules of the 1991 land reform in Baba Säat.[49] Käbädä* stated in the interview that he had received 4 *t'emad*. This, I believe, was according to the official rules in Baba Säat. In addition, in other contexts, including in some of the survey data, 4 *t'emad* appears as the standard holding for husband and wife, as in my model above.[50] On this basis we might expect that the standard allotment would be 1 *t'emad* of house-near land and 1 *t'emad* of distant land for each adult, and double this for a married couple, in other words one *geber*.[51] This is well exemplified by Sisay Bälaynäw. Since he was very recently married, he and his wife received land in separate areas, with each receiving 1 *t'emad* of house-near land and 1 *t'emad* of distant land.[52]

It is puzzling that none of the interviews specifically covering the rules of the reform support this simple picture. There are also a number

45 This case has been described in some detail in Ege and Yigremew (2002: 17–19).
46 D9693: 9, Käbädä*.
47 D9422: 9, Mäsärät Kenfä.
48 The quote is from memory. I believe the peasant in question was Alämu*, but so far I have not been able to locate it in my notes.
49 See also Aspen's account in Chapter 6, reporting typical peasant discourse on the reform, with information that is not easy to convert into a clear description of the process.
50 See D9691: 1–2, Däreb Däräsä; D9664: 2–4, Sisay Bälaynäw.
51 See also Teferi (1998: 64) for a similar pattern.
52 D9664: 2, Sisay Bälaynäw.

of contradictions in these interviews, and certainly many gaps in the information. It is too early to seek to establish an authoritative picture of the reform, which may have varied even within Baba Säat itself. Let me recount the information from one well-placed informant called Mulugéta*. The following is an abridged, paraphrased and somewhat reorganized version of a four-page interview:[53]

> According to the guidelines, husband and wife would receive one *t'emad*, or 50 metres by 50 metres of land; this would be increased to 50 metres by 75 metres if it was of medium fertility and 50 metres by 100 metres if it was infertile.[54] A woman above eighteen years or a man above twenty years got *gemash geber*. Household size was also considered, and eight children would lead to one extra *t'emad*.
>
> The land reform was 'uprooting' (*ser näqäl*), meaning that nobody could claim any land by previous ownership rights; it was all up to the team. People were told in no uncertain terms that those who opposed it would be imprisoned, and therefore the reform could be implemented effectively.[55] They did not make any registration of household members and land holdings.[56] Since the team consisted of nine local peasants, they knew who had a lot or a little land. All registered land claimants got land, and some ten *t'emad* was set aside as 'reserve'. This was later distributed to people who returned to Baba Säat after the reform. Persons who had been party members under the Därg (EWP) should not get land if they were not present,[57] but their family members were entitled by the same rules as others. In Baba Säat there was only one such person.[58]
>
> The land redistribution was equal. The house-near land was measured by the rope. Distant land was given jointly to eight household heads and sixteen children; the sixteen children equalled two heads, and thus the total group equalled ten household heads. This group was assigned twenty *t'emad* jointly, or slightly less if the land was fertile.[59] The group would divide the land among themselves. If the household had more than one child, these were taken into account. There was no favouritism, and the team was not influenced by kinship relations.

The last statement we do not take too seriously; after all, our informant was the team leader. There is overwhelming information to the

[53] D9662: 1–4, Mulugéta*. To indicate a certain distance to the original, I recount the story in third person plural, rather than the first person plural used by the informant.
[54] Many accounts stop here, giving the impression that this was the only land received. This is the source of the common misunderstanding noted above.
[55] Such warnings will have had great weight in Baba Säat, where the disaster following the resistance against the Därg was still quite fresh in people's memory.
[56] This is quite surprising and must have created considerable problems. The reason for this could be that Baba Säat was short of literate peasants who could act as secretaries. This is in contrast with my evidence from Yefat, but it was probably a widespread problem.
[57] And if they were present, they would be arrested and taken away, and were thus not present.
[58] This quite limited discrimination is a major contrast with the 1997 reform in the southern Amhara zones. In Baba Säat, peasants were even permitted, after some haggling, to elect a previous chairman, *Qés* Ert'eban Negusé, as chairman under the new regime, something quite unheard of in Yefat.
[59] *Bäräha* land would often be less fertile than the house-near land; thus, the point of departure was apparently land of medium fertility.

contrary, although that information does not necessarily apply to his team.

This is the only interview which mentioned assignment of distant land to a group. In addition, the information provided by Mulugéta* on the handling of land for children differs somewhat. Another informant claimed that for children, land was added to the main parcels: nothing for the first child and 2 *kend* per additional child. If the husband and wife were assigned 3 *t'emad*, 50 metres by 50 metres each, 2 *kend* would be added to each of these if they had two children. *Kend* is usually translated as cubit (48 cm), but in this case 24 *kend* equalled 50 metres. By this account it would take thirteen children to double the holding from the basic *geber*.[60]

From the account of Mulugéta* it would appear that the basic *geber* corresponded to 1 *t'emad* of house-near and 2 *t'emad* of distant land. In the other interviews, there is information conflicting with this, but it is virtually impossible to disentangle it. Several informants also described the fertility conversion rules as 50 metres by 50 metres, 50 metres by 75 metres, and quite strangely 100 metres by 100 metres for fertile, semi-fertile and infertile, respectively. I rechecked the last figure, but the informant insisted.[61] Against such a background, there seems to be ample room for manipulation and playing with the figures, as long as the land was seen to be measured using the rope. In any case, the mathematics needed to calculate the size of the irregularly shaped parcels of land are well beyond the curriculum of Baba Säat Elementary School, which few, if any, of the distributors had completed.

The EPRDF land reform is quite difficult to understand if we take the information literally. However, if we disregard what appears to be errors in the available descriptions in the research literature, as well as in my interviews, the impression is that it was remarkably standardized in its basic design, with little room for the local community to shape the rules. This may have led to much unofficial adaptation in the legal grey zone, and beyond. The land tenure system established was also rather complex. The 'nose of this hippopotamus' is visible in the Indicator Survey, where some households reported that they were paying three land taxes, some often in another commune. There is little doubt that the reality was even more complex, e.g. with land registered in the names of children who lived in Addis Ababa or elsewhere. Some of the practices were according to the current 'law', some were in a legal

60 D9695: 5, Magegnät Sheshegu. In a number of interviews, as well as in the literature, the mathematics do not add up.

61 D9684: 7, *Qés* T'ägaw Täfära; rechecked in D9685: 1; see also D9643, Adeno Shefäraw. The same information was also gathered in neighbouring Chebena (D9675: 2, Mäsfen Aligaz). The same figures are reported by Aspen in Chapter 6. It is difficult, however, to accept this information. One possible explanation could be that these figures did not have much meaning for the interviewees. Perhaps they were the theoretical rules they had been taught and could easily repeat, but when it came to the actual assignment of lands, they may have just used their good sense.

grey zone, and some would probably lead to land confiscation if they were officially known. In such a situation, information becomes sensitive, and it may not be desirable that an outsider understands too much.

Although it may be difficult to say exactly how much land a peasant has, the various attempts to cover up information may tell us a lot about the land tenure system, the lack of trust and the need to hide information from outsiders in general and from higher administrative levels in particular. This is an important part of the land tenure system in itself and should make us treat survey data with some caution; it may also provide some entry points into the various aspects of peasant land tenure.

In this chapter we have traced land tenure history in what used to be a remote part of the highlands. In contrast with Gojam, the traditional *rest* land tenure of the imperial period here was not replaced by the *dersha* system under the Därg. The key variable seems to be the way the reform was implemented, due both to the civil war in the early phase and to perhaps a certain lack of government interest in these bleak highlands. We have also seen that Baba Säat turned out to be a remarkably equal society, a process that started with the Därg land reform and culminated with the EPRDF land redistribution of 1991. The latter reform was implemented all over the northern half of Amhara in the last years of the civil war. In the next chapter, Aspen investigates developments in an area not so far from Baba Säat, but in a rather different ecological situation, with both lowlands and, above all, a roadside market village with a certain urban atmosphere and more scope for inequality.

6

Rich and Poor: Land and Wealth in Mäqét, North Wälo

HARALD ASPEN

INTRODUCTION

In the Amhara highlands, the household is a key economic institution, being the basic unit for production and consumption. It is an autonomous unit, but with numerous links to other households, through kinship, work, and other rights and obligations through formal or semiformal institutions (see Aspen 1993). In the previous chapter, Ege explored the history of land tenure in a rural community in the extreme highlands of North Wälo. In his analysis of Baba Säat, Ege found that the society was remarkably equal, as a result of the 1975 land reform and the 1991 EPRDF land redistribution. In this chapter, the community under investigation is also in North Wälo, but further west and, in contrast to Baba Säat, centrally located along the major highway that connects the community to the big markets in Gojam, Tegray and Addis Ababa.

The topic here is the distribution of key resources and how this affects patterns of relative wealth and poverty in the peasant community, specifically in Jerelé commune. North Wälo, where Baba Säat and Jerelé are located, is the region that became emblematic for Ethiopia as a poor and famine-ridden country, or, as Gill (2010: 3) has expressed it, 'the iconic poor country'. Wälo was hard hit by the 1984–85 famine, and was for many years afterwards a recipient of international 'emergency aid' (cf. Aspen and Ege 2010: 1). Detailed knowledge about the peasants' rights to and use of land, and the strategies they employ under shifting political, legislative and climatic conditions, stands out as an extremely important prerequisite to combating new crises and the prevailing insecurity and poverty in the northern highlands.

In this chapter, I present a glimpse of how some of these elements are related in survey data collected in North Wälo around 2002. My ambition is to analyze how key resources are distributed in the peasant population and to explore what patterns of relative wealth and poverty can be discerned. I mainly discuss how land, together with a few other key resources related to farming in the northern highlands – in particular manpower and draught power – are distributed between households and how they are managed, in relation to variables commonly used as indicators of productivity and wealth. The analysis shows that there are tendencies towards greater differentiation in the more 'urban' part of the commune (Arbit), while in the rural wards the situation resembles that of Baba Säat, as described in the previous chapter by Ege. In this chapter, an overall picture of Jerelé is presented, while the specific tendencies of growth and a development towards a more urban economy and orientation is dealt with in the following chapter (Chapter 7).

JERELÉ COMMUNE

Jerelé commune is located in the south-western part of Mäqét district in North Wälo. The majority of the population live off agriculture. Most live directly from farming. A small, but apparently growing, part of the population depends indirectly on agriculture, through trade and trade-related activities (see Chapter 7). Jerelé is the name of one ward (*got'*) in the lower part of the commune, but it is also the official name of the administrative unit as a whole, comprising several wards. Although Jerelé ward has lent its name to the whole commune, it no longer serves as its centre. Even if a new building is constructed close to the school in Jerelé to house the commune administration office, the role as the centre has for all practical purposes been taken over by Arbit, to the extent that in everyday parlance the commune might just as often be referred to as 'Arbit' as 'Jerelé'. In the following, I refer to the commune as Jerelé, and to the specific ward with the same name as 'Jerelé ward'.

In contrast to Jerelé ward, which lies in a typical rural environment, Arbit also had the appearance of a 'centre': it lies on the highway from Wäldiya to Däbrä Tabor, it hosted a weekly (Friday) market, and consisted of a cluster of dwellings, stores, a few kiosks and 'cafeterias', and a mill. As such, it resembled a number of other small market villages along the road, all of which held weekly markets on alternate days. Arbit also hosted the representatives of the state – the agricultural and health extension workers. The office for official business, including the commune administration, was located in Jerelé ward but was little used. Meetings with officials from the district level were usually arranged in Arbit, rather than in the less accessible (and inaccessible by car) offices in Jerelé ward.

Jerelé itself stretches along the highland plateau, and also includes the steep escarpment and lowland areas to the north. The altitude of Jerelé ranges from about 2,900m (Arbit ward) to 2,400m (Jerelé ward) and is lower further north. The descent from Arbit, on the plateau, to places like Jerelé ward and Mäqärqariyat, is steep and dramatic, and outright dangerous in the wet season. The difference of around 500m in altitude between the higher and lower tracts of the commune also implies great ecological differences. While the highland is relatively plain and fertile, with flat fields interspersed with quite a few lush green eucalyptus plantations, the lowland is drier, with many signs of depletion, as testified by the shades of grey that colour the landscape.

In such a varied ecology, the conditions for livelihoods in general – and for agriculture as a source of living in particular – also greatly vary between the different parts of the commune. As such, the area largely mirrors North Wälo, where ecological variation is extreme over short distances. An additional factor is infrastructure, in particular proximity to the road system. The survey data, which I shall return to shortly, may to some extent reflect these differences, but they are not aimed at providing a complete picture of conditions in Jerelé, Mäqét or North Wälo. The lowlands proper were omitted from the survey, which concentrated on three sub-sections of the commune: Arbit, Galadäjän and Mäqärqariyat wards.

Arbit ward comprises the settlement around the marketplace. The market, and its location literally on the highway, have contributed to a steadily increasing population in the little 'town', which has further speeded up since the survey was conducted, due to a massive upgrading of the infrastructure (see Chapter 7). Galadäjän ward also lies on the plateau, bordering the escarpment to the north, while most of Mäqärqariyat covers the escarpment and the lower tracts below it (north-east of Galadäjän).

Agriculture on the plateau is characterized by relatively flat fields, with a dominance of rain-dependent crops typical for the highland (wheat, barley and pulses), large tracts of grazing fields, and an increasing presence of eucalyptus cultivation for sale. Eucalyptus logs are bought by middlemen and exported on large trucks to urban centres such as Mäqälé, Däsé and Addis Ababa. Peasants refer to eucalyptus as 'vegetables' (*atkilt*), which in turn is synonymous with cash crops. The demand for eucalyptus not only provided a means of cash income for peasants who cultivated them – it was also a source of income for daily labourers who carried the logs to collection points at the road and loaded them onto the trucks (see also Chapter 7).

The peasants who farm the land on the highland plateau depend on the application of fertilizer. 'Without fertilizer we get nothing', an informant in Galadäjän exclaimed, adding, 'But when we use it, even if we cannot use the recommended quantity, it gives good product'.[1] Application of UREA/DAP fertilizer has doubled the harvest of highland plots, according to a representative of the district's Ministry of Agriculture. Due to the cost of fertilizer, however, peasants tend to apply less than the recommended quantity.[2]

While fertilizer had become an integrated part of highland agriculture, it was not commonly used in the lowland. During a field visit in Jerelé some years later, a peasant said: 'The soil is very old, that is why we produce less. We do not use fertilizer here; it is in the highland that

1 NW 1: 107, 14.03.2003 (see the Bibliography for information on my field notes and archives).

2 Most only apply about half the recommended quantity, according to the specialist (NW 1: 106, 14.03.2003). This was in 2003, however, and attitudes and practices have changed, with fertilizer becoming more accepted and used in subsequent years.

they use that. For one, it is very expensive – but also the soil, if we use fertilizer, it may get dry soon'.[3]

LAND

Informants from different places in Mäqét have described two major land redistributions: the first by the Därg, around 1980;[4] and the second by the EPRDF in 1991. The land redistribution that followed the land reform appears to have been a series of events which took several years, from about 1978–79 when the users of the land were registered, to the actual redistribution (*shegesheg*[5]) which was completed as late as 1984.[6] The EPRDF redistribution, in contrast, is consistently dated to 1991 by all informants in Mäqét. Informants who had relatively more land before the revolution told the same story: while the Därg reform reduced their land holdings to some degree (especially if they had relatively more land, or if they had land in more than one commune), the 1991 EPRDF redistribution left them with even less. During the EPRDF redistribution land was classified in three quality/fertility categories, and each household received a certain combination of these categories. In contrast with the Därg reform, there was no clear-cut system during the EPRDF redistribution of shares for individual family members, although the size of the allocated land could increase if the family was large.

Evidently, land tenure rules and practices in the Ethiopian context are neither clear-cut, nor without great local variation (see Chapter 2). It is also problematic to try to differentiate between local interpretations of the rules and how they were in fact implemented. Sometimes the two periods (Därg and EPRDF) may also be confused by informants and researcher alike. I obtained an account of how the EPRDF redistribution was regulated and implemented based on a group interview with three commune leaders who attended a meeting at the Mäqét district's Ministry of Agriculture (MoA) office in June 2002.[7] The three men were assigned by one of the MoA district officers to explain to me how the 1991 redistribution had been implemented. We should therefore be

[3] Arbit 1: 153–4, 25.02.2010.

[4] See Aspen and Ege (2010) for brief accounts of the Därg land redistributions in three other communes in Mäqét. In Jerelé one informant explained that he received his land from the Därg in 1984 (Arbit 1: 71–5).

[5] On the concept of *shegesheg*, see Chapter 3.

[6] This was the case in Debeko commune according to an informant (Aspen and Ege 2010:73). In Dänkäna commune an informant explained that 'the land reform transferred the land ownership to the tillers (*märét lä-aräshu*), and they continued to plough the same land up to the distribution', which started in 1977 and was completed the following year. Land was distributed in a way by which 'each family member got 2 *t'emad* land' (Aspen and Ege 2010: 51). In general, the descriptions of the Därg land distribution have much in common with the '*dersha* system' described by Ege in Chapter 3 in this book.

[7] NW 1: 79–84, 08.06.2002.

cautious in interpreting their account as a description of actual practice, as it may well be a normative and politically correct representation of the rules. To the extent possible I have compared it with information from peasants elsewhere in Mäqét district (see also Aspen and Ege 2010, and Chapter 5 in this book).

At the EPRDF redistribution husband and wife together received one plot of good quality close to their house (*wäjäd märét*), and could also be allocated land from the two other categories (middle and low quality land)[8]. One plot of good land measured 50 metres by 50 metres, medium land was 50 metres by 75 metres, and poor land 100 metres by 100 metres. If the family had more than one child, they would be allocated additional land. If there were adult children in the household at the time of the distribution (boys over eighteen years, girls over twenty-four years), they had the right to receive their own land (as one-person households, 25 metres by 25 metres). Each family had also the right to a plot (20 metres by 20 metres) on which to build a house, if they did not already have one.

According to the representative from Dänkäna, there was no land left after they had distributed to all the households according to the rules, while the representative from Qemqem explained that after the first round was completed, two (of the originally seven) members of the distribution committee were assigned to distribute the remaining land equally to everybody.[9]

Another source, from Agrit commune (north-west of Jerelé), explained that one share of land had been defined as 3 *kitar*, equal to 50 metres by 50 metres. 'Even households as big as 10 members would only have the right to get a portion of three people', he said, but any individual older than twenty-three or eighteen years (men and women, respectively) was also entitled to one share of land.[10]

AN EXAMPLE FROM ARBIT

A case from Arbit illustrates how things actually became after these rounds of reallocations. In 2002, Welätaw Fäläqä lived in a relatively new house, at the outskirts of Arbit town.[11] He was the head of a large household, with ten members in total. Five of the household members were adults: Welätaw (forty-two years) and his wife (thirty years), his mother (sixty-six years), and his oldest daughter Bayu (twenty years) and her husband Däsé (thirty-eight years). Bayu and Däsé had married ten years ago, and just had their second child.[12] Däsé had no

[8] The terms used were *mähalägna märét* (middle quality land) and *ch'ench'a märét* (low quality land).

[9] NW 1: 82, 08.06.2002.

[10] NW 1: 11, 30.05.2002.

[11] NW 1: 84-9, 08.06.2002; ISHouseholds #1096.

[12] Even if it was a rough estimate by the family head that Bayu and Däsé had married 10 years ago, it seems likely that Bayu was formally married to her

land of his own and lived by sharecropping. The couple shared the space in Welätaw's house with the rest of the family, including the kitchen. They used the wood for cooking in common, but food was not shared and they ate separately. In the survey, this extended family was considered as one household. The way they had organized their cohabitation – living under the same roof but eating separately – indicates that they were, at least symbolically, two separate households, which was the ideal cultural norm.

In the survey, we recorded Welätaw as having 4 *t'emad* of farmland. In the informal talk we had with him, however, we obtained more detailed information. He told us that he had land both in the lowland and on the plateau near his house. The land up on the plateau 'is 1 *t'emad*, but sometimes it is 1.5–2 *t'emad*', he said, alluding to the dynamic character of the land measurement unit (a *t'emad* is the size of land that a pair of oxen can plough in one day). The land in the lowlands was about the same size. In addition, his mother had about 0.5 *t'emad* of land in the lowlands, where he also had some grazing land of about 0.5 *t'emad*. Since the land that belonged to the household was formally registered as belonging to two individuals, Welätaw and his mother, they had to pay two annual land taxes.

The land holding of this household was apparently the result of a combination of historical periods of land tenure change, even though officially the land that individual farmers controlled was regarded as having been allocated to them by the EPRDF redistribution. In other words, as described in the previous section, all the land in the commune was distributed in 1991, but in most cases, much of the land (but far from all) was actually returned to the previous holders. The local conception of the post-1991 redistribution was therefore expressed as loss of land, rather than as (re)allocation of land. A statement by a peasant in Arbit, Teleq Berihun, illustrates this. When he was asked about his mother's land, he explained it had belonged to the family since the Därg land distribution in 1975, but that there had subsequently been a 'new' distribution by the EPRDF. He said, 'The land is the same, even if it has become smaller'. Somewhat contrary to this, he also stated that his mother had obtained land for herself and his younger brother through the EPRDF redistribution, and that this was the first time his brother had received land 'since he was too young that time [at the 1984 redistribution]'.[13] Others present at this group discussion commented that Teleq himself was lucky as his land had remained the same since the

(contd) husband before she had reached maturity. Early marriage, especially for girls, is a well-known practice in this part of the country. It seems common for the young wife to move to her husband's family, while in this particular case, the girl Bayu remained with her natal family while her husband Däsé moved in. Usually, when a girl is very young, the consummation of the marriage will be postponed, and the husband and wife live together as 'sister and brother' under the protection of the older generation (Berihun and Aspen 2010).

13 NW 1: 3802.06.2002. The notion of 'share' is obviously at work here (see Chapter 3).

time of Haylä-Selasé; Telaq's land was *rest*[14] – an inheritance from his father (*yä-abat wers*).

Similarly, Welätaw also held land which he categorized as *rest*. He said that his plots in the lowland 'was [sic] the property of my father during the time of Haylä-Selasé. The size of the land was reduced at the time of the Därg, and it shrunk even more now by the EPRDF'. Welätaw had originally lived in the lowland but had moved up to the plateau 'just after the EPRDF take-over' for health reasons.[15] Here he had then been allocated land by the EPRDF redistribution in 1991.

The procedure was that land plots were measured by rope (*gämäd*). One *gämäd* was 40 cubits (*kend*) long. The share for husband and wife was 1 by 4 *gämäd*. At the time of the EPRDF redistribution it seems that Welätaw had two children. He explained: 'I got 6 *kend* [later explained to be 6 *kend* by 4 *gämäd*] for one child, even if I had two – one of them was not counted for. If they had been four, we would have got 12 *kend*. Now I have eight children, but only one of them has been counted for, the others are counted with me'.

Welätaw had two oxen and a cow and needed grazing land for the animals. He had two sources of animal fodder: one was his own plot of grazing land in the lowlands, and the other was a share of a formerly common pasture field (*yä-gara*) in the highland of Galadäjän, next to Arbit. This pasture field used to be 'just common', but after EPRDF came to power, it was divided into shares which were distributed among the original users on the basis of their cattle ownership. A committee had been established, which assessed ownership of cattle and beasts of burden and distributed shares of the pasture accordingly.[16] The specific parts of the pasture used by each individual right-holder rotated annually, to even out differences in produce over time.

Even if Welätaw ploughed the land both he and his mother had direct rights to, it was not sufficient for sustaining his household. Consequently, Welätaw had a sharecropping contract with an elderly woman who had previously lived in Arbit, but after falling ill, she now lived in the district capital Felaqit. He rented two plots from her, one in the lowland and one in the highland, in total about the same amount of land as his own. The woman was a relative of Welätaw's wife – her elder brother's widow. In this area, the usual sharecropping agreement was *yä-ekul* (equal shares of the produce), and this was probably also the case here. In addition to sharing the produce with the land owner, Welätaw was also responsible for covering the land tax for her and the cost of the fertilizer used on her land.[17]

14 See Chapters 1 and 5 for more discussion on *rest*.

15 NW 1: 87, 08.06.2002

16 According to Welätaw, owning two cattle gave 2 *kend*, three cattle gave 3 *kend*, and so on.

17 Welätaw complained that even with the application of fertilizer, production was lower now than it used to be during the time Haylä-Selasé and the Därg, when they did not apply fertilizer. 'The land has become very old', he said.

What does Welätaw's case tell us? Perhaps most of all, it describes an intricate system of land rights, where some land holdings remain from the historical period when *rest* was the principle for land access, and other land holdings are the result of the two major events after the revolution: the Därg land reform and the EPRDF redistribution. Welätaw's household more than doubled the land they farmed by using sharecropping agreements,[18] and in this case, the agreement was made between distant relatives.[19] The size of his household was relatively large, and with two male adults and a pair of oxen it was probably at its peak development cycle. Welätaw's failing health perhaps announced the start of the gradual demise of his household in its present form. 'I used to be a strong farmer – I was the best in my ward', he complained, 'but after I got sick I have become very weak. All my body parts are sick and aching. This is the consequence of the hard work'.[20]

Welätaw's household was assessed to be relatively wealthy in the survey (with a 'P-score' of 6, see discussion below). It is important to note here that 'relatively wealthy' refers to the specific context of Arbit, where living standards were generally very low. This household lived under hard conditions, often on the brink of starvation, but their total resource base nevertheless made them a little more resilient. They had somewhat larger food security margins than households with fewer resources and who consequently scored lower on the 'wealth' indicator (P-score). In the following section, I present data from the survey and seek to identify some of the factors which affect whether a household scored high or low on the wealth indicator. In other words: what variables can explain why some households are relatively wealthier in the available data?

THE SURVEY[21]

The survey I conducted covered 574 households in total.[22] In principle, it included all the households in the three wards described above, as the research assistants went from house to house and interviewed the household head or some other knowledgeable member of the household.

[18] In addition to the sharecropping agreement between Welätaw and his wife's relative, his son-in-law, Däsé, was also a sharecropper. The details about his sharecropping arrangements are not known.

[19] I did not systematically gather data on kinship relations between sharecropping partners in this study. In Gänät, North Shäwa, I found that two-thirds of sharecropped plots were tilled by non-kin (Aspen 1993: 46).

[20] NW 1: 86, 08.06.2002.

[21] Some preliminary findings from the Jerelé survey were presented in an earlier publication (Aspen 2011). In that publication, the full data set was not employed, and consequently there is a slight discrepancy between figures reported here on the same variables, while the general structure and pattern of the data remain unaltered.

[22] The total number of households in the commune was 1,290, as reported by the district in October 2000 (Ege and Yigremew 2002: 49).

A striking, but unsurprising, feature of the household data is the high frequency of female-headed households in Arbit (43 per cent), compared to the other two wards (15 per cent and 18 per cent, respectively; cf. Table 6.1).[23] This small 'town', or rather village, of Arbit attracts women, many of them divorcees or widows, who seek to exploit the economic niches typical for urban settlements, of which the production and selling of local beer is the most common for women.[24] Although the variation in sources of livelihood is larger in the more urban setting than in the countryside proper, the great majority of the households – including in Arbit as well as the female-headed households – were registered as land tax payers (i.e. at least one of the household members was registered as a land holder). More than 80 per cent of the households in Arbit were land tax payers,[25] not much less than in Galadäjän and Mäqärqariyat, where about 90 per cent of the households in each ward paid land tax.

The emergent 'town' of Arbit obviously represents more varied economic opportunities for people, but judging by the frequency of land tax payers, land seems to continue to be the backbone of livelihoods here as well. But paying land tax does not necessarily imply active farming. In this context, it simply means that a member of the household is responsible for paying land tax for at least one 'tax name' – the 'tax name' being the person registered in the tax list as the owner of the land for which tax is imposed. It was not uncommon for the tax name to be that of a deceased person's. Widows would in such cases be responsible for paying the land tax in the name of their deceased husband, in whose name the land was still listed. Some households were responsible for more than one tax name (Welätaw, as described above, paid the tax for the lands listed in his mother's and his own name and covered the land tax for the woman he sharecropped for as well). Others shared a tax name, i.e. they paid tax only for the share of the land of a tax name which they controlled. The tax payments that were registered in the survey were of the tax imposed on owned land, and not on rented land.

It seems to be common for a woman to keep 'her share', i.e. (half) of the land that was originally registered as hers and her husband's at the EPRDF redistribution, including after a divorce. In other words, the '*dersha*' system (see Chapter 3) appears to have been operational under the EPRDF system as well. In a number of cases, single or remarried women stated that they had kept a share of the land they had with their former husband, for which they paid their share of the tax. The land was not necessarily located in Jerelé; if the women moved to Jerelé after

23 The detailed tables are found at the end of this chapter.

24 A similar trend was found in the small urban settlement around the market in Debeko commune in Mäqét, where 58% of the households were headed by women, compared to 20–22% in the purely rural neighbouring ward (Aspen and Ege 2010: 74; Aspen 2011: 134).

25 This was true for both male- and female-headed households where 16% of male-headed households did not pay land tax versus 18% of female-headed households.

their divorce, they would still have land in their original commune, where it would be ploughed by sharecropping agreements. 'I rent a room here in Arbit', a 45-year-old woman explained. 'My land is in Wadla. I divorced my husband, gave my land by sharecropping [*mägazo*], and returned here, to my birthplace'.[26] Another woman of the same age stated: 'I came here two months ago; I rent a house here. [I moved here in order] to live close to the market and the mill, since I am weak. I have rented out [my] land by *mägazo*'.[27] A third woman, fifty years old, was able to establish herself with a little business: 'I came from Wadla [district]. Here I live in a rented house, and sell *aräqé* and *t'äla* [locally produced liquor and beer]. I have given my land by *mägazo*'.[28] Apparently, the ban that was implemented by the Därg against holding land outside one's commune of residence (*mofär zämät*, cf. Chapter 3) was no longer in operation.

The Indicator Survey included a variable which was the research assistants' assessment of the relative wealth, in local terms, of the household in question (P-score range 1–10). The highest score in Arbit was 7, the lowest 3. The average for Arbit was 5.4.[29]

The three women mentioned above all lived alone. Two of them were neither rich nor poor by local standards, while one was relatively poor (P-score 3). Twenty-two households in Arbit were classified as 'rich' (P-score 7) and 21 as poor (P-score 3). In the rural wards the majority was classified as poor (P-score 3), while in Arbit the picture was more varied, with only 16 per cent classified as poor (cf. Table 6.2).

The general picture that emerges is one of relative equality in a rather poor population. In Arbit, there were larger groups at the higher end of the scale compared to the rural wards, but despite the presence of a number of merchants and salaried workers, no one was classified as 'very rich' – the highest score was 7. Even more striking is the absence of the very poor in the survey data from Arbit. That a small percentage was classified with P-score 2 (very poor) in Galadäjän, and a larger proportion, especially of female-headed households, in Mäqärqariyat may be as expected. The ecological conditions are most difficult in Mäqärqariyat, and it is the most isolated (distant from road and centres) and rural of the three localities. It is also possible that the variation in livelihood sources for single, independent women in Arbit has had the

26 ISHouseholds #1097. The woman lived alone and was registered with 1 *t'emad* of land. She was categorized as poor (P-score 3). She had moved from Arbit and married somewhere in Wadla, where she was also registered as the landowner together with her husband. After her divorce, she retained her right to the land in Wadla but returned to live in Arbit.

27 ISHouseholds #1098. This woman came from Qäläbas, a ward in Jerelé. She had 2 *t'emad* of land, lived alone and was categorized as 'middle' in terms of wealth (P-score 5).

28 ISHouseholds #1104. This woman had 2 *t'emad* of land and 0.5 *t'emad* grazing of land. Her P-score for wealth was also 5.

29 Average P-scores for male- and female-headed households in Arbit was 5.6 and 5.1, respectively. The two other wards had lower scores: Galadäjän, 4.2 (male) and 3.4 (female); Mäqärqariyat 3.5 (male) and 3.2 (female).

greatest effect on migration from areas closer to the town, which may explain the relative absence of very poor female-headed households in Galadäjän compared with Mäqärqariyat, as well as the absence of such households in the data from Arbit.

Incidental variation due to the subjectivity of the research assistants may have had an effect on the data, but this is not likely because the same team, when conducting a similar survey in 2003 in another small 'peasant town' in Mäqét (Gäbäyäw Mändär in Debeko), classified a number of households there as very poor (P-score 2), and even used category 1 (extreme poverty) (Aspen and Ege 2010). My guess is that if the same survey was repeated in Arbit today, after the quite rapid expansion of the town, both ends of the scale would be employed, perhaps particularly its lower end (see Chapter 7). Gäbäyäw Mändär in Debeko differs in ecology from Arbit, and is also likely a much older settlement than Arbit, which grew up around the market that was established around 1960. In addition, Gäbäyäw Mändär seems to have become overshadowed by Gashäna, the small town which has developed at the junction where the road towards Lalibäla now departs from the Wäldiya-Däbrä Tabor highway. Arbit, by comparison, is relatively distant from Gashäna and 'competes' with other small settlements of equal size along the road. So Arbit today seems more dynamic and geared towards growth than Debeko.

As mentioned above, even in the most 'urban' setting, the majority of the households, including female-headed ones, had land. In Arbit, where one would expect to find more individuals without land than in the purely rural areas, 82 per cent of female-headed and 84 per cent of male-headed households paid a full land tax, while some of the remaining households paid a half land tax. As one would expect, in Galadäjän and Mäqärqariyat most households paid land tax (92 per cent and 90 per cent, respectively).[30]

WEALTH INDICATOR AND HOUSEHOLD RESOURCES

As expected, there is a positive correlation between wealth and key household resources (cf. Table 6.3). This is particularly evident for the land asset and the number of household members. There is less correspondence between the P-score and the other variables. Manpower and oxen, both critical for farming, do not show an increasing tendency with increasing wealth ('adults' refers to adult male labour). One should keep in mind that the 'wealth' variable is not simply a reflection of how much resources or assets a household controls (although it will have an effect on the assessment), but is just as much an expression of the enumerators' subjective assessment of the household's condition. The enumerators observed the condition

[30] In Galadäjän, 91% of male-headed households and 97% of female-headed households paid tax, while in Mäqärqariyat the respective figures were 91% and 89%.

of the actual household – i.e. how big (or small) the house was, the general state of the house and its inhabitants, how they were dressed and carried themselves, and how the house was equipped. As a result, correspondence between a high P-score and resource endowment had a number of exceptions.

One example illustrates this well: the household of Ayähu Gälana in Arbit.[31] This household had five adult members, with three oxen, three cows, 5.5 *t'emad* of plough land and 2 *t'emad* of grazing land. They had, in other words, relatively good resources, but their P-score was not more than 6 (upper middle by local standards). The most probable reason is the overall size of the household, comprising twelve members, of whom seven were considered children. Three of the adult members were taxpayers: Ayähu, his wife's mother, and one of his wife's brothers. The two other adult members were his wife and another of his wife's brothers (for details, see Table 6.4).

Unfortunately, this is all we know about Ayähu's household. It would have been interesting to know more about the household's land history, the background for the inclusion of in-laws to this extent, and the position of the wife's brothers in the household: what were the strategies behind this assemblage of people and resources? What the example reinforces, however, with the limited information we have is that strategies and adaptations to make ends meet are both intricate and multifarious. Moreover, it exemplifies the general trend that larger households control relatively more resources – which likely makes them more resilient than smaller households. This is also reflected in the P-score; with the exception of Arbit, the lowest averages of P-scores are found among the smallest households.

CONCLUSION

In this chapter, I explored some aspects of the relationship between key resources, household size and relative wealth of households in Jerelé. The Indicator Survey provides some clues about the relationships between key variables in the peasants' livelihoods. It was used to identify groups and clusters of households of particular interest – specifically female-headed households and households which stand out as special in terms of size and/or resource endowment. The data were collected from three administrative sub-units of Jerelé commune, among which there were some ecological differences. The lowland/highland dimension may have had some effect, but this cannot be firmly decided due to the lack of accurate information on ecological variation in the data. The most prominent difference was the proximity to the road, market and 'town', where Arbit stands out in contrast with the two other localities as having a higher frequency of female-headed households and a higher wealth ranking.

[31] ISHouseholds #1108.

There is a clear positive correlation between household size and wealth, which can be explained with reference to productivity and resilience (well-off individuals attract more relatives for support). Land and other resources must be viewed in relation with other elements in the resource budget, such as the relationship between the number of productive members and dependents, and the availability of alternative sources of livelihoods. The number of oxen and the land size cannot be used as indicators of wealth alone. They do influence the general condition of the households to some extent but may be counteracted by the conditions for productivity and consumption. In this study, we also found that most households in the small town of Arbit retained their relation to agriculture, especially by keeping their land rights in the community. Such land is commonly rented out in sharecropping agreements. In the next chapter, we take a closer look at how dynamics of growth, increased differentiation, and heightened expectations for the future influenced land tenure issues in Arbit.

Table 6.1 Households by gender of household head

	Ward			
Gender of head	*Arbit*	*Galadäjän*	*Mäqärqariyat*	*Total*
F	55	34	39	128
M	74	197	175	446
Total	129	231	214	574
% female heads	43	15	18	22

Table 6.2 Wealth indicators (%)

P-score	*Arbit*		*Galadäjän*		*Mäqärqariyat*		*Total*
	F	*M*	*F*	*M*	*F*	*M*	
2	0	0	2.9	0.5	10.8	3.6	2.2
3	23.6	10.8	79.4	47.1	70.3	64.1	48.6
4	0	0	2.9	5.3	8.1	8.4	5.0
5	34.6	22.9	8.8	34.9	10.8	22.8	26.4
6	23.6	50.0	0.0	5.8	0.0	0.6	11.2
7	18.2	16.2	5.9	6.4	0.0	0.6	6.7
Total	100	100	100	100	100	100	100
N	55	74	34	189	37	167	556

Table 6.3 P-score and resources (average values)

Hamlet	*Land*	*Oxen*	*Cows*	*Hh size*	*LPP**	*Adults*	*P-score*	*(N)*
Arbit	1.42	0.26	0.24	3.70	0.38	0.69	5.40	128
Galadäjän	3.34	1.00	1.11	3.84	0.87	1.03	3.75	101
Mäqärqariyat	1.81	0.86	0.95	4.52	0.40	1.05	3.48	21
Total/average	2.19	0.71	0.77	3.83	0.55		4.57	250

*LPP: Land per person, in *t'emad*

Table 6.4 Adult members of Ayähu's household

Relation	*Age*	*Gender*	*Oxen*	*Cows*	*Land**	*Grazing*	*Tax*
HH Head	41	M	2	1	3	1	1
Wife	25	F	0	0	0	0	0
Wife's mother	50	F	1	2	2	1	1
Wife's brother	32	M	0	0	0.5	0	1
Wife's brother	21	M	0	0	0	0	0

*Land in *t'emad*

7

Rural Land and Urban Aspirations: Future Orientation in a Time of Change

HARALD ASPEN

In our exploration of peasant land tenure in the Amhara highlands, we have so far analysed key issues in traditional peasant settings, some of which date back several decades, including the pre-revolutionary and Därg periods. The analysis of (in)equality in Jerelé commune in the previous chapter (Chapter 6) showed a higher degree of differentiation in the little market town of Arbit, when compared to the neighbouring rural wards. The situation in Arbit in many ways mirrors the winds of change which have been blowing across rural and semi-urban communities throughout Ethiopia since the early 2000s, with seemingly increasing speed (see, for instance, Ege 2015 for an account of recent transformations in a community in North Shäwa).

This chapter takes a closer look at the transformations that could be observed in Arbit around 2010, and which had consequences not only for land tenure, but also for the general attitudes towards the future among peasants, traders and officials alike. A series of noticeable changes affected the general conditions for people in this small 'town', which in turn opened new and alternative imaginings of the future.[1] In many ways, the fast and profound developments in infrastructure – by which the town literally became connected to a world associated with modernity, through electricity, mobile phones, telephone lines, and a greatly improved highway – people also became 'connected' to alternative futures, different from and for many more promising than rural, peasant life. Economic growth and relative peace during the first decade of the new millennium not only boosted the Ethiopian government's 'will to improve' (cf. Li 2007), but also stimulated transformative changes (cf. Dwyer and Minnegal 2010: 632).

The developments in the little roadside settlement of Arbit which are treated here took place from about the end of the Eritrean-Ethiopian war (1998–2000) until 2010 (see also Chapter 6). This chapter is based on my acquaintance with the area since October 2000, when I first visited as a member of a small team of researchers on a rather exten-

[1] This chapter was developed as part of the 'The Hot Lava Edge of Cultural Flows: Global Social Inequality and the Anthropology of Uncertainty, Contingency and Future Orientation' (Norwegian Research Council project #222821), and I am grateful for comments from project participants on various occasions.

sive explorative trip to North Wälo.[2] I made several follow-up visits and fieldwork in Jerelé commune in 2002, 2003, 2006 and 2010.[3] The end of the war with Eritrea in 2000 also had significant impact on the topic of this chapter, namely the increased pressure on rural land for non-agricultural purposes, occasioned primarily by demobilized soldiers. With retirement allowances in their pockets, they were in a position to pay for plots of land, as well as to build their new homes and to start small trade businesses on the land. When I first observed this in 2002, the new houses of the demobilized soldiers, although few in number, were easy to spot along the highway, with their conspicuously virgin look. The wooden parts of the wattle-and-daub houses were light in colour and the corrugated iron roofs were clean and shiny. All this signalled new buildings, which was reinforced by their square modern forms, a consequence of the shift to using corrugated iron sheets instead of grass as thatching material for the roofs (cf. Aspen 2007: 78).

These observable changes appeared to herald the beginning of a decade of more profound changes, in Arbit and in Ethiopia as a whole. It was to become a decade of growth and development, to the extent that in 2009, *The Economist* declared the Ethiopian economy to be the fourth fastest-growing economy in the world that year (*nazret.com* 2008). As a matter of fact, in 2010 I was unable to identify the new houses of the ex-soldiers I had visited eight years earlier, regardless of the fact that I knew they were situated in the vicinity of the market place, and close to the road. The physical appearance of the environment was quite radically changed. There were new houses 'everywhere' and renovation work on the road, which was ongoing in Arbit, also altered how things looked. The little town had obviously grown.

Officially, it is only the district (*wäräda*) capital, Felaqit, with its adjacent twin town Gäragära, which has an urban status, although a number of settlements exists along the 'Chinese road' which can pass as small towns. In 2000, the population of Felaqit/Gäragära was 6,022, representing 2.73 per cent of the district's total population.[4] A decade later, the urban population, still limited in official statistics to Felaqit/Gäragära, had doubled to 11,750 (CSA 2007: 12). The general impression was that a number of localities along the road had seen a rapid growth

2 The team consisted of Abdulhamid Bedri Kello and Yigremew Adal from Addis Ababa University, and Svein Ege and myself from NTNU. Our general aim was to gain some first-hand impressions of North Wälo. The specific aim was to compare what we found with South Wälo and North Shäwa, where all of us had already done extensive work. The data which the team was able to gather on this trip were later presented in Ege and Yigremew (2002). See also the map of North Wälo in Ege (2002b).

3 My earlier fieldwork was conducted in four different communes in Mäqét. In addition to Jerelé, these were Debeko, Tiweha and Dänkäna. For the last three, see Aspen and Ege (2010). This chapter is primarily based on my field notes from 2010 (Arbit 1, Arbit 2), supplemented with notes from fieldwork in 2002 and 2003 (NW 1, NW 2). (See the Bibliography for information on my field notes and archives.)

4 Ege and Yigremew (2002: 41, 49).

in population, judging by the quite impressive physical changes, particularly because of the big increase in the number of houses observed along the highway. This was true for all the small towns, most of which had a weekly market, from the highlands in the east, starting from Dänkäna and Adisgé, towards the somewhat lower tracts to the west, where Agrit, a major eucalyptus-exporting town west of Felaqit, had gone through a particularly remarkable transformation and growth.[5] It seems that the growth had been given a tremendous boost since 2002, triggered by a high level of activity along the road. The road was now renovated and upgraded from a narrow, very dusty, and slow road, to a broad and fast tarmac highway. The work on the road was, as before, done using Chinese manpower and machinery, supplemented by a rather large local workforce, and was about to be completed in 2010 after several years. Another great development, which likely also provided labour opportunities, was the construction of electricity lines to Felaqit and beyond, connecting not only Felaqit to the electricity supply network, but also the smaller towns along the road which had been without electricity up to about 2009.[6] The third striking change within the last ten-year period was the rapid spread of the use of mobile phones connecting people to a more or less reliable network; while this did not directly influence the physical appearance of the settlements, it had radical consequences for communication in general, and for trade in particular. At about the same time, Felaqit was connected to the telecommunication system by telephone lines. This made obsolete the previous satellite telephone office in the district capital, which had been powered by large solar cell panels, but the development was likely cherished mainly by the government officials in the administration.

The improved infrastructure certainly speeded up development trends which were already visible prior to the new investments. We observed one of these on our first visit in 2000: namely the relative density of tree plantations, especially in Felaqit and increasingly towards Agrit (Ege and Yigremew 2002: 10), and the numerous trucks loaded with tree trunks bound for the bigger urban markets, particularly Mäqälé in Tegray. The importance of trees seems to have increased sharply in the period, and had become an important source of income. In 2003, the head of the Finance Office of Mäqét district said that the tax revenue from trade in trees was 'not very impressive' but increasing. Tax was imposed on middlemen (people who bought logs from the producers and sold to bigger traders), but there was a plan to tax producers directly too, according to the Finance Office head.[7] While indigenous trees were

5 This observation is based on a short visit I made to Agrit in March 2010. The transformation of the town was so profound that I was only able to recognize Agrit by its surrounding landscape, which was familiar to me from previous fieldwork in the area.

6 Prior to the connection to the national electricity grid, Felaqit was supplied with electricity by a generator for a couple of hours every night.

7 The plan to tax producers had not yet been implemented in 2010, as far as I know.

to a large extent extinct on the plateau, plantations of eucalyptus had become widespread. In 2010, a 'model farmer'[8] in Jerelé, who lived in Arbit but had land in the lowland part of the commune (Qola Qalabas ward), explained that with the help of district development agents, over one million trees had been planted, and that he himself had 500 trees on his land.[9]

ARBIT MARKET AND VILLAGE

The stories told by local informants about how Arbit emerged as a market, some of which I present below, were perhaps coloured by the atmosphere of growth and development at the time when I collected them (in 2010). Typically, the anecdotes and stories described development from barren wilderness to growth, civilization and control. The most elaborate story was told by Däsalägn,[10] a well-established trader in his fifties and one of my key informants in Arbit over the years. According to Däsalägn, the market in Arbit 'has always been here', but this was immediately corrected to 'at least since 1968, when I was a shepherd'. Däsalägn shared that the place had been plagued with robbers and bandits (*shefta*) in earlier days. The following is a slightly edited version of how Däsalägn told the story of Arbit:

> This was a place where many bandits came and robbed people, from Gaynt', Dawent, Lalibäla. ... Just like people today meet to trade, that time bandits met here. Two district governors gathered the people and elected twelve men to protect the area. Daily, six men were assigned to protect the environment. People who passed had to pay ten cents each to them and they shared it. After that the bandits stopped.
>
> Because there was nobody here, it was like wilderness. They gathered here. That time traders passed by mule, to Gondar, Däsé, Addis Ababa, Baher Dar, with honey, and were robbed by bandits.
>
> The traders transported their goods, lentils, etc., by mule, and when they stopped here to rest, they slaughtered an ox and stayed here for three days. The bandits knew this. This was during Haylä-Selasé, I may have been six-seven-eight years old. That time we collected firewood for the traders and they gave us roasted grain. After these twelve men were elected and bandit activity stopped, the district governors discussed, and marketing started.
>
> This was long before the road came. There was disagreement between two of the district governors, both wanted the market to be named after them. It

[8] After 1995, the 'ruling party undertook a massive recruitment drive among [the rural] elite'. 'Model farmers' were to be turned into 'vanguards', who 'automatically became members of the party, and vice versa, peasant members often, if not systematically, became model farmers' (Lefort 2012: 684).

[9] This man was obviously an exceptionally industrious farmer. He owned two mills, was engaged in the grain trade, and had planted vegetables, fruit trees and different kinds of indigenous trees (such as *wanza* and *gerar*) on his land. For this he had been rewarded, at regional state level, by Prime Minister Meles Zenawi as a development fighter ('*yä-lemat arbägna*'), and given a medal and a T-shirt as material tokens of his status.

[10] All my informants' personal names are pseudonyms.

> was decided by lottery. The winner was Wärät'a S'agäw, and the market was named Wärät'a Gäbaya Arbit – this is still the name. Before, the specific place name was Dudta.[11]
>
> The road construction started in 1980 or 1981 and finished about 1985. But there was a road from Baher Dar, during the time of the Italians, to Kon, Wägäl T'éna, Kutabär, Däsé, Addis Ababa. The route now is different from then. Before the Chinese road, we had a road for people and donkeys from here to Wäldiya.

Alämu, an older man perhaps in his sixties, lived in a house which, compared to most other dwellings in the town, was of quite high standard, with cement covering the walls and urban-style door and window shutters. It was situated along the main road and close to the market. Alämu testified to the story of the growth of Arbit from 'nothing', by claiming that he had been quite alone in the area some twenty-five years earlier:

> I have lived here for twenty-five years. I was alone at that time. All this surrounding land was my farmland. When I was young there was no market, no houses, here. There were very few eucalyptus trees, at distant places. The market started about 1968, in Haylä-Selasé's time. After that, some people began to construct the houses. I had my house at the other side then, in Mäläy. That house was taken during the EPRDF land redistribution because I had this one. First I gave the house to my relative only to live in it, and now her grandchildren live there and have taken the land. They are distant relatives. I had much land before the *shegesheg*. I was vice-chairman in Mäläy when they came. They came in 1989; the *shegesheg* was in 1991.

Alämu also had his own theory about the road from Gashäna to Lalibäla. According to him, it was by accident that the important road junction from the Wäldiya–Wäräta Road to Lalibäla was located in Gashäna and not in Arbit:

> This place was called Duduta before. Barta (the road construction company)[12] asked where is Duduta. ... The foreigners thought that Duduta was Gashäna and made the road to Lalibäla [from Gashäna]. We heard that the plan was to make the road from here, seventeen years ago. We are waiting but we have lost hope.

The expectations of growth and development had certainly received a boost by the recent, rapid changes. That Arbit had not become like Gashäna was depicted as an unfortunate historical accident in the

11 This is how I have noted the place name as pronounced by Däsalägn. Another informant (Alämu, discussed in the following paragraphs) said that 'this place was called Duduta before'.

12 I have not been able to find references in the literature to a road construction company called *Barta*, or Bärta. Birhanu Teferra wrote to me in September 2009 saying: 'From what I know of the Woldya–Woretta Road, it was the result of a project agreement between the Imperial Ethiopian Government of Emperor Haile Selassie and the Peoples' Republic of China of Chairman Mao Tse Dung. The agreement was an outcome of a visit by the Emperor to China in 1972–73, I believe. The construction was started during Haile Selassie's period (went on up to 1981). It was completed during the early years of the Provisional Military Government (Därg); so it was inaugurated during the time of the Därg'. According to Gascon (2010: 394), 'the Chinese rebuilt the Däse–Wäldiya–Gondär' road during the Därg.

narrative above, but this did not quell people's ambitions for the place. One reason was the impact of the already mentioned electricity and road upgrading. There had also been a shift in the local administration's attitude to urban growth. Only a decade earlier, the local administrations at commune and district level were strictly opposed to any tendencies towards 'urbanization' of the area. During my fieldwork in Arbit in 2002, the chairman of the commune reported that 'the commune committee wants urbanization to be stopped; it is destructive for agriculture and tree production'. The standard view was that it was a 'problem that poor farmers sell land. Poor become poorer, traders richer'. The ban on house construction on agricultural land had been strictly implemented until recently. An officer of the Mäqét district branch of the Ministry of Agriculture (MoA) indicated that houses had been illegally built in 2000, but building was now allowed.

Within the district administration of 2003, the policy regarding land sales, including in areas close to the road, was clear. According to the acting district administrator, selling and buying land was forbidden. There was a particular focus on the tendency for people to buy small plots of land in order to construct houses on them. The reasons given for the ban were that: (1) it involved selling land, which was then not allowed; (2) people were moving closer to the highway (popular plots for house construction were near the road); and (3) land scarcity: 'Land is scarce; it has to be used for agriculture, not for unproductive settlement'. The district administrator firmly claimed that urbanization was in conflict with the prohibition of land selling, but also stated that 'in general we encourage people in each commune to live close to the road, each (commune) has a small town. In Arbit, we allowed the commune to give land to ex-soldiers for house building'. These rather contradictory but concurrent statements may be seen as typical illustrations of a turbid situation. The law was clear, but development trends pulled in an opposite direction. It is also noteworthy that the MoA officer in 2002 stated that it was allowed to buy plots of land for house construction (which was wrong in principle), while the highest district authority, a year later, expressed that it was still illegal, yet simultaneously something to be encouraged.

TOWARDS URBAN LIFE

The changes which I observed in Arbit in 2010 were striking. Compared with my first visits at the beginning of the decade, the most conspicuous feature was that of *urbanization*, and hand in hand with it, the expectations of *modernization*, to paraphrase Ferguson (1999). The signs that pointed towards urbanization were the physical changes. These were the increased number of houses around the marketplace and along the road, the electricity and telephone poles, cables and streetlamps, the small retail kiosks that advertised their presence by exhibiting plastic cans and domestic utensils in bright colours, a number of places where coffee, food and drinks were sold, and the modern tarmac road that connected it all together. Most of this was directly related to trade, which flourished around the marketplace and the adjacent compounds of the traders of some scale.

One of the biggest compounds belonged to *Ato* Däsalägn, who was one of the major and most experienced merchants in Arbit (whom we met earlier in the chapter). By local standards, he was a rich man, to the extent that he could afford the cost of sending one of his sons to a Catholic boarding school in Addis Ababa. At the peak of his career, he owned two warehouses, one in Gäragära and another in Arbit. He had in total five trading licences for various items, such as coffee and grains, and paid tax accordingly to the government. He complained, 'Now, EPRDF opened trade for everybody – people trade but they don't pay tax' (Aspen 2009). Däsalägn had rented out his warehouse in Gäragära until he sold it in 2006, but he kept the one in Arbit for his own use. He stored sacks with grain and onions in it, perhaps two or three tonnes in total. In 2006, after selling the warehouse in Gäragära, he bought a mill in Arbit. The seller was a younger trader who had built it some years earlier but had decided to leave Arbit and settle in Gashäna, where there were presumably better business opportunities. Däsalägn's oldest son was now in charge of operating the mill.

Although Däsalägn was a well-to-do person and had substantial property, he led a simple life. If he was better-off than his neighbours, his inconspicuous lifestyle contributed little to signal that. It was rather in gesture and attitude that he appeared as one used to giving orders, and when travelling to markets like Yänäja, he would ride his mule, thereby demonstrating that his status was higher than that of the peasants, whose means of transportation was, as always, their own legs and perhaps a donkey or two for the goods. Neither did his immediate family who lived with him stand out to any extent, perhaps with the exception of a good pair of leather shoes that his youngest son received from an elder brother in Addis Ababa. However, his relatively unassuming lifestyle did not challenge his status as a 'big man' in the community – he was an employer, a trader, and a man who was entrusted with important work for the local church. Neither Däsalägn nor any other of the merchants in Arbit owned a car, but many of them, particularly the younger ones, mentioned this as a much desired next step in their career.

The Arbit market had grown to become a major centre for onion trade, and Däsalägn's compound was used by traders and their middlemen to collect, weigh, and store large quantities of onion bags before they were transported to the markets in the big towns. Däsalägn's large compound was situated at the roadside, opposite the market. It was only the highway that separated the compound from the market place. The buildings in the compound consisted of two dwelling houses, the warehouse, and a stable where he kept his mule. The warehouse was now being used to offer storage, against a fee, to a number of merchants in need of a transit store for the agricultural products they had bought at the Arbit market to send elsewhere, or for products that had come from other districts to be distributed for sale in the local markets. Däsalägn also had a scale, on which traders, for a fee, could weigh the sacks of onions, grain, or pulses before storing them or sending them off in a typical medium-sized Isuzu lorry. On busy market days Däsalägn usually sat by his scale in his compound, with traders queueing in front of him with their sacks of grain, garlic, pulses and onions. Middlemen and smaller traders had balance weights with them for weighing smaller quantities when buying from peasants at the market, but they depended on Däsalägn's bigger scale to weigh the larger sacks that were ready to be stored or transported.

The store and the scale were sources of a steady, although limited, income for Däsalägn, who collected fees from his clients for the use of these services. It was common to see the lorries outside his gate, surrounded by a group of strong men who worked to load and unload the vehicles, under the supervision of the person in charge of the goods. This could be the merchant who owned it, or the driver who acted on behalf of the owner. Although there was hectic activity in the compound on market days, it was the income from the mill that brought in steady income for Däsalägn. This was his source of livelihood, and also what paid for his children's education. He was starting to experience competition from electric mills, which were cheaper to operate than his diesel-mill and hence was also cheaper for the customers. Däsalägn had adjusted his prices to the same level as the electric mills, and was preparing to change to electric milling as soon as electricity became available.[13]

FORMALIZING LABOUR

The relatively recent establishment of an association, or 'labour union', for the group of porters (*yä-wäzadät derejet* or 'workers' association') may be taken as one of several indications of an increasing trend of urbanity – if we associate it with economic specialization and an extension or development of civil society. According to the chairman of the association, it was the labourers themselves, together with the merchants, who had taken the initiative to regulate this particular labour and service market, around 2006. The need for regulation was explained by the high and sometimes chaotic competition among unskilled workers for the odd job of loading and unloading trucks. That people from the 'countryside', sometimes fortified by drinking beforehand, got involved in the competition for the jobs, was emphasized by

[13] There was a good deal of frustration in Arbit because the connection to the electricity network had been long delayed. Several months before my fieldwork in March 2010, Arbit had been connected for a couple of days, but was then cut off because of a destroyed transformer. The small town was without electricity during my whole fieldwork period, but the electricity was reportedly back on the day I left the area.

both workers and merchants as a particular reason for the need to regulate the work. The chairman of the association explained:

> Many people try to get work, and we were fighting for it. ... People also came from the countryside to work and sometimes they stole the bags. ... People were fighting to get work – when the cars stopped here, some people from the countryside had been drinking *t'äla* and hit the car with their sticks, and broke the window [of the car].

The merchants and the car owners, the owner of the store, and the labourers all had, in this situation, a common cause and a reason to organize a hitherto unorganized economic activity in the town. This distinctively urban activity (paid work connected with trade and transportation) was seen as being threatened by what was described as the unruly forces of men from the rural areas. They could not, however, organize themselves at their own will. The union chairman explained that local government institutions had to be engaged for their agreement to the plans:

> We, together with the merchants, took the initiative to regulate this work. First the merchants selected our members, those of us whom they trusted, and they gave the list to the commune. ... Now we control it ourselves, together with the police and militia. We cooperate with the police and we have meetings with them. Now nobody else but us can do this kind of work. If we think we need extra hands, we can hire people we trust for that particular job.

Through this step, a division was established between organized town life and the perceived rural threat of disorganization. The quote below is from Däsalägn, who talked about the workers as a group the merchants had to organize:

> There was much disturbance before they were organized. Peasants came and tried to work but lost the loads and spilled it, so we took initiative to organize them. We talked with each other and with the commune and organized them. We sent the labourers to the district and they brought back a letter, a permission to organize themselves and to work. The permission to organize was [necessary to obtain]. This was in 2008, or 2009. Since then we have had peace. If a peasant comes to work, he cannot.

The grassroots workers' association in Arbit was apparently a registered organization, with a management committee consisting of a chairman, vice-chairman, secretary, cashier and controller, listed members by application, and an insurance fund.

The work was hard and intense; the bags they carried from the car to the store (a distance of 20–30m) could weigh up to 150kg each, at a payment rate of 0.20 birr. The payment was made to the group for the total amount of work done. In the words of the secretary of the association:

> We divide the total in equal shares. If one of us cannot carry 150kg, another can do it. There are also some of us who work one day on the car, sending the sacks down, but do not carry. The next day they will carry and somebody else is on the car. Some also arrange the sacks in the store one day and carry another day. We take turns, so that over time the work and the payment are distributed evenly.

The porters' association had elements akin to a labour union, a shareholder company, and a self-help organization for a particular segment of the population. The secretary of the association explained:

> If somebody wants to become a member he will first have to bring a letter from his commune that he has no land. Then he has to pay some money, to contribute to our capital that we keep in the credit association for the security for our members. The amount will depend on how much we have in the bank, he will have to pay 1/14 share [if fourteen members]. Now we have 2,000 birr. If, for example, my mother dies, they will contribute from the capital. Before, when one lost a family member, we paid 70 birr, but now we have increased it to 100 birr.[14] [A new member] has to prove that he is poor and that he has no other work, so that he doesn't need to go to other places for work but work with us and help his family.
>
> There is a Safety Net programme, which helps people by giving them work. We also help each other like the Safety Net programme. It is the commune that requires us to ask for letters: many people try to get work, and we were fighting for it. We asked the commune for regulation and this became the instrument. Now the commune supports us and the traders trust us. If a load comes from Gojam, we take the bags and store them. We take responsibility.

The secretary of the association also saw their work in a development perspective: '[it contributes to] two things: it creates work and it helps the town to grow'.

The organization of trade in Arbit is a fascinating study, as it involves middlemen (*dälala*), informal credit, transport deals, storage, etc. In many of these small towns (and in bigger towns as well) one can see groups of men 'hanging around', seemingly only killing time, but who may well be working hard, negotiating deals, arranging transport and storage, or comparing prices.[15] Many of these men are 'trying' urban life as the first generation; some succeed, while others barely survive; a small minority become success stories. The few 'success stories' were the merchants who had become 'big' and influential locally. The most successful in Arbit was Däsalägn, who owned the store, the scale and the mill; another was the younger trader who sold the mill to Däsalägn and moved to Gashäna in search of better opportunities (Aspen 2009).

The development and organization of the trade and labour market in Arbit is also a story of urbanization. It is the story about in-migration to the centre, while it also concerns urbanization as a process of organizational change, creating a border between what is conceived as urban and ordered versus the depiction of disorder represented by 'peasants' or rurality. Another important point is the conflation of local government and local organization and initiative. The workers' interest in organizing was approved by the commune and district authorities, and also directed towards a self-help association, in which only men who

14 100 birr was equal to USD 7.50 in March 2010 (www.xe.com).

15 I owe thanks to my colleague Dr Abdulhamid B. Kello, an economist at AAU, for making me aware of this point. Some years ago, when we passed a group of seemingly idle men around one of the many plazas in Addis Ababa, he explained to me that these people were actually working as middlemen in small businesses in the locality. See also Eleni (1999).

could prove they were poor and without land or other sources of income could be members.

The principles of solidarity, which the members claimed were regulating their group, may well have been self-activated regardless of any pressure from the authorities. One group member was described as someone more interested in drinking than working: 'He is unmarried, starts in the morning without food, with *koräfé*, then *t'äla*, then *koräfé* [local alcoholic brewages]. He is a porter, but is satisfied when he has earned 10 birr, then he goes to drink'. Another group member described him like this:

> He is also a member, but he is not so strong, so we cover his share [of work]. If he is poor and has nothing to live by and we don't help him, he will die. No, he is not old, it is because of his life that his hair has become grey.

In this section, I used the example of the labourers and traders and their need for organization and order to suggest that the process of urbanization in Arbit (as elsewhere) was not only a matter of population movement and density; it also had to do with changes in people's mentality and aspirations. The expansion of trade, the higher degree of organization of trade and labour, and the great improvements of the local infrastructure – providing better connections to a wider network of commerce and communication – all contribute to increasing expectations for Arbit as a centre with urban, rather than rural, qualities. In the next section I discuss how this also affected matters concerning land and land transfers in Arbit.

RURAL LAND AND URBAN ASPIRATIONS

The history of Arbit starts with the history of the market, and trade continues to be the attraction and a major resource of the small settlement, although strong links to agriculture persist (see Chapter 6). The improvement of the highway may not have contributed to increased trade activities in the short run. It had been, after all, fully operational before, but it was dusty, bumpy and slow for travelling on. The upgrading was in essence a reconstruction, with the road becoming a modern highway that offered comfort and speed. The immediate effect was a sense of new opportunities, and in combination with the physical improvements it certainly stimulated growth in the longer run. Also prior to the infrastructural upgrade, after the fall of the Därg, trade had grown due to increased security and peace and the general economic growth in the country, and specifically because of the increased importance of trade in wood and tree logs from the area.

This trade had its own logistics and scale. Most of the logs were bought in large quantities through middlemen and exported from the area on big lorries. In contrast, the Arbit market was a traditional weekly market with a variety of agricultural products. The majority of the sellers were peasants offering their own agricultural products, which were sold directly to consumers in small quantities or bought in bulk by middlemen. Most peasant sellers preferred the latter kind of customers as they could conclude their sales in one transaction.[16] Many traders in Arbit were engaged in both the tree market and the more traditional sectors such as grain and onions, while merchants of a certain scale tended to specialize in one or other of the commodities. They were typically active at a number of the markets in the area, each market operating on different weekdays.

One major market in the vicinity of Arbit is in Yänäja, a much older and bigger market towards the south-western part of the plateau, about eleven kilometres from Arbit.[17] The Yänäja market also contributes to the trade in Arbit. Although it is accessible by trucks in dry weather, the common means of transportation is by foot and beasts of burden. Many people visit Yänäja on its market days, and on their way home from Yänäja many make a stop in Arbit for refreshments, to conclude or follow up deals they have made, and to visit relatives and friends.

In Arbit, the marketing activities, together with the kiosks and the several places where coffee and drinks were sold, added to the urban flavour of the town.[18] In comparison with the peasant population living in the surrounding countryside, the inhabitants of the town had a much wider repertoire of livelihoods, although the great majority also had a link to farming, often through land still kept and farmed by themselves or by sharecropping arrangements. Another typical indicator of the degree of urbanization was the high frequency of female-headed households (see Chapter 6). Informants in Arbit were clear that life in town was highly preferable: it was easier, offered better access to a variety of foodstuff from the market, and was generally cleaner (Aspen 2011: 136).[19]

The situation I described above was one where people found themselves in transition between rural and urban conditions, not only in physical terms but also mentally, or attitudinally, and where old standards and values were rapidly challenged and changing. Modernization and development were primarily associated with the growth of the small town and proximity to the 'centre', and things connected with it were particularly attractive. The owner of a little shop at the market place expressed this explicitly: 'It is during the last four years

[16] According to Däsalägn, peasants preferred to sell to the small-scale middlemen who operated at the market, using tin cans (*t'asa*) as measurement, instead of selling directly to the bigger merchants, because they were not familiar with the scale involved.

[17] I measured the walking distance with a GPS when I visited the Yänäja market in March 2010.

[18] A number of simple restaurants (*megeb bét*) had been established to serve the labour force working on the road, a few of which were still operating but with regular service limited to the market days in Arbit and Yänäja on Fridays and Mondays, respectively.

[19] Similar responses are reported by Baker (1994: 82–4) from informants in three rural towns in South Wälo, such as 'life is easier', 'daily work is available', 'trading possibilities', and 'clinic services'.

that the growth of the town has taken place. When *selet'ané* [civilization, modern life] comes, peasants come and buy and build houses. The road, the electricity, the telephone line, these are the things that make it attractive.'

The increased demand for land for non-agricultural purposes should be considered in light of the sharp and sudden change in opportunities and horizons of expectations which took place at the local and the national scene at the same time. This is the topic of the remaining part of the chapter.

LAND SALES

The *ad hoc* arrangement that allowed demobilized soldiers who wanted to settle in Arbit to buy land, as described earlier in the chapter, represented the beginning of an increasing trend of buying and selling land for housing purposes. While the land purchases made by ex-soldiers were temporarily allowed by the authorities, other transactions had less support in the administrative or legislative system, as I show in this section.

One of the demobilized soldiers who established himself in Arbit was Zäwdé, whom I interviewed in 2002. He had bought a piece of land beside the main road, and was trying to establish himself as a wood and grain trader. Upon demobilization from the army he had received an allowance of 5,000 birr, of which he had spent 1,050 birr to buy the land, with the rest to cover the costs of the house construction. In addition to the trade, he was a sharecropper, ploughing with oxen that he rented for 20 birr per day.[20] He had paid 100 birr to the landowner as *gubo* (lit. 'bribe') for the contract (in addition to giving the landowner a share of the crops).[21] One of his neighbours, Adisu, also had a relatively new house beside the road. He and his wife had come to town in 1994 from the 'distant countryside' (*ruq gät'är*).[22] Their livelihood was trade in grain and wood, and their little compound was filled with trunks of eucalyptus. Among his household members was a young boy who was hired to work for an annual payment of 250 birr in addition to food and lodging.

Adisu was not a demobilized soldier, but one of the young men who had started a trade, little by little, based in the rural areas. A gradual

[20] 100 birr was equal to USD 11.88 in June 2002 (www.xe.com).

[21] The share of the crops is not specified in my notes. Zäwdé's household was covered by the Indicator Survey that we carried out in Arbit in 2002. There he is listed with a household of five members, including himself (32 years) and his wife (22 years). According to this source, he had neither animals nor land, and did not pay land tax. But he was classified as relatively wealthy by local standards (P-score 6. For a description of the Indicator Survey method, see e.g. Ege and Aspen [2003: 19–20]).

[22] This household was also covered by the Indicator Survey, registered with seven household members, two oxen, 2 *t'emad* of land and 1 *t'emad* of grazing land, and as a land tax payer. Its P-score was 6. Adisu was thirty-five years old in 2002, and his wife was twenty-eight.

building up of both the scale and his ambitions had eventually enabled him to move to the town with his family. Young men like Adisu, and the demobilized soldiers, with cash in hand and without the opportunity or inclination to return to the countryside and a life of farming, seem to have been catalysts for the evolving urbanization and urban land market in Arbit (and elsewhere along the highways).

It was the effect of this that I observed in 2010, when I was unable to locate the two compounds of Zäwdé and Adisu, mainly because the physical appearance of the environment had so radically changed. But not only had the town grown, there had also been a shift in the official attitudes to the growth of Arbit, at least at commune level, as indicated earlier. Now the standard view among people in the little settlement seemed to be that many of the land transfers that actually took place were indeed illegal but were necessary and wanted, and that it would have been good if the land transfers could have been legalized by administrative measures. More specifically, what was commonly expressed was a need for change in the administrative status of Arbit from that of a rural community to a municipality or town administration.

The chairman and the administrator of the commune listed two ways of transferring land under the current system (in 2010), which were not exactly illegal (but also not, it seems, regarded as strictly legal): (1) The land owner builds a very small house on the land, and sells the house on the land. He may also plant some trees and sell them. To sell a house including land, and a house and trees, is legal. But empty land cannot be sold. (2) An agreement is made under long-term rent conditions, or rather, in practice, plots of land are exchanged, not rented: i.e. a person who has land close to the road exchanges it for land elsewhere belonging to someone else.[23]

The views that the local leadership now expressed regarding land transfers were much more pragmatic than what was represented by the commune leadership eight years earlier (see the statements by the then chairman given earlier).[24] Now the commune administration welcomed the urbanization of Arbit:

> For the development and improvement of the town and in the interest of the people, it would have been better if we had a municipality administration. Although the land sales are now illegal, people systematically sell by the means we have mentioned. With town status, land selling and house construction could take place in a legal way.
>
> There is a plan to change the status. We are asking the district officials about that and they also believe this [should have been done] but the problem they raise is that if this place changes its status into a town and is administered by a municipality, they fear that many peasants around here will lose their land and will have to be compensated with cash or with land elsewhere. Now the town is expanding, whether they believe it or not, it is expanding illegally. We ask them to legalize the town.

[23] From an interview conducted in February 2010.

[24] It seems that while the former chairman could only express the official position, the political atmosphere in 2010 permitted, to a greater extent, the local leadership to voice attitudes at odds with official policy.

The chairman of the Land Administration Committee in the commune said that since the 1991 land redistribution, two kinds of land had been distributed to the 'landless and orphans', namely: (1) land of people with no inheritors; and (2) land that had been categorized as communal (grass-)land (*yä-gara märét*). Since 1991, he said, the amount of the latter kind of land had been reduced because shares from communal land had been distributed to people for private purposes: 'If it can be ploughed, they plough it, or [else] they plant eucalyptus trees [on the land]'.

In 2008, the commune had distributed plots of land to about forty to sixty people from a field of communal grazing land along the main road in Galadäjän, close to Arbit. A new, small settlement had grown up there with a number of residential houses. The plots were just big enough for house construction: 'We gave it to about forty landless people to build their houses and start their own business. [The plots are] not big enough to plough, only for a house'. This land allocation seems to have had an unusual motivation for a rural commune administration. Instead of thinking of land in terms of agriculture, land was now allocated, at a rather big scale, for house construction only. It was followed up by further incentives for the development of a more urban lifestyle and livelihood: 'We organized about twenty young people among them and they wanted to start to produce rugs.[25] They have not yet started production. Now they are also in conflict about the border of the land of another peasant'.

By distributing land in a way that created new, dense settlements, and also initiating processes that were meant to support non-agricultural income-generating activities, the local administration gave direct backing to the urbanization process, on a practical as well as an attitudinal level. It seems that the ethos of modernization and development was concretized in action that aimed at building town-like structures and livelihoods. In people's minds, it was civilization that was coming, as opposed to what was now perceived as unruly and undeveloped rural conditions – similar to what was expressed by the porters when they narrated the establishment of their association.

All this also had an impact on people's attitude towards land transactions, and particularly the value of land. A number of informants expressed great expectations about their land in Arbit and how much it was now worth versus when they had appropriated it. One was a relatively young man engaged in trade as a middleman and transport facilitator. He had bought a plot of land two years earlier for 3,000 birr and now, he claimed, he could sell it for 5,000 birr 'to cover my expenditure for driving lessons'. Another was the owner of a compound just in front of the market place, where he also had a little kiosk. He had bought the plot of land, with a small house on it, a year earlier for 6,000 birr. Now,

25 Woven wool rugs in a variety of patterns are commonly produced and offered for sale in the area. Racks with rugs exhibited for sale are a common sight along the roadside from Arbit towards Agrit.

he claimed, the plot of land alone could be sold for 16,000 birr, with the value of the buildings on top of this amount. A third merchant estimated his land to be worth 50,000 birr, fifty times the amount he had paid for it about a decade earlier. Yet another owner of a plot close to the road claimed he could sell it for 200,000 birr. It seemed that the sky was the limit for what could be expected in terms of the value of land located close to the road and the market place. According to a number of informants, it would be even more profitable to have such land if the formal administrative status of Arbit changed from a rural to an urban community with municipal status.[26]

Even if the estimates of 'urban' land value were somewhat inflated, the value of the land was nevertheless increasing. A related major issue was the matter of the (il)legality of land transfers for house construction purposes. One of the informants cited above thought that if the Arbit settlement became administered as a municipality, it would assure his status as the owner of his house, which meant he would be able to sell it legally at a higher price. In his understanding, a sale under the present regulation would be illegal in formal terms and therefore carried risk, so the price would reach 'only 30,000–40,000 birr' – as opposed to a legitimate transaction under a different (urban/municipal) legislation, which he believed could fetch 'maybe 100,000 birr'. According to him, because the land transfer had not been registered officially, it was still registered in the seller's land certificate. Accordingly, my informant did not pay any land tax for the plot. Although he did not believe that his neighbour intended to 'grab the land', he expressed a feeling of uncertainty regarding his ownership to the house on the land.

The value of land in Arbit was obviously rapidly increasing, but the growth was curbed by doubts about the formal validity of the transactions, which involved risk of confiscation, either by the authorities, or due to a breach of contract by the seller. The rise in prices had led to a growing number of disputes, conflicts and court cases over land. The perceived risks were associated with the formal legal system, and these could be countered by appeal to tradition. A number of informants emphasized that agreements were made according to custom, which also involved written contracts attested by witnesses. In addition, many residents in Arbit had received their plots of land from relatives. 'We lived in Mäläy [commune in Wadla district] until eight years ago', a woman explained, when she then moved to Arbit where her mother had land. 'She asked me to come and take the place. We took it and built this house. "Come and get a site in town", she said'. Her mother lived in a smaller house in the same compound, which she shared with two other women who rented rooms from her.

The space between private agreements following tradition and those following formal, legal requirements, became open to disputes and conflicts in the situation of a rapidly increasing demand for and value

[26] This was prior to the proclamation regarding urban land (Ethiopian Government 2011), which presumably had great consequences for the value of urban land holdings.

of land. Transactions that had been made only a few years earlier were now felt to have been disadvantageous by the seller, and some tried to annul agreements and get back the land.

The district court dealt with forty-one cases related to conflict over land in Jerelé commune from June 2008 to July 2009. A number of cases were related to the ongoing certification of land. According to the Chief Justice of the court, many of the cases were brought by women, who in his view were often 'victims', i.e. at the losing end when conflicts over land occurred. Perjured evidence against female claimants made the court helpless, he said. He also mentioned the land of deceased persons, presumably without inheritors, which commune authorities had distributed to landless people, but where claimants had then come forward as inheritors to contest the decision.

The general principle to be followed, according to the Chief Justice, was to legally register any transaction worth more than 500 birr, and in particular land and houses. 'To come and register is the starting point', he said. '[People] have little awareness about the law. Agreements truthfully made by people were respected before, but now, when prices increased, they do not do that anymore'. It may be correct that people had 'little awareness' about the law, but I would also argue that the law and the application of it were not necessarily clear and straightforward. Instead of risking contracts being scrutinized by the authorities, with an unpredictable outcome, people preferred to do things in the customary way. Mistrust and lack of confidence remained the characteristic relationship between peasants and the government.[27]

The issue of legality was evidently not clear to the parties involved in disputes, nor to the population at large. At the lowest level of administration, it seemed that agreements that had been made 'by custom' (*bä-bahel*), without the involvement of formal, legal authorities (the court system) were fragile and easy to contest. According to the chairman of the commune Land Administration Committee, some individuals would take the agreement to the commune court and sign the agreement there. This did not necessarily guarantee the legality of the contract, however, because of the regulation that the commune court only could deal with matters of a value up to 1,500 birr, and that matters relating to land had to be dealt with by the district court. It seems, therefore, that there was also discord between the commune level court and that of the district. The commune court is an arbitration court without legal professionals, and might therefore make decisions that would not stand the test of the higher, professional court at district level.

In the district administration, the general rhetoric was that land sales were forbidden because it could create a new capitalist class of landowners and an increasing number of poor, landless people. This is of course the official position on land ownership by the current government in Ethiopia and is not specifically related to the pressure of urban growth in Arbit. But when the specific needs of Arbit were discussed

[27] Cf. Aspen (2002: 69) and Lefort (2010).

with officials, the same arguments were presented, rather mechanically. The pressure on land for non-agricultural purposes was high along the road, and particularly at comparatively central places like Arbit. High prices could be tempting, but some people were able to resist the allure, for some time at least.

For example, a family in a small house close to the 'centre' of Arbit did just that. They expressed that their strategy was to protect their land from expropriation. To that aim they had moved their house closer to the road in order to ensure a continued use of the land for agriculture. However, their strategy could well have been to mark their rights to the land in the expectation of a value increase and a future sale instead of outright expropriation.

The family had some land close to the road, but they had previously lived at some distance from the road. Six years earlier, they had abandoned their old dwelling and moved to their plot close to Arbit along the dusty roadside, because they 'wanted to preserve the place. This was our ploughing land. The town – if this is [to become] a town, the place could be taken as town land'.[28] They had a small, traditional grass-roofed house, round in shape, which the family shared at night with their herd. Their cow, calf and three sheep all spent the night in the house, while the five family members slept in the loft just above the animals' backs.[29] The contrast between this small cottage and the new, square houses with shiny corrugated roofs nearby was a striking illustration of the changes that were taking place in the community.

CONCLUSION

Over a ten-year period, Arbit went through a transformation of many dimensions. It grew physically, with an increased number of dwellings along the road and around the market place, and it attained an increased sense of centrality, which came with a tremendous improvement of its infrastructure – the road, the telephone system, and, not least, regular electricity. In general, the tint of urbanity that the little settlement around the market place had enjoyed around the turn of the millennium was now, about ten years later, more apparent and with stronger colours. There was a clear attitudinal change among local government representatives, who had turned from a position in favour of prohibiting urban growth, in order to protect agricultural interests, to that of expressing the need for urbanization and urban

[28] The informant here was the brother of the owner of the house and land in question. He had his own house nearby; he had built it with equal shares with a companion (*yä-ekul*); he provided the land while the companion built a house on it, with two rooms. The house builder owned one part of the house, and the land owner the other.

[29] The family consisted of an old, childless woman, her stepson's daughter and the latter's husband and two young daughters. The little house was the only building they had.

legislation. As such, they were in line with local businessmen, who also expressed the same interest, and seemed optimistic about what the future could bring.

Arbit was far from being a town in official terms; it was not even close to the official definition of an 'urban centre',[30] but for people in this part of Mäqét, it represented a marked difference from the countryside and was frequently referred to as the 'town'. With the benefit of having had the opportunity to do research, even if intermittently, in the same community over a period of almost a decade, it has been possible to detect not only physical changes, but also alterations in people's expectations of change. The story of Arbit is a tale not only of new opportunities, but also of new opportunity horizons. The perceived possibility for an alternative future represented by the emergent town – to establish an urban environment with economic activities different from that of the traditional peasant's – stands out as a vision that is shared by local government officials, small and big merchants, and people at large. Ambitions are high, for the status of the town, for the value of land and houses, and for the furthering of 'modern life'.

The state (or government; *mängest*) has a long history in Ethiopia, and certainly continues to be an extremely important agent of change in the country (see, among others, Mains 2012; Ellison 2006) in ways which can best be described as social engineering, or what Scott (1998: 87) has labelled 'authoritarian high modernism'. The state is a major agent of social change, with stick and carrot, force, compulsion and incentives. The results are clearly visible; not only are there many signs of economic growth, but the future orientation also seems to have changed. In the words of the kiosk owner in Arbit, quoted earlier: 'Civilization [modern life] has come to us'.

Arbit, in the year 2010, showed signs of change towards a more formalized and market-oriented society. An acute problem was occasioned by the fact that while the economic value of land rapidly increased, the judicial regulation of land excluded it from being a marketable property. In the next chapter, Ege points out that in such a situation, with a high economic value on land but a zero price, illegal practices are likely to emerge. In Arbit people found ways – not always strictly legal – to price the cherished land, both in actual transactions and in their conceptions about the value (and price) of the land in the future. In the current analysis, the value of land was related to non-agricultural usages. Later on, however, with higher outputs from agricultural land, the same process of market orientation and monetization also appear to have manifested itself in rural areas (Ege 2015).

30 '... "urban centre" means any locality having a municipal administration or a population size of 2000 or more inhabitants of which at least 50% of its labour force is engaged in non-agricultural activities' (Ethiopian Government 2011: 6221).

8

An Unstable Land Tenure System

SVEIN EGE

THE LAND ISSUE IN THE CURRENT CONTEXT

For decades, Ethiopia was associated with famine. In recent years, it has become associated with spectacular economic growth. The GDP figures are impressive, but of even more importance is the growth in the agricultural sector and notably in food production.[1] The changes outlined by Aspen in Chapter 7, in what used to be the famine-struck rural backwaters of highland North Wälo (cf. McCann 1987a), are indicative of the growth and, increasingly, the transformation of the Ethiopian economy.

This astounding success must necessarily affect the way we frame the discussion about Ethiopian land tenure policy. It could be argued that this contentious issue has now finally been laid to rest: the current land tenure system is no hindrance to economic growth and welfare; indeed, it may be the guarantor for growth with equity. In this chapter, I shall argue the opposite.

When I first visited Ethiopia, in 1981, I presented my plans for a study of land tenure to a senior Ethiopian professor in the social sciences. His reaction was that land tenure was not of interest any more. It had been settled by the land reform of 1975 once and for all. It should be pointed out that although I did not agree, this view looked much more sensible in 1981 than it does now with the benefit of hindsight. The government also considers the land question to be settled, and after the certification programmes of the early 2000s, many observers seem to agree. My view, however, is that there are built-in contradictions in the system of state land ownership, and it is therefore unsustainable in the longer run, or if it is sustained for political reasons, there will be significant social costs.

As social scientists we are used to criticizing, yet often without presenting the underlying alternative that is implicit in the criticism. Is

[1] About 80% of the population currently depends on agriculture, an unusually high figure for Africa. Poverty reduction is therefore intimately connected with agricultural growth. Dessalegn (2008: 230) aptly argued that rurality equals poverty, and peasant empowerment therefore equals empowerment of the poor.

the alternative more viable or less problematic than what is criticized? In this chapter, I take a more positive stance by outlining the basis for an alternative policy. This is challenging, as any land tenure policy in Ethiopia is likely to lead to specific problems. Writing this chapter is therefore a matter of honesty, making clear my thinking and thus exposing it to criticism. Being a historian, I set the argument within a long-term view of Ethiopian development and land tenure history. My hope is that the analysis can contribute to the debate regarding a stable and productive land tenure system, whether one agrees or disagrees with the specific points made.

The basis for my argument is partly my reading of the literature, which includes many more ethnographic studies than covered in the preceding chapters, socio-political studies of land tenure, the reports of economists and various proposals for reform. It also takes into account the contributions presented in this book: the farm model, peasant land rights understood as conditional private property, the low level of rural inequality, but also the intrusive state and challenges of development. The general thrust of these other chapters, and of my argument, is that certain peasant rights do exist, and we need to understand these rights and the related peasant strategies. This is a platform from which I propose some simple principles of reform, or 'reform' since the changes proposed are modest, albeit with potentially significant systemic implications.

My views are also strongly coloured by impressions and information gathered during years of fieldwork. Since the late 1970s, I have researched Ethiopian history and society, conducting regular fieldwork since 1989, especially in the Yefat area, but also in Wälo. During this time, I have talked with hundreds of peasants and lived for extended periods in peasant communities. What I have heard, read, seen and discussed during these fieldwork studies form the primary basis of my thinking. In this context, I focus on the properties of the land tenure system, and the documentation of the empirical claims I make is therefore rudimentary. As always, these claims could, and should, be challenged by empirical research.

I have approached the issue of land tenure starting from the farm and what it would take to create and maintain a healthy agricultural structure. I sometimes refer to this as 'the peasant perspective', which does not mean that all peasants would agree with my specific points, especially if asked in a typical survey format. My argument is based on the peasant situation but it also takes into account much wider concerns than what may often underlie a peasant's immediate response. It is a refined peasant perspective in the sense that peasants tend to agree after we have discussed the matter for some time. Attitudes to land sales serve as an illustration. It was common for peasants to repeat the official position and express opposition to a policy position to permit land sales, but after being asked some critical questions, they usually reached the conclusion that if they had full ownership rights, land sales might in fact serve the long-term interests of themselves, the community, and the development of Ethiopia. It is especially easy to convince youngsters who start out arguing for a new round of land redistribution that they would be better served by the right to buy land, the flip side of the right to sell.

Much of the critical literature treats the Ethiopian government as the adversary. My argument is not against the state, but rather for the state to find its proper role. The state would gain much by engaging in dialogue with peasants, more so than the current command-based participation approach. The aim should be to arrive at a land tenure policy that is sustainable over time and which has generalized local legitimacy. The fact that fundamental land tenure issues periodically return to the political agenda shows that this is not yet the case.

THE PROBLEM

The discussion above raises two questions. First, we must assess whether there really is a need for further land reform, or whether the current system already satisfies, to a reasonable degree, future demands. In this section, I argue that current land tenure, even in its latest version after land certification, produces problems that cannot be solved without overcoming the limitations inherent in state land ownership. This takes us to the second question: what should be the principles of the alternative system? For a land tenure system to work well, the following three elements are necessary:

1. Tenure security: the operating unit must have good security of future rights as this is essential for good management and investment decisions.
2. Legitimacy: the laws must have generalized legitimacy so that breaking the law is seen as deviant behaviour, and not something many have to do simply to stay alive.
3. Sustainability: the system must be sustainable over time, and not just a reform that solves the problems of the day, as has repeatedly happened in the past.

The current land tenure system fails on all three accounts.

There are two basic narratives about the trajectory of Ethiopian land tenure, in which differing views of land tenure under the Därg play a pivotal role. In my view, peasant land tenure under the Därg can best be described as conditional private property (see Chapters 3 to 5), set within the official system of state land ownership. The EPRDF maintained the essential features of this system, notably state-peasant relations where ultimate state control over land was the central political nexus. The Ethiopian state after 1975, including the current EPRDF period, fits well within the picture of authoritarian high modernism (Scott 1998: 87).

The standard narrative differs. There are several strands of it, and I shall deal only with the economics literature due to its current dominance. In this standard view, peasant land tenure under the Därg was shaped by periodic land redistribution, which generated great tenure insecurity. After the fall of the Därg, the EPRDF initiated a more market-friendly policy. This culminated with land certification and new land laws, which led to improved tenure security and to a better-functioning rental market. The result was higher production, more investments in the land, and better livelihoods for the poor, notably women.[2] Although the theoretical arguments appear to point to the superiority of a free-market system, certification and land rentals seem like a workable compromise (Deininger *et al.* 2003b: 10–11; Berhanu Gebremedhin *et al.* 2003: 1–3; Holden *et al.* 2009c: 294). Because the view of the present is coloured by a particular view of the Därg period, such a conclusion lies near at hand.[3] However, if we analyse the current hybrid property system on its own terms, it seems questionable whether it is truly sustainable over time.

There are major contradictions in the current land tenure system, and as long as these persist, it will continue to be unstable and likely to generate problems – problems which are only temporarily solved by *ad hoc* solutions. In the following, I discuss these contradictions under the following points:

1. Null-price of land: land has a high economic value, but ownership rights are acquired for free by the lucky ones. Illegal practices are likely to follow.
2. High stakes: everybody is entitled to land according to the constitution, but not everybody will receive land. There are very narrow margins between receiving a fair land endowment and being excluded from the landowning system. This results in intense competition.
3. Dispersion of rights: partible inheritance means that farmlands *tend* to disperse. Marriage makes people move, often over distances too long to rationally farm all the land where the individuals might have a stake. There is thus a structural tendency towards a costly farm structure.
4. Insecurity: an unstable system generates tenure insecurity, even after formal land certification.

With these problems as a backdrop, I formulate a proposal for land tenure reform using the following main ingredients:

1. Do no harm: my proposal is based on the current system of peasant farming and only seeks to reform what is absolutely necessary. The key is to vest the peasants with formal rights for what they already practice – in other words, to clarify the concept of ownership, or to reduce the conditionality in conditional land ownership.

[2] For some relevant historical summaries, see Deininger *et al.* (2009: 59–60), Holden *et al.* (2007: 3), Benin (2006: 223) and Dercon and Daniel (2007: 2).
[3] Bruce *et al.* (1994: 60–2) also saw tenure security combined with permission to rent out the land as a workable compromise.

2. Right to sell: landowners should have an absolute right to sell their land, with due respect for the rights of other family members or legitimate right-holders.
3. Right to buy: local farmers should have the right to buy land, up to the legal maximum holding; other potential buyers may be excluded. The precise rules should be locally adapted and modified as the economy develops.

On this basis, I seek to sketch a viable land tenure policy where private property rights are set within a flexible regulatory system in order to counteract any negative consequences that might develop.

THE ALTERNATIVES

The broad policy alternatives are: (a) state ownership with regimented development; (b) a free market system based on privatized holdings; or (c) peasant entitlement within a regulatory framework.[4]

The advantage of state ownership, as argued by the government, is mainly to protect poor peasants against market forces. This has a strong paternalistic flavour, since it means that the peasants have to be protected against their own decisions by a presumably more responsible state. We might also add as advantages the protection of the environment by regulating and commanding the subject peasants. Finally, state land ownership is a key ingredient in the policy of forced economic transformation. Until about 2005, most researchers seem to have accepted that state land ownership had failed, but the country's more recent economic success cannot be easily dismissed. State land ownership may be viable, but comes at a high cost for the peasants in economic terms if policies fail on a grand scale, and above all in the authoritarian political environment and social unease which tends to accompany such systems. Therefore, what I have presented as advantages here could just as well be seen as disadvantages: limited peasant rights and a command approach to environmental protection and economic development.

Turning to the privatization of land rights, the advantages of this policy approach have been summarized as follows:[5]

[4] See Berhanu Abegaz (2004: 328–33) for a parallel classification. The major difference is that he referred to the third option as an intermediate solution, which may be correct but is too vague to be helpful. The only purpose of his category may be to include Dessalegn's (1994b: 13–16) proposal for 'associative ownership', although he then dismisses it as 'populist' without serious exploration. My own alternative is obviously close to that of Dessalegn's, although not identical.

[5] See Berhanu Nega *et al.* (2003: 110), Deininger *et al.* (2003a: 1) and Holden *et al.* (2009d: 14).

1. Incentive for investments: the land market provides the owner with the security that he will reap the fruits of any investments in the land. It therefore becomes more rational for him to invest in good land management.
2. Allocative efficiency: land is transferred from less efficient to more efficient owners, and thus the total production increases.
3. Collateral: when land can be sold, it can also serve as collateral for credit. This can lead to capitalization, by which a farmer can use the value of the land to increase his operational capital and still keep the land for farming.

A free market may create dynamism, but there are pitfalls. Those who argue against the right to sell land highlight the danger of distress sales and mass exodus from the countryside. I have my doubts about this, but it is nevertheless an important issue which I shall deal with separately in the next section. I also take this potential threat into account in the reform proposal. In our context, it is important to note that 'the market' is far from a simple and clear category, and specifically, while I emphasize the right to sell land, this right to sell does not necessarily imply a free land market.

The entitlement option aims to create a vibrant peasant economy. While the first two options prioritize either the state or the market, entitlement aims to strengthen the smallholder sector – in this context by land titling, a process which goes well beyond land certification.[6] My proposal fits into this category. It starts from the farm, reforms only what needs to be reformed, and seeks to align the interests of individual peasants with wider social concerns.

THE SPECTRE OF THE MARKET

The debate over Ethiopian land tenure has mainly been focused on presenting market arguments in critical opposition to government policies. However, the advantages of the market (outlined above) are questionable. There is widespread agreement about the importance of tenure security, but the other two points about allocative efficiency and collateral are controversial. If the effect of the land market is to transfer land to more efficient users, it means that some users are losing out. This may be economically sound policy in terms of GDP growth rates but undesirable for social reasons, and has the potential to threaten political stability. Similarly, using land as collateral implies that an indebted farmer may lose his land. It is not difficult to draw up some frightening scenarios in the case of a major famine.

[6] The recent reforms in Ethiopia consisted of certification and registration of holdings, with no or very little land titling in the form of formalizing the holders' ownership rights. Here I agree with Dessalegn (2008: 219). See also the Amhara land law (Amhara Regional Government 2002 E.C.), discussed briefly in the next section.

The government argument plays on these fears: if peasants are given the right to sell their land, there will be many distress sales, increased migration to towns, and concentration of land ownership in the hands of the rich. This threat seems plausible, and I have met a number of researchers arguing along the same lines.[7]

However, there is surprisingly little empirical evidence pointing in this direction. In Ethiopia, I can think of none. The experience that usually comes to mind is the CADU project in Arsi which, due to its technical success, led to a considerable eviction of tenants by landowners who preferred to operate their farms by modern methods (Ståhl 1974). However, those evicted were not small farmers operating their own farms but landless tenants, a legacy of the conquest of the south in the late nineteenth century. Another example sometimes mentioned is Käfa. Pausewang (2004: 3) argued that the experience of the small coffee producers there was proof of peasant eviction, but again, this was mainly the result of the state selling off the peasants' land, not the peasants selling their own land. The land could be sold precisely because the actual farmers lacked secure property rights.

In addition, on the international scene, very unequal land ownership is the legacy either of a feudal past or of colonialism – both cases being created by forms of conquest, with typical examples from Asia and Latin America, respectively. The contrast between the agricultural structure of England and France is also telling. Eighteenth-century France was more aristocratic than England, but today the contrast between the French peasant farms and the large landed estates of England is striking. Although it has been two centuries since the French Revolution, the land market has not yet concentrated farmland into the hands of a small stratum of large farmers or capitalist entrepreneurs. The lesson seems to be that when peasants control the land, rural social structure is remarkably resilient.

If peasants are given the right to sell land, active farmers will buy it. There is widespread agreement that smallholder farming is efficient (e.g. EEA 2002: 4; Chiari 2003: 13), and investors usually find it difficult to compete on purely economic grounds.[8] Even apart from the competitiveness of peasant farms, land is of such a high value to local farmers that they are not likely to sell their land. Some non-farming landowners would be candidates to sell, while active farmers in the same locality would be the most likely buyers.

These issues are weakly covered in the research literature, but there is some empirical evidence from my own fieldwork to support this assertion. My impression from a number of cases of land sales in Yefat in the late imperial period is that the buyers were not investors but active farmers, often tenants who sought to improve their own

[7] This position is more easily found in conversations with researchers than in the literature itself, but see Chiari (2003: 93–5), Pausewang (2004: 3) and Degefa (2005: 163–5).

[8] The real danger is in investors using political channels to exert pressure, but in this specific case the state is the problem, not the solution.

position. The typical sellers, on the other hand, were not farmers, but individuals who were selling off land rights originating in the feudal past.[9] Furthermore, evidence from later periods illustrates the competitiveness of peasant agriculture. State farms under the Därg were less productive than the peasant sector, and current commercial farms may not be much more productive than the peasant farms.

During my fieldwork in Yefat, I never heard of any active farmer selling off his land.[10] Instead, the sellers were youngsters who had gained access to some land, too little to even attempt to establish a farming household. A few active farmers mortgaged their land in order to set up an urban enterprise. At the time, the area was edging very close to famine, but farmers went to great lengths to avoid distress sales, which they knew would permanently cripple both their current household and the future of their children. These attitudes are also expressed in the survey of the Ethiopian Economic Association, according to which only 5 per cent of the respondents thought they would sell any land, if allowed. In case of distress, they would prefer to rent out some of their land (EEA 2002: 49).

CONTRADICTIONS IN LAND TENURE POLICIES

Who owns the land in Ethiopia? The 1975 land proclamation abolished private land ownership, and from then onwards land formally belongs to the Ethiopian people represented by the state. On this basis, it has often been argued that the peasants have only usufruct rights (e.g. Dessalegn 1984: 29; Makonen 1987: 126; Birhanu and Mamo 2010: 11). Peasants are reportedly fully aware of this situation, and in a 2001 survey 84 per cent responded that land belongs to the government (EEA 2002: 46). This was during a heated political situation and the peasants' response seems to capture the contrast between well-known policy positions – the government versus the opposition, rather than the property rights structuring the daily life of peasants, the focus of the current book.

To refer to peasant land rights as only usufruct rights is, however, against everyday usage. When asked about who is the owner of a specific parcel of land, peasants respond with the name of the local landowner, not the state. Similarly, the survey reports of the Central Statistical Authority routinely refer to 'Private Peasant Holdings' (e.g. CSA 2000: 17). The peasants have more than usufruct rights, and it is common to find peasants who can trace their holding history for some generations. These rights may be labelled 'possession', somewhat more limited than full ownership, but I find it terminologically

9 The cases are from lower Ayné and Wäyra Amba, the area I know best. They were not part of a targeted investigation, but something I stumbled across in people's life histories.

10 This might be challenged by evidence from lower Yefat, an area characterized by many land sales in the mid-1990s and where distress sales might be an interesting hypothesis.

simpler and even more precise to refer to the peasants as land *owners*, although within the limits of conditional land ownership as described in Chapter 3. The concept of usufruct rights, on the other hand, is better reserved for the rights of those renting land from the landowners.

The peasants are the owners of the land, and this is how the local economy works. However, state policies may at any time evict them from their holdings. Furthermore, since land is formally owned by the state, peasants cannot sell their land. While this seems logical, it is less clear why they cannot sell whatever rights they have, except for the obvious fact that these practical rights are so strong that selling them would amount to land sales. This is the basic contradiction in Ethiopian land tenure.

Peasant usufruct rights are not the only theoretically problematic issue in the standard description. The concept of state land ownership points towards a political system but is not very helpful for understanding land ownership rights, because the state does not in any meaningful way own the land. By land ownership we usually mean the right to use the land, the right to exclude others from this use right, as well as a variable package of transfer rights. The state has these rights in the case of state farms, and the existence of this category illustrates that peasant farms exist under different property rules. Any attempt by the state to take over peasant farms would be experienced by peasants as eviction, not as the legitimate owner exercising his right. Rather, the system of general state ownership is a legacy of the despotic state.[11] It has been taken over by the modern developmental state, for different purposes but with much the same state-peasant relations, based on control and orders rather than the provision of services required by the peasants.

State land ownership and smallholder agriculture operate according to different rationalities. This problem could logically be solved by the state taking over practical ownership rights, as the Därg attempted to do to some extent and with disastrous consequences. The other obvious alternative is to formalize the ownership rights of the smallholders, but this means that the state has to relinquish its claim to own all land on behalf of the people. The non-resolution of this contradiction unduly limits the rights of the real landowners and creates fundamental uncertainty about future developments. This introduces a considerable element of risk, not ordinary economic risk but something bigger – and fundamentally unpredictable. The example of the Amhara land redistribution of 1997, a shocking experience, is a perfect illustration of this risk (see Ege 1997b).

Some practical consequences can be seen in the land legislation of the Amhara Regional State contained in a booklet apparently distrib-

[11] I here refer to a system of government, not the popular pejorative meaning. The image of despotism is very prominent in Darkwah (1975: 112–13), where the king of Shäwa was described as a benevolent despot, in control not only of all the land in the kingdom but also the lives of his subjects.

uted to all rural communes (Amhara Regional Government 2002 E.C.).[12] Elements of these laws point towards improved tenure security, but the basic thrust is towards tighter state control, which means weaker rights for the peasants. While Proclamation No. 133 of 2006 pays lip service to the constitutional rights of all peasants to get land, the emphasis is rather on good land management (Proclamation, Preamble). Regulation No. 51 of 2007 takes the control aspect one step further. Its stated aims are to establish a land administration system, a land use system, documentation for all holdings, protection for women, disabled and orphans, and to create conducive conditions for investors (Regulations, Art. 3). Tenure security and the rights of peasants are not mentioned here, but the latter are mentioned in the next paragraph which basically only restates the Proclamation. Current government policy is based on a large dose of modernist attitudes, interspersed with paternalism and an eye towards what might be appreciated by donors; it is not based on tenure security, land titling or the belief that peasants by and large are competent and responsible actors.

Null-price of land

Land has an inherently high economic value. The most common land rent is probably the half share, often without the landowner contributing any input. On the other hand, ownership of this land is a right which is non-tradable and therefore without any economic value expressed in a price. This is most clearly revealed in the compensation rules, by which land confiscated for public purposes is not compensated, with only buildings and other investments made on the land being compensated. While this is obviously unfair, to compensate for the land itself would put a price on the land, which officially it does not have. To fully resolve this problem is difficult within the current system.[13]

To sell land is illegal but may be very tempting, especially in peri-urban settings (Chapter 7). Assigning a high-value item a null-price is simply not realistic. It is not surprising that a person who has decided to leave the area may seek to recover some of the value of his land through arrangements amounting to sale, usually at a low price due to the risk faced by the buyer. Both parties lose out in the current situation.

Even worse is the fact that illegal practices become legitimate in the eyes of the peasants. Currently land transactions are more closely monitored than before, not the least due to certification, but sales still happen. So I asked a peasant leader whether he would report the cases

[12] The booklet contains Proclamation No. 133 of 2006, Regulation No. 51 of 2007 which further specifies the rules, and undated Guidelines. The first two are in Amharic and English, while the Guidelines are in Amharic only. The various regional land laws have been extensively commented upon in the literature. Holden (2008: 22–4) provides a very useful overview.

[13] Recently, the government issued compensation rules for when land is expropriated for public purposes; however, peasants complain that the level of compensation is still rather arbitrary and unsatisfactory. The main problem is that the money received by the peasants cannot be used to buy other land.

of land sales we both knew of and, as expected, he stated that neither he nor anyone else would report such cases.[14] The occurrence of land sales and similar practices have ebbed and flowed, but as long as current policies are maintained, illegal sales will exist, and where there are illegal practices, corruption may follow. This has a corrosive effect on the rule of law. Sales can be reduced by control measures, but these are costly, have a negative impact on state-peasant relations, and often provide even more opportunities for corruption.[15]

High stakes

The principal way to obtain land is through inheritance and related practices. Land may still be assigned by the commune, but this practice is now so limited that we can disregard it in the current context. Even under the Därg, what was labelled as land redistribution was to a large extent simply to confirm the farmer in the land he was already cultivating, often inherited from parents.[16] Current allocations mainly refer to house sites for a few youngsters and maybe a small hillside area to be farmed jointly. With few exceptions, those who do not inherit land are permanently excluded from the category of landowners. There is thus an acute process of eviction from the rural areas. If a similar number of landless had been produced by peasants selling their land, we would have regarded it as an acute social problem and solid proof of distress sales.

In order to understand peasant land tenure we need, above all, to understand inheritance. To my knowledge, there is no study of this important topic and the following are just some brief points.[17] The principle underlying the current Amhara legislation is partible inheritance,

[14] D11057, Diary: 19.11.2014 (the Bibliography contains more information on my field notes).

[15] Illegal land sales are probably found everywhere, but it is most acute around expanding towns, due to two opposite tendencies. The real land value greatly increases, but the likelihood that the peasant landowner can keep the land declines. Since the land is officially without a price, it is better to sell for whatever one can get to those who are in a position to push their claims. See Aspen's description in Chapter 7, as well as Mitiku *et al.* (2005: 29–32).

[16] In some of the literature, there is a strange opposition between commune land and inherited land, as if they were separate categories. In fact, all land was formally allocated by the commune. On the other hand, the typical way of obtaining such land was to first inherit or receive it from one's parents, and then have this transaction formally registered with the commune. After certification, the role of the commune has been replaced by the formal court system.

[17] Hoben (1973) analysed one particular inheritance system, but the book is more about system properties than a careful investigation of the variation of peasant practices. The same applies to my description of the *dersha* system in Chapter 3. These two studies refer to the imperial and the Därg periods, respectively, and there is an urgent need both for system descriptions of the post-certification period as well as good ethnographic and life-history accounts, in order to capture the flavour of peasant life. In Ege (1997a; 2017), I discuss inheritance practices and conflicts, but these are case studies, not systematic investigation of inheritance.

regulated by the state. There are a number of highly specific rules, and while each rule may appear sensible – e.g. to protect the interests of widows or minors – the effects of the totality are somewhat unpredictable for the peasants. Potentially overlapping rights seem to have generated a great amount of conflict. Some inherit nothing, some a share of the family estate, and some inherit several land holdings. For many youngsters with farming ambitions, this is almost a life or death struggle, aggravated by the fact that there are no other ways to get land. Due to the high stakes, such conflicts often become very bitter.[18]

Dispersion of rights

The Ethiopian farm is not a trans-generational economic enterprise. Partible inheritance makes it a much more dynamic and temporary unit. The dominant pattern, but far from the only one, is for a young man to marry and settle on the land of his parents, getting a very small parcel of land from them. The wife may receive land from her own parents, but often this remains a latent right or expectation, especially if the young couple lives far away. When their parents die, however, they may expect to inherit their respective shares, equal inheritance still being the basic principle (although it is under considerable pressure).

If we think in model terms, we can see that after a generation or two, this system becomes untenable. Family holdings become scattered, the operational plots may become small or they have to be owned jointly. I find it difficult to believe that a society can operate in this way for a long time. In a case I observed in Yefat, two sons were registered as the formal inheritors of a farm, but each of them headed a group of other siblings with locally accepted equal rights. There was considerable tension both between the two sons and within the groups.[19] The management of such rights becomes a challenge, and it is remarkable that only a few years after a comprehensive land certification we see the emergence of a new, somewhat informal, property system operating 'beneath' the official one.

Both the peasants and the administration will seek to find solutions to the worst consequences of the dispersion of rights. But it is likely that there will be a tendency towards fragmentation and complicated joint property rights.[20] Within the current system, grey-zone practices is the easiest solution for the peasants, while land redistribution is the easiest short-term solution for the state. The right to buy and sell land is an obvious alternative.

18 This description is based on impressions from my fieldwork in 2014 (D11057, Diary: 17.11.2014 *et passim*).

19 D11001, Interview about land inheritance case, 09.08.2013: 3.

20 Fragmentation has been somewhat of a red herring in the literature, but was probably not much of a problem after the 1975 land reform. The inheritance system, however, potentially leads towards fragmentation, which either takes place or is counteracted by other practices. Redistribution may work towards fragmentation or consolidation, depending on the specific rules.

Tenure insecurity

In theory, Ethiopian peasants have absolute tenure security, without any time limit, but this principle is contradicted by the right of all peasants to receive land. At least one of these principles must give way, and in the past both have been breached. State land ownership and a history of authoritarian practice create insecurity.

Absolute tenure security is a contradictory concept, unless it is taken to mean some form of bondage. The Ethiopian peasant is free to move, but at the risk of losing his current land holding. For tenure security to be truly meaningful, it must include the right for the holder to decide when and how to end these rights. From the perspective of the farm, the right to sell the land is an integral part of tenure security. According to Deininger *et al.* (2003a: 18) transfer rights have more impact on investments than tenure security *per se*. Without the right to sell, peasants cannot be sure that they will reap the fruits of their investments. The promise of compensation for land improvements if the land is confiscated is hollow, due to past practices and also because it is difficult to assess the impact of good land management. Improved fertility of the land through years of labour can easily be regarded as an inherent characteristic of the soil.[21]

Land certification should in principle lead to tenure security, but instead it has apparently led to the spread of tenancy and thus to increased insecurity for much of the land. The current land tenure system – i.e. absolute tenure security with access only by inheritance – is rigid and therefore likely to result in an increasing incidence of land rentals up to a certain level. Some reports have found that about 30 per cent of all households rent out land (Deininger *et al.* 2011a: 4; Devereux *et al.* 2005: 123; Gebrehawariya and Holden 2011: 47). Others report somewhat lower figures (Benin and Pender 2009: 219; Deininger *et al.* 2008: 80).[22] The problem inherent in this situation has been clouded by the fact that many of the landowners are poorer than the tenants, at least when economic status is measured by farming assets, which is a common but problematic practice. While economists have focused on the positive contribution of the land rental market, this is both one-sided and short-sighted. The pro-market argument that tenure

[21] This certainly happened in the 1997 Amhara land redistribution, and may well happen again. Thus, if the land registers are updated through a new round of measurements, it could lead to confiscation of land which was 'hidden' in the first round. In previous rounds of land distribution and assessment, a *t'emad* of low fertility was considered large (see Chapter 5). If this land was developed and is now fertile, more than half the parcel could be liable to confiscation. Rumours about a future GPS-based round of certification fit well into this picture. Certification and its follow-up has thus created new types of insecurity.

[22] There is considerable variation between localities, and aggregate data tend to cover up this variation. It is also difficult to compare data for trends and ecological variation because the reference point of the figures varies: share of households, share of land, renting in, renting out, or unspecified 'participation in the market'.

security is important for investments applies to the farmer rather than to rentier owners. It would therefore appear that a high share of tenancy is a problem rather than the ultimate solution.

Finally, the ownership structure also leads to instability. In recent years inequalities have been rising. This has resulted in a situation where many youngsters continue to ask for new land redistribution. Even though official policy is firmly against new rounds of land redistribution and most youngsters have lost any real hope for redistribution, the issue easily pops up in conversation. The very real problems faced by young people lead to considerable insecurity among those who feel exposed if there were a new round of redistribution. Thus, Deininger *et al.* (2011b: 320) found that even in communes where certificates had been distributed, the fear of losing land had only decreased from 23 per cent of respondents in 1999, just after the Amhara land redistribution, to 19 per cent in 2007. In communes where certificates had not yet been distributed, the fear of losing land had actually increased over the same period, from 20 per cent to 28 per cent.[23]

TOWARDS A SUSTAINABLE LAND TENURE SYSTEM

No one knows the future trajectory of the Ethiopian land tenure system. It is likely that it will ultimately move towards some sort of private property system, but redistribution to solve growing problems within the agrarian structure cannot be excluded, even in those cases where current laws have called a halt to redistribution. Laws can be changed – in Ethiopia very rapidly – or they can just be ignored. Furthermore, a simple decision to enforce stricter residence requirements, or specific land management, or to measure the lands again, could lead to very significant redistribution of land rights without breaching current laws. As long as the land tenure system produces serious problems which can find a short-term solution through a redistribution, this option is more than a theoretical threat. For years to come, peasants are likely to feel a considerable amount of tenure insecurity.

The other danger is an extreme free-market reform. In my proposal, which centres on the right to sell land, I do not refer to the benefits of the market, partly due to the ideological overtones of such an argument, and partly because I do not find the market terminology very helpful in capturing peasant practices. It is common for economists to talk about transaction costs, with a rather diffuse reference forcing us to try to retranslate this back to actual peasant practices. These costs are rarely precisely described, and so far, I have not seen any attempt to quantify them. The main point, however, is that many of the peasant transactions are ill captured, even misunderstood, when analysed as market transactions. First of all, the relevant partners are often so

[23] Surprisingly enough, the thrust of the Deininger *et al.* (2011b) article is on improved tenure security. I have argued that tenure insecurity may have increased as a result of the recent reforms (Ege 2017).

limited that this becomes, at best, a very special market, the features of which would have to be properly described. But above all, there are so much emotions, considerations for others, communal economy and customs involved that the price mechanism – key to the market principle – may not be very relevant. There are of course market elements in the transactions of peasants, but they are highly variable and often not dominant.[24]

The farm perspective

Rather than arguing from the point of view of the efficiency of the market, my starting point is the peasant farm in its current configuration. A primary concern is tenure security, an element that most researchers seem to agree on. Simply stated, in order to make it rational for a farmer to invest in the land, he needs security that he will benefit from the investment. At the current stage of development, of the three main pro-market arguments only the tenure security argument is relevant for Ethiopian peasant agriculture.[25]

Seen from the perspective of the farm, a key aspect of tenure security is generational transfer. Both parents and children should know that their future on the farm is assured if they so desire it. The partible inheritance of the northern highlands is here a challenge because it tends towards fragmentation in every generation. This could potentially be solved by legally limiting inheritance of land to the oldest child. The inheritance system may be moving in this direction in areas of great land shortage, which is not without its problems.[26] In any case, imposing such a change would be an extremely radical reform, dispossessing most children. Changes in the inheritance system could well lead to the feared mass exodus to towns.

The current proposal is not really a proposal for reform of peasant land tenure, but for recognizing widespread peasant practices – to bring them from the realm of shadowy practices into the open where they can be monitored and, if need be, regulated. Ethiopia here differs from much of the rest of Africa where land titling has often meant a move from some form of communal land tenure towards private property rights, a much more challenging process with obvious openings for land grabbing and corruption. By contrast, in Ethiopia it is a question of moving from conditional to largely unconditional private ownership rights for peasants.

I deal with the issues in a rather practical way, informed by my understanding of Ethiopian peasant society. Logically, and even more so practically, there is a difference between the right to sell and the

[24] There is a large body of literature in economic anthropology dealing with differences in economic systems, much of it going back to the contributions of Polanyi, Chayanov, and the Marxist debate on modes of production.

[25] See the earlier discussion on the three main theoretical advantages of the market: tenure security, transfer to more efficient producers and collateral.

[26] We found some tendencies in this direction in Ch'orisa, South Wälo (Ege and Aspen 2003: 89–90).

right to buy, and I therefore examine each element in turn. While the ownership debate in Ethiopia has mainly been about the right to sell land, my interest is more in the right to buy.

The right to sell land

The peasant land owner should have freehold rights in the sense that he or she has the full right to sell the land. If this infringes on the rights of others (e.g. family members), their consent would be needed. This has several benefits. First of all, it is a precondition for real tenure security. Secondly, it brings land sale and similar practices into the legal realm, which facilitates good land administration and hinders the erosion of state legitimacy when the state seeks to prohibit practices that have local legitimacy. Thirdly, the price of land will increase due to the removal of risk, to the great benefit of those landowners who decide to move out of agriculture (e.g. by selling inherited land to a co-inheritor). Fourthly, and most importantly, it contributes to the maintenance of a healthy ownership pattern by allowing owners to readjust their assets. Farmers are willing to pay more for land close to their homestead than for distant land. The same applies if someone sees new opportunities, e.g. fruit cultivation on waterlogged land unsuitable for grain production, or tree plantations on steep hillsides. To buy and develop such land is a dream for some enterprising youngsters, and this option could significantly contribute to development and welfare.

The counter-argument is obviously that peasants may be so poor that they will sell out and become paupers in the towns. I have dealt with this argument earlier in the chapter. Certainly, there will be cases of individual tragedies, but it is highly unlikely that these will be more frequent than what is regularly produced by the current system. For instance, after the 1997 Amhara redistribution, some people killed themselves or died shortly due to extreme stress and bitterness caused by the events. Some youngsters received land while others were, in practice, disinherited. Some single persons were permitted to hold 12 *t'emad*, while some households of eight or more had their holdings reduced to 4 *t'emad*, all according to the official rules, thus producing inequality in land per person at least in the range of 1:24 (Ege 1997b: 135). Such authoritarian practices must be kept in mind when we consider the argument that the right to sell land will lead to distress sales and evictions.[27]

Even apart from redistribution, there are tragedies due to family conflicts over land, enhanced by a quite unpredictable legal system. Furthermore, many have land rights that are simply too small for a farming livelihood. They therefore opt for an urban life, perhaps far away, but continue to receive some small benefit from their land as long as they are permitted to keep it. Both they and their tenants are insecure. By the current laws of Tegray, if someone is away for more

[27] Därg practices of evicting peasants for afforestation projects, producer cooperatives or other development initiatives are equally relevant.

than two years, his or her land should be confiscated and assigned to more worthy farmers. In Amhara there is currently no such rule, but land rights of absentees do remain tenuous and are highly vulnerable to policy changes.

There are many ways to lose land; it is better to let the peasants themselves choose how and when to relinquish their rights. If they can sell their land, they may also obtain the means to buy new land elsewhere or to create alternative livelihoods, which is after all the main element of economic transition and development.

The right to buy land

The right to sell logically implies the right to buy, but there are significant differences. While every landowner should have the right to sell, there should be limitations on who can buy, and there should be a limit to the size of the holding. In the land reform legislation of 1975, the upper limit of a holding was 10 hectares, while in the current Amhara legislation it is 7 hectares for non-irrigated farmland in the highlands. This is flexible thinking which allows for sufficient dynamism in the foreseeable future. The specific limits should of course be adapted to the needs of the times, and if the total economy develops and becomes more urban, the legal maximum could be moved upwards. It could also be possible for a commune to set the locally accepted maximum below the national limit. For instance, in the middle Yefat area of intensive *t'éf* farming, peasants seem to agree that 3 hectares (or rather 12 *t'emad*) is a fair maximum in the current situation. The key point is that the resulting system would be shaped by the local agricultural and social system and, not the least, by local legitimacy.

Setting a limit on the size of holdings leads to considerable challenges in defining who should be reckoned as legitimate landowners. Strategic peasants will exploit any weakness in the system, as they have amply demonstrated under past and current property regimes. The obvious candidate for landowner is the peasant household, but the definition of the household has suffered from considerable manipulation in the recent past. Thus, individuals have been counted as households in terms of land rights, giving the real household land rights well above what would have been due if they were counted as just one household.[28] The best solution is probably to provide a sensible definition of the household and let the local community decide who is eligible through ordinary political and judicial processes. It is then not a case of beating the rules imposed from above, but of maintaining social justice within the community. An alternative – a realistic option based on the experience of the *dersha* system outlined in previous chapters – would be to link the maximum holding rights to individuals, via household size,

[28] One recent case is the practice of allocating 2 hectares per household in resettlement areas. Savvy peasants move as individuals, obtain the land, and then marry (Mitiku *et al.* 2005: 34). Official rules to treat some individuals as households greatly contributed to the surprising outcome of the 1997 Amhara redistribution (Ege 1997b: 122-3).

which annuls some of the games peasants can play with the definition of a household.[29]

Seen from the perspective of the farm, the most important benefit of permitting land sales is the possibility for farmers to buy land, not so much for accumulation, but for agricultural rationalization. Currently, operated farms often consist of the farmer's own land – which is fairly secure but not enough for sustenance – and land rented in by short-term agreements, with extreme tenure insecurity. Own holdings, at least in some cases of TPLF-style land redistribution, could consist of parcels far apart, and the competition for rented land is currently so intense that farmers are willing to take land more than two hours' walking distance away. In such cases, readjustment of the holding by the individual farmers would lead to more efficient agriculture. This could also make it realistic for able youngsters to build up a farm, something which today happens by chance rather than by strategy. Such policy would limit out-migration, instil more hope, and channel additional labour into the development of their land and future livelihoods.

The counter-argument to the right to buy land is that it may lead to land concentration. As indicated above, there is not much empirical evidence to support this fear. Under conditions of peasant agriculture, it may not be profitable to invest in farmland for farming purposes unless the owner intends to farm the land himself. However, a policy to stimulate development by letting investors and enterprising peasants buy up land, with the argument that they will introduce better technology, would indeed be a reason for concern.[30] There is of course great need for improved farming methods, but from the point of view of equity, and also almost certainly efficiency, good extension work would seem preferable. Despite all the criticism that can and has been levied against government policy and administration, this aspect should be considered a tremendous success in view of recent agricultural growth.[31]

The cap on land holdings will in itself prevent any major land concentration. It would also make sense to limit the right to buy land through some form of residence requirement where outside investors are excluded. In the current stage, the priority must be to strengthen peasant farms by consolidating lands and letting farmers build up a viable holding. Transactions that contribute to this should be allowed, while selling land to outsiders could be controlled by appropriate local regulations.

29 A specific concern is peri-urban lands, which must be tackled separately in a way that protects the interests of the peasant landowners exposed to expropriation.

30 In addition to the pro-market argument, emphasis on the need for social differentiation by stimulating a yeoman or kulak class would seem to fit in here (e.g. Dessalegn 2008: 347–51; Devereux *et al.* 2005).

31 In my paper on economic transformation in Armanya, Yefat (Ege 2015), I show that the process is driven locally by enterprising peasants, often poor, exploiting opportunities that are ultimately created by improved infrastructure provided by the government.

Technically, these are not easy issues and blunders have been made in the past. It is not advisable to demand residence in the commune because this would in many cases make it impossible to buy nearby land located in another commune. It would also logically lead to the loss of land rights if the owner moved out of the commune – currently quite a common practice – or it would open up the system for cheating by faking residence for only as long as it was necessary to obtain the land title. Such challenges can be addressed, however. The formal regulations should not be unduly limiting, but give the commune the necessary tools and then allow for local discretion within a set of national rules – basically, allowing practices that are seen as legitimate locally and which strengthen the local community, or at least do not unduly weaken it. Again, there will certainly be problems, but probably no more than today, and serious problems can be tackled through targeted policy. The basic point is to bring national legislation in tune with local legitimacy and create an enabling environment, rather than the control approach which has characterized Ethiopian land tenure since the 1975 land reform.

Berhanu Abegaz (2004: 333) doubted the capability of community institutions to be trusted with any regulatory functions, apparently based on a negative view of the commune under the Därg. Similar criticism was raised by Pausewang (2004: 8–9) against the current commune leaders. It is true that there is little difference in local leadership in the two periods, despite the enmity between the Därg and the EPRDF at a higher level; but in my experience average peasant leaders in both periods are much better than their reputations suggest, although they are certainly not without fault. There is actually considerable social capital in the local community, even more than can be officially admitted. Local officials often have to play a double game: professing loyalty by towing the party line, while acting at a lower level to protect community interests as much as possible. The latter remain the secrets of the local community.

Tax system

The tax system is an integral part of land tenure both due to the documentation aspect and to the economic effect of the land tax. Before the land reform of 1975, the main document of ownership was the tax receipt. A person could own land in many different locations and there was no cap on the amount of land owned. The land holding was whatever land, potentially from very different sources, the person controlled.

With the land reform and the subsequent adjustment of holdings, the landowners were organized into commune peasant associations. The practical expression of membership was the land tax, and each household had one, and only one, membership. It was illegal 'to accumulate tax names'. This was a logical consequence of the commune peasant association approach, but over time, it created a rigid system. Through various processes, including bad luck, some ended up with small holdings; holdings that were not, contrary to the literature, likely to grow much by redistribution; and holdings which could not easily be combined, even if the combined holding would not be in any way excessive. The problem was aggravated by a regressive tax, basically 20 birr per holding irrespective of size.[32]

The landholding system resulting from the recent land registration is rather similar, although there are some interesting opportunities for a more flexible policy. The land is registered per household, and the tax is also per household. However, in the case of inheritance and related practices, it is envisaged that the holding may be divided, and presumably a new holding – with parcels of lands originating from different previous holdings, typically the parents or other old relatives of husband or wife – may emerge. The limit on the maximum size of holdings indicates that the system, in unspecified ways, may allow for an increase in holdings. Peasants still seem a bit hesitant about these changes and prefer to vest inherited land in a family member who can, if need be, appear as an independent household. It may take some time until the inheritance rules are well enough established to be generally trusted.

It has been pointed out in several reviews of land certification that the registers only provide a snapshot of the present and were not developed for a dynamic situation (Mitiku *et al.* 2005: 15–17, 39; Deininger *et al.* 2007: 8, 13, 18).[33] This problem would become acute if land sales were to be permitted. The land registration system and land tenure management would be simpler with records of parcels of land, based on the pattern of the imperial regime, rather than the current registers of households with their land. The proposed records would require less updating. Even more importantly, it would remove any doubts about whether a person could combine two tax holdings, since the link between tax name and household, a legacy from the Därg land reform, would be broken. Anyone would be free to combine lands in any way they chose, within the regulations regarding purchase of land and up to the maximum legal limit for land holdings.

There is no reason to expect any significant problems of tax evasion. If there is something Ethiopian peasants want to do, it is to pay tax for as much land as possible, albeit as small an amount as possible. This is linked to the tradition of using tax receipts as proof of ownership. After the land reform, tax payment continued to be a precondition for land ownership. Under my proposal, a landowner needs to renew his claim every year to each specific parcel of land by paying the related tax. This worked under the imperial regime with a quite limited modern admin-

32 Occasionally there were extra, graduated taxes according to the wealth of the taxpayers, but taxes remained relatively lighter on larger holdings.

33 A radically different and much cheaper approach would have been a register of deeds, i.e. registering only the transactions in land, without prejudice to any other rights in the land (Deininger and Feder 2009: 243–5). This would have prioritized the dynamic aspects of the land tenure system and downplayed, or even ignored, the control aspect of the current land certification.

istration and it should not be too difficult today, given the increased administrative resources.[34]

The land tax should also be progressive rather than a flat rate per holding. Currently there is some increase of the land tax by holding size, but in such a way that the tax on the first unit of land is much higher than the tax on the last unit. The tax per *t'emad* is 40 birr if the holder has only 1 *t'emad*, 19 birr if the holder has 4 *t'emad*, and 13 birr if the holder has 10 *t'emad*.[35] This is socially unjust. It also creates some unsustainable effects from the point of view of state revenues. If holdings are merged, right up to the maximum limit, there would be a very significant decline in revenue, to a third or probably even less. This is the opposite of the desired effect; larger holdings should be able to carry a relatively larger tax burden per unit of land. Finally, the tax system can, in conjunction with any legal cap on holdings, be used to steer the pattern of land holdings in the desired direction.

CONCLUSION

Despite recent success in agricultural development and widespread praise for the land certification programme, the current system of land tenure is unstable. In the past, there have been periods when the land issue has seemed to be settled, only to re-emerge with force at a later time. In the long run, Ethiopian land tenure is probably heading for privatization, which in some ways returns it to the trajectory it followed half a century ago, but now operating under very different conditions due to the equalizing effect of the 1975 land reform. The road may, however, still contain some unexpected twists and turns, potentially costly to the society and tragic for some individuals.

The proposal given here, emphasizing that peasants should have the right to buy and sell land, may be labelled as pro-market, even neo-liberal, but the motivation and the specific formulation is very different. My concern is not the blessings of the market, but the need to promote vibrant peasant communities. Peasants should have the right to sell land in order to solve some very real and highly predictable contradictions within the current system – above all the inter-generational dynamics and the paradox of null price for a highly valuable asset like land. This is also the most effective, and perhaps the only way to give them the confidence that they will reap the fruits of any investments they make.

[34] This can be contrasted with the current vision of a highly technical land register which will certainly strain administrative resources and may well break down.

[35] D11138, Information on the land tax in 2014. In the commune in question, there was no holding above 10 *t'emad*, and the information therefore stops here. But holdings can legally be as large as 28 *t'emad*, and this most probably strengthens my argument. See also Aspen and Ege (2010: 5) for tax data from North Wälo in 2003.

There are counter-arguments, like the fear of concentration of ownership or mass exodus from the countryside, but these are largely unfounded and the residual problems are quite manageable by appropriate regulations. Private property logically includes the right to sell, but it does not have to mean a market unfettered by social concerns. There is nothing unique in a regulated land market, as this is probably, with plenty of local variation, the most common land tenure system in the world.

9

Conclusion

HARALD ASPEN

Ethiopia is still mainly a rural society. It is also one of the world's poorest countries, despite rapid development in recent years. There is good reason to believe that these two elements are linked, as indicated by repeated famines that have hit the rural, food-producing areas. Serious efforts to change this situation started in the late imperial period and became key policy aspects under the Därg and later the EPRDF. There is widespread agreement that the measures in the imperial period were too little, too late, while those under the Därg were often tragically misguided. Those of the EPRDF, still evolving, are up for discussion.

Most Ethiopian farmers are smallholders. For centuries, the rights and obligations of peasants in the land they farm have shaped Ethiopian society. Much changed with the land reform of 1975, but for the peasants concerned, these rights are as important as ever. These rights are, in our view, so much more than what can be covered by the term 'usufruct rights', and even if we were to accept the term as a fair description, one would still have to specify how, and under what conditions, peasants practice these usufruct rights. In order to develop its economy, Ethiopia will certainly require large investments. By contrast, good land tenure policy is not expensive, but bad policy can be very destructive, as amply illustrated by some of the programmes under the Därg. Policies are most likely to succeed if they emanate from a good understanding of the concerns and the practices of those to be reformed. It is therefore a problem that the land tenure practices of Ethiopian peasants have not been much studied.

In this book, we seek to contribute to the relevant body of knowledge in two ways: firstly by the specific descriptions and arguments we provide, and secondly by asking for more research, not the least to assess and challenge our own arguments. We hope that even those who disagree with our specific arguments may agree to the need, even urgency, for improved knowledge of peasant land tenure. We focused on the Amhara region, which is probably the region best covered in the research literature. We demonstrate that even here, there has been virtually no research on peasant land tenure practices. For the rest of Ethiopia, the literature is even more fragmentary. As indicated in the introduction, the same seems to hold for much of Africa.

This book operates on three levels. Firstly, it is permeated by its emphasis on peasant agency. This is a perspective, not a research finding. It is, however, a perspective that emanates rather naturally from our disciplinary backgrounds. We believe that this approach is an essential element (although not the only one) if the aim is to understand peasant actions, but it has been rather weakly represented in the literature on land tenure. Secondly, we advance some specific arguments, where the *dersha* theory is the most relevant. Apart from the particulars, the general aim here is to open the space for research by challenging widely held beliefs. While the *dersha* theory itself is based on practices in one community, it is probably applicable to many more, but the available literature does not permit us to specify its extent with much precision. This is, however, not the key point. By challenging the periodic redistribution theory, we believe we have opened the topic up for further empirical research, and not just in the Amhara region. This takes us to the book's third level, which is the rich world beyond the models. We need studies characterized by ethnographic richness and the willingness by researchers to question common assumptions, assumptions that shape all of our work but which are rarely sufficiently checked by critical research. In this way, ethnographically oriented research can complement, challenge and enrich the more macro-oriented studies based on large, perhaps nation-wide, samples. The latter type of research could make an important contribution by paying more attention to, and seeking to bring out and better understand, regional variation. Good research is, we believe, a never-ending dialogue between local realities and the models we develop to summarize and describe the practices observed.

A strong motivation for writing this book has been the disparity between standard accounts of Ethiopian land tenure and our own observations. Starting from the last few years of the Därg period and up to the present, we have spent many shorter and longer periods of time in various peasant communities in the Amhara region, first in Yefat in North Shäwa, and later, after the fall of the Därg, also in South and North Wälo. It is now more than four decades since the revolution and the ensuing land reform, while our close acquaintance with Amhara peasant society has lasted for nearly three of these decades. In this book, we have capitalized both on our formal field material and organized data sets, and on the relatively intimate knowledge about local realities in the Amhara highlands we have gained over the years.

Chapter 2 discussed the status of knowledge about peasant land tenure in Ethiopia in general, and the Amhara region in particular, and it pointed to the weak empirical basis for the general understanding of this fundamental element of the Ethiopian economy. Ethnographic studies, including our own, have tended to be coloured by the immediate topics of the day. In the late Därg period, typical examples were the intrusive state and its various forceful campaigns of villagization, war conscription, afforestation, and collectivization. After the EPRDF takeover, key issues which emerged were, among others: the re-organization of administrative set-ups and state control systems, the implementation of a multi-party (nominal) democracy, and more recently the land certification programmes and development-oriented investments in infrastructure, extension services and new agricultural inputs.

How peasants practised land tenure received less attention. The result of the focus on state policies was a never-challenged, general acceptance that we had a fair understanding of peasant land tenure. The image of peasants with usufruct rights only, suffering from frequent redistribution of their lands, was not, however, supported by studies detailed enough to show how such a system, or variants of the system, operated in any specific area. Such a generally accepted interpretation, apparently applicable to all of Ethiopia, but without clear reference to any particular area, is difficult to falsify. Any aberrant case is easily seen as just a deviation, without implications for our general understanding. In this book, however, we have tried to change this situation by showing that the standard interpretation is not well grounded in evidence, and that the case we describe seems to fit communities in several parts of the Amhara region, perhaps also beyond – where it may also be helpful in attempts to isolate the key features of other peasant land tenure systems.

The standard view of periodic land redistribution under the Därg was outlined in Chapter 3. This view was to a large extent built on Dessalegn's (1984) book about the land reform, a study based on fieldwork in 1981, only a few years after the reform started, which was too early for a full description of land tenure practices taking place over time. The book has been of great importance for anyone interested in land issues in Ethiopia after the revolution. However, more often than not, its description of redistribution has been understood as an empirical description of the land tenure system as it actually worked during the Därg period across the whole of Ethiopia, rather than as a very early model formulation. Gradually, a creeping feeling of uneasiness about the validity of the standard view of periodic land redistribution – when confronted with actual, observed practices of peasants in the Amhara highlands – urged us to deal with the model as just a model, and to examine our own and others' ethnographies to see how the model related to reality. Much of this book has therefore been a critical check of our own old assumptions about peasant land tenure (e.g. Ege 1990; Aspen 1993). Here, we have revised our previous views, basing our general formulations on our own fieldwork material, as well as on our critical reading of the research literature and acquaintance with Ethiopian culture and society.

Another important work, of particular interest for students of Amhara land tenure, is Allan Hoben's (1973) study of a local community in Gojam. This has become a standard reference work, dealing in particular with inheritance (*rest*) rules in pre-revolutionary Amhara. It describes a land tenure system as it actually worked in a local community, but has since – like with Dessalegn's book – been referred to by practically everyone (with the essential exception of Hoben himself) as a model description of Amhara land tenure, or even communal land tenure in northern Ethiopia in general.

Both books have had great impact on later studies of land tenure in Ethiopia, but they are different in scope and ethnographic detail. Dessalegn's study covered four communities in different parts of Ethiopia, the analysis was held on a rather general level, and fieldwork was undertaken in a period of great upheaval. Hoben's study is a typical ethnographic, in-depth study of a community at a certain time and place. The importance of both studies is unquestionable – our understanding of land issues in Ethiopia would be much poorer without them. However, both works are limited in scope (although in different ways), but have been used to represent issues far beyond their initial pertinence.

Ethnographic studies approaching the calibre of Hoben's are hard to find for the period after the revolution. We have therefore made extensive use of our own material, supplemented with that of Yigremew's from Gojam, in addition to other publications of relevance for our topic which were available to us. Our primary material presented in this book is from a few scattered sites only, and although we claim that our current arguments are compatible with the evidence reported in the literature, it would not only be hazardous, but also against the basic motivation of this book, to claim that the system we describe applies everywhere. What we do claim, however, is that our arguments and evidence seriously challenge the existing model. We therefore need more research on peasant land tenure practices, preferably grounded in specific communities, in order to move from general statements of regional variation to showing what these variations were and why they existed. Such a research agenda also has considerable policy implications. In Chapter 8, Ege sought to demonstrate how this could work, by linking our understanding of peasant land tenure practices with some principles for a policy discussion.

Throughout this book, peasant initiative, inventiveness and creativity have been contrasted with the curbing effects of the often brutal and capricious power of the state. Peasant agency has often modified state policies. This can best be observed on the local level. Universal policies may take on a local flavour as orders and rules are translated within local culture and conditions, and perhaps bent to the interests of the community or persons within the community. Sometimes, breaches of the rules were kept hidden, at least nominally, from the authorities, and local practices developed their own logical consistency in the grey zone between legislation and custom. Customary practices should not, however, be confused with 'traditional' or 'cultural' as something inherited from an unchanging past. Custom can rather be understood as something that gradually develops in an environment of incentives and limitations – an 'opportunity situation' in which tradition and culture, together with state power, ecology, and a number of other factors, are integral parts.

Peasant ingenuity, as well as long traditions of accommodating state interventions, are important elements in understanding land tenure today. They should also be taken into account when future land policies are considered. Chapter 7, which covered approximately a decade of more or less grey-zone negotiations about land rights and transactions in and around an expanding market village, centred on an account of attitudinal changes among peasants and local leaders alike. The most acute problems of the semi-urban population, whose attachment to agriculture and rural life was still a prominent aspect of their lives, resulted from the land legislation. In this setting of rapidly rising prices of land, the contrast between the value of land on the grey-zone land market and the fact that the land possessed by peasants had no legal price (see also Chapter 8), was especially acute. Towards the end of the period covered, it seems that peasants and administrators agreed on what was needed for the future development of the area: new land legislation which gives the landowner the legal right to sell the land in officially recognized ways and thus provide tenure security for the new owner, i.e. security both for the land and for his investments in the land.

While the shortcomings of the current land legislation is most visible in peri-urban areas, they are even more important in the rural areas, be it for peasant welfare or for economic development. The work of peasants on their own farms – notably good land management, terracing, as well as investments in new farming systems – are huge resources for the development of the country. The rights of peasants in the land they farm shape the incentive structure under which they operate. The periodic redistribution theory implies an open-access system in which good farm management would not make much sense. State land ownership gives the state a large leeway in its interventions in the peasant economy, and here we believe that less is more. Although the situation has improved in recent years by the introduction of specific land legislation (for the first time since the land reform), it is rather questionable whether the current land tenure system can be maintained over time. Although lands have now been registered, there is still considerable tenure insecurity, indicated by the persistence of practices to cover up some land tenure practices. Although peasants now have certificates for their parcels of land, they still know, arguably more so than ever, that the land belongs to the government and may be lost in any future reform.

The land issue figured prominently in the early 1990s, until it was seemingly settled by the 1995 constitution. Then, in the 2005 elections, when the opposition was allowed considerable political room, land tenure again came to the fore, only to be taken off the table as the government chose a more authoritarian path. Since the late 1990s, the government has sought to address the land issue through a flurry of land laws and regulations, but the basic, underlying problems have not been addressed. Since 2015, Ethiopia has suffered from considerable unrest, largely due to the authoritarian approach of the developmental state in dealing with peasant land rights. This led to a political crisis in early 2018, and in April 2018 a new government was formed, promising a more inclusive policy. In the few weeks that have passed,

Prime Minister Abiy Ahmed has sent strong signals that he wants to accommodate the full spectrum of political interests and create a basic consensus about the Ethiopian development path. Despite the many challenges ahead, this has created considerable optimism about the willingness to address them.

Ethiopia is currently one of the most rapidly growing economies. A remarkable feature of current policy are the ambitious plans to extend railways, dry ports and industrial parks to many parts of the country, instead of concentrating the modern economy around Addis Ababa alone. This may create the conditions for somewhat broadly based industrialization, but here also the government is facing land tenure issues. There are numerous reports in the press about peasant complaints of land taken for railways, industrial parks, or urban expansion, even resulting in killings. These are not easy issues, and the government has not yet shown its hand on how to deal with them.

An even greater challenge is the vast rural hinterland, the main concern of this book. The approach here by the state has so far been a stream of paternalistic, top-down development initiatives, often based on government control of land. The peasants have been issued with land certificates, which entitles them to compensation if the land is confiscated, but their current rights in this land are tightly circumscribed and the future remains ambiguous. This limits the contribution of the peasant sector to the economy, and even if the rest of the country develops, in the worst of cases, large swathes of rural Ethiopia may remain as pockets of extreme poverty, perhaps with increasing social malaise, large outmigration and rural unrest. In the short run, the problems in the hinterlands may not seem acute, but the long-term wellbeing of Ethiopia depends on giving the peasant farmers real tenure security and control over their own lives.

Postface

KJELL HAVNEVIK

This book is about peasant agriculture in Africa, the dominant production regime of the continent. The average size of African farm holdings is declining over time, representing a threat to peasant farmers. In a survey of landholdings in Ethiopia, Malawi, Kenya, Mozambique, Rwanda and Zambia, it was found that 25 per cent of small-scale farming households were approaching landlessness (Jayne *et al.* 2010). This finding challenges the general claims of the high availability of unused or under-used land in the region.

Beyond size, there are wide variations among smallholder farmers in Sub-Saharan Africa. Some could be described as rural residents, since they mainly farm for subsistence. Others cultivate chiefly for the market and are commercially oriented. In practice, they may function as enterprises and may be highly productive both in terms of labour and land productivities. Research from several African countries indicate that about 10 per cent of the smallholders belong to this category (Djurfeldt *et al.* 2005). There are many variations between these extremes.

Land tenure is a critical factor for peasant farming regimes. On the production side, land tenure has implications both for agricultural yields (i.e. production per unit of land) and for agricultural labour productivity (i.e. production per peasant). It is important to distinguish between these two productivities for understanding the potential role of agriculture to contribute to the development of other sectors of the economy, as well as for its implications for labour absorption and migratory flows. Agricultural yields do not reflect the surplus produced in agriculture. The latter is signalled by the labour productivity which, if positive, may contribute not only to the subsistence of rural people and inputs in the farm economy, such as seeds for the next season and fodder for animals (particularly important in the ox-ploughing peasant agriculture of the Ethiopian highlands), but also food and other products for the urban population, industries and exports.[1] This helps us

[1] The relation between labour productivity and agricultural yields is specified by the following equation: Production(P)/Labour(L) equals Production (P)/Area (A) x Area(A)/Labour (L) is central for our understanding of both the constraints and the potentials for agriculture to contribute to rural and national development (see Morell 1997).

understand that it is not only the size of investments in agriculture that matters, but also their character. Of particular concern in Ethiopian-type economies is how investments can raise agricultural labour productivity in a labour-intensive manner, both through investments directly in production and in rural-based processing of crops and diversification of the rural economy. The issue of how peasant land tenure is related to investments, a central topic of this book, thus becomes highly pertinent.

A problem that has faced most African countries over time is a combination of a low level of agricultural yields and low labour productivity when compared to other continents. Thus, there was rarely an economic surplus for investment in other sectors, which could have widened the base of the economy and made it less susceptible to the influences of global economic conjunctures. In periods where agricultural surpluses did emerge, most African states used the surplus for their own benefit, in a context of inefficiency linked to monopolization and bureaucratization. At times, the state and external donors created an economic alliance, which excluded the peasants. The economic surplus of peasant production was thus expropriated, used by the state, and did not contribute to improvements of peasant production conditions. Rather, peasants and smallholders were seen to be inefficient and backward, without sufficient knowledge and motivation to improve their livelihoods. These top-down, negative and ill-informed conceptions of peasant production regimes have during the last decades once more contributed to a shift by African states, including Ethiopia, towards attracting and facilitating large-scale agricultural investments on their land, often in the hands of external interests, and to the detriment of peasant producers and pastoralists (Matondi *et al.* 2011; Ståhl 2015).

The persistent focus on problems in agriculture over time is closely connected to the inability of the state and the economy to broaden its economic base and through this process absorb labour – peasants, tenants or workers – from agriculture into other sectors. In a context of rapid population growth, as in Ethiopia, and limited growth of the non-agricultural sectors, the rural population has limited exit options in terms of alternative employment. In this context, migration to cities increases social and economic problems, including crime, as can be seen most clearly in some Latin American countries. In Brazil, nearly 80 per cent of the population live in cities marred by high levels of unemployment and crime, while, on the other side, there are large unpopulated rural regions dominated by large-scale mechanized agriculture, which requires abundance of land but hardly any workers. Even the processing of agricultural produce, such as sugar cane, is highly automatized.

This book is an important contribution to our knowledge and understanding of peasant land tenure in Africa, with its detailed discussion of conditions in the Amhara highlands of Ethiopia. Today the country has a population of about 100 million, with 85 per cent living in the rural areas, primarily engaged in peasant agriculture. What happens to agriculture and the rural areas will therefore have an impact on Ethiopian national development – on the production conditions of peasant agriculture and the way it is connected to the wider economy, both on the input and output sides. Thus, land, investments, labour supply, household processes, tenancy relations, technology, markets and infrastructure are all of great importance. The argument of this book is that peasant land tenure – historically and in the future – will be a determining factor for the development of Ethiopian agriculture, as well as for the welfare of rural people. This outcome is again contingent upon the development of the relations between the peasant sector and the Ethiopian state, which is the ultimate owner of all land, as is the case in many other African countries.

It emerges from the book and other sources that Ethiopia over the last decades has seen the rise of a state with developmental features, contrary to that of most African countries. Ethiopia has recorded a sustained economic growth rate of nearly 10 per cent over several years, and the Ethiopian state seems to have an ambitious plan for expanding economic growth and for the modernization of society. What takes place in Ethiopian agriculture will be central to the possible sustenance of this process. The role of peasant land tenure, particularly in view of the large rural population, will here be central.

Under what conditions can peasant land tenure provide opportunities for the generation of an economic surplus, without leading to a massive out-migration of rural people? What type of agricultural production regime(s) can balance these concerns, and what are the priorities of the state in this context? Chapters of the book argue that the Ethiopian state, although developmental, is of a despotic character. This is linked to the unwillingness of the Ethiopian state to abdicate from its ultimate ownership of all Ethiopian land, which gives it a basis for heavy-handed interventions in peasant land tenure. Such a context creates an underlying fear or uncertainty among the peasants as to control over their land, and thus their willingness to invest in it.

The book's overview of central historic literature on Ethiopian agricultural change and land tenure provides an important foundation for its analyses and arguments. They are often based on longitudinal empirical fieldwork in a limited number of sites in the Amhara highlands. The attempt is to understand peasant conditions as they appear 'to us' (the authors) in the local economy. The 'us' comprises both Norwegian and Ethiopian researchers with a longstanding commitment and interest in Ethiopian land tenure and society. The composition of 'us' has helped create conditions for research that gave good access to peasant views, perspectives and conditions. This is in contrast, as argued by the book, to the large-scale surveys (of, for instance, the economic discipline) which have become increasingly dominant over the last decade, most often unaccompanied by systematic and direct fieldwork.

The research approach of the book, including its longitudinal character, reveals a deep understanding of the dynamics of peasant land tenure over time, which is rich in observations, descriptions and analyses. The empirical foundation of the research makes it possible for the authors to review and assess to what extent standard analyses of Ethiopian peasant land tenure stand up against their empirical findings in their own fieldwork areas. A conclusion, which seems also to have incentivized the production of the book, was that the empirical studies of the Amhara highlands led to 'a feeling of dissonance', i.e. that the research of the authors did not fit well into key elements of the standard interpretations dominating the view of Ethiopian peasant land tenure.

The book takes upon itself to provide an alternative understanding of peasant land tenure in the Amhara highlands. Although the book's empirical studies emerge from some sites in the Amhara highlands, the argument is made for the need to make generalizations about its agricultural system in order to challenge the received interpretation. It is argued that there exists few detailed studies of the period of concern. Overall, the longitudinal character of the analyses opens up a comprehensive understanding of long-term processes, such as land redistributions and their implications, including state interventions of different kinds (e.g. the creation of agricultural producer cooperatives, settlements and villages). The authors are careful in distinguishing causes and impacts that relate to peasant land tenure reforms from those that are connected to other types of interventions. The researchers, in their use and analyses of the information received from peasants and local representatives (in surveys and interviews), are cautious and reflective as to the reliability of the information and data collected. This is made possible due to the empirical approach including visits over time to several of the sites of investigation.

The historical developments leading up to the Därg land reform in 1975 is laid out so that it gives an understanding of how the south and the north may resemble each other in terms of ecology, but not in history. The Amhara highlands, being the base of the creation of the Ethiopian state, was a conquering region, although much of the Amhara highlands, including the sites studied in the book, remained extremely poor.

A few chapters of the book describe and analyze an emerging process of rural urbanization and what it may mean in terms of the broadening of economic opportunities, changes of attitudes and perspectives of the future. Hence, interesting insights are provided into the process of change and modernization. It is argued that this is part of a key transformation, although robust structural economic and social conditions are still in their infancy. The construction of roads, the increased supply of electricity and the spread of mobile phones, however, are correctly – in my opinion – identified as important contributors to modernization. In addition, we know that the construction of dams for power generation and irrigation, including peasant irrigated agriculture, have expanded rapidly in several regions of Ethiopia, contributing to the potential for economic and social transformative development (Zeray *et al.* 2018; Atakilte 2018)

One argument of the book is that standard analyses are often grounded in descriptions of land tenure based on general accounts of land policies. It is argued that this is insufficient for revealing mechanisms at local level. One stylized standard interpretation is that periodic land redistributions under the Därg led to considerable tenure insecurity among the peasants. The book, on its side, argues that there were no systematic and periodic land redistributions. The land tenure system under the Därg should rather be understood as conditional private property with peasants commanding strong land rights within the local community. Other specific developmental policies by the intrusive state, like the drive for cooperatives, villagization and forest projects, created variable degrees of resentment and tenure insecurity. Hence, there is a misconception of the causes of insecurity. The book advances the *dersha* system as an alternative theory to explain the elements of land tenure that have commonly been taken to support the periodic land redistribution theory. The *dersha* theory shows that peasant land tenure was well regulated. In the late Därg period, land transfers were mainly linked to household processes. It is argued that if left alone, it might have developed into some form of private property system (see also Platteau 1996). In general, the book argues for more emphasis on the role of inheritance for explaining the dynamics of the peasant land tenure system.

The *dersha* theory points towards a new understanding of the dynamics of the peasant land tenure system. For instance, it could help explain why the process of land registration and certification programmes from the late 1990s onwards did not necessarily lead to increased tenure security. If the past was characterized by great tenure insecurity due to periodic land redistributions, it would have been logical that land certification would result in enhanced land tenure security. There is limited evidence to support this, however, and the book argues that other factors may have impacted on the land tenure system. The book points towards intrusive interventions by a developmental state that caused tenure insecurity, and this type of insecurity could not be addressed by registration and certification programmes alone.

As to the standard argument in the research literature that land reform abolished rural class relations and the feudal aspects of Ethiopian society, the book fully agrees. However, there also exists a significant research literature that deals with the emergence of kulak tendencies. Based on the peasant farm model put forward in the book, it is argued that what may appear as incipient class formation, such as the unequal possession of oxen, a key item of farm capital, is largely linked to household processes, the growth and dissolution or decline of the households.

Attention to peasant household processes is also seen to be important for the understanding of tendencies linked to the peasant production regime. The land reforms led to a rather equal society in terms of access to land. However, the cycles of peasant households led to a substantial rental of land. Rental or sharecropping arrangements often occurred in situations where the landowning household was in a downward phase of the household cycle. This could have been caused by such factors as divorce, old age, or death or loss of household members. Hence, the capacity of the household to till the land declined. Other households were entering cycles of abundant access to labour (children), and these households were in need of more land for ensuring their subsistence. In this way, the tenant increased his cultivated land but had to share between one-third and half the produce with the landowner. The total outcome was cultivation of more land than if each owner had tilled only his (or her) own land. However, the redistribution of the produce through sharecropping or tenancy agreements also mitigated against the creation of an agricultural surplus. On the other hand, it helped to ensure household subsistence for both parties to the deal. Thus, both the equal land-owning structure and tenancy agreements tended to equalize household incomes.

A major challenge in such a context is how to increase the agricultural surplus for investments in other economic sectors so that the economic base of the country can widen in a way that inhibits a massive exodus of people from agriculture and the rural areas.

Based on this book, it could be argued that reform of the Ethiopian land tenure system is the key to increasing the agricultural surplus. However, could other factors such as agricultural strategies, state intervention, international conjunctures, etc. be of similar importance for inhibiting the creation of an economic surplus? Must the development strategy of a country, including that of Ethiopia, not address in a balanced way challenges facing several key sectors and their interconnections? This takes us to the role and character of the Ethiopian state and state-peasant relations, issues that will continue to generate debate.

In Chapter 8, it is argued that the current land tenure system generates problems which cannot be resolved without removing limitations inherent in state land ownership. Principles of an alternative peasant land tenure system are outlined which, it is argued, could function well. One may ask if it is realistic or relevant to 'think away' ultimate state ownership of land in drawing up alternative principles. Another approach could perhaps be a modified peasant land tenure system in which ultimate state ownership of land was retained. Such a system might induce investments in agriculture that could create an economic surplus at the same time as peasants and rural people attained employment in a growing rural economy.

Select Bibliography

Only sources and works directly relating to the chapters of this book are included. Official sources are listed together with books and articles below.

PRIVATE ARCHIVES

The relevant materials in Ege's and Aspen's private archives are available for consultation in Trondheim upon request.

Aspen: Fieldwork diaries

Arbit 1: Field diary, Arbit (Jerelé), February 2010.
Arbit 2: Field diary, Arbit (Jerelé), February–March 2010.
NW 1: Field diary, North Wälo May–June 2002 and March 2003.
NW 2: Field diary, North Wälo March–April 2003.

Aspen: Survey

ISHouseholds: Indicator Survey in Jerelé February 2003 (data file 'Meqet IS 2.mdb').

Ege: Notes

Notes are referred to by their ID number preceded by 'N'. All notes are stored in my database 'Notes.mdb'.

Ege: Surveys

Survey 1989. 'GM survey', data, explanations and calculations linked to N6779.
Survey 1994. 'GMS survey', land parcel history.
Survey 1994. (GMS: Household 347: Land 946 'Däläl') Lägäsä Täshomä, 24.02.87 EC.

Ege: Documents, interviews and diaries

These materials are all located in Ege's archive under the document number 'D'. They comprise handwritten copies of documents (in Amharic), his assistants' interview notes (in Amharic), as well as his own field diary (in English). Interviewees' real names are used, except for when a pseudonym is required.

Ege: Documents and interviews from Ayné, North Shäwa

D186 'Yä-märét dälday komité mäzgäb' [1970 E.C.]. (Referred to in the text as the Registers of the Land Equalizing Committee).

D3080 S'ägayé Eshäté, 'Märét däldayoch ...', key informant interview 11.10.86 E.C.

Ege: Interviews and diaries from Baba Säat and Chebena, North Wälo

D9221 Baba Säat tax list, copied from Guba Lafto *wäräda* Ministry of Finance Office, 11 June 2002. The list was the current one and can be taken to refer to 1994 E.C.

D9333 Berhanu Bétä, 'Report on Baba Säat', 12 Säné 1994.

D9422 Mäsärät Kenfä, 'Notes', 23 Genbot - 14 Säné 1994.

D9643 'Yä-märét shegesheg', 5 Hedar 1996.

D9644 Ayänäw Gäbré, Interview, 6 Hedar 1996.

D9648 Mola Agazhu, 'Ersha, mert, beder-ena yä-gulbät sera', 8 Hedar 1996.

D9650 Amarä Yazäw, 'Yä-rähab zämän', 8 Hedar 1996.

D9651 Ayälä Mola, Interview, 10 Hedar 1996.

D9652 Wärqé Mälaku, Interview, 10 Hedar 1996.

D9654 Sheshegu Aqatä, Interview, 11 Hedar 1996.

D9656 Yaläw Kälkay, Interview, 12 Hedar 1996.

D9658 Täfära Ejegu, 'Bä-Haylä-Selasé yä-märét yezota', 13 Hedar 1996.

D9659 Täfära Ejegu, 'About land tenure', 26 Hedar 1996.

D9661 Sisay Adisu, 'Liqämänbärenät, yä-märét shegesheg wä-zä-tä', 14 Hedar 1996.

D9662 Mulugéta*, 'Yä-1983 märét shegesheg', 14 Hedar 1996.

D9663 *Qés* Ert'eban Negusé, Interview, 14 Hedar 1996.

D9664 Sisay Bälaynäw, 'Yä-1983 märét shegesheg', 14 Hedar 1996.

D9675 Mäsfen Aligaz, 'Adis yä-märét lek', 17 Hedar 1996, Chebena *qäbälé*.

D9681 Wärqu Kasaw, 'Beder', 21 Hedar 1996.

D9684 *Qés* T'ägaw Täfära, 'Selä-83 yä-märét deledel', 19 Hedar 1996.

D9685 *Qés* T'ägaw Täfära, 'Selä-83 yä-märét deledel', 19 Hedar 1996.

D9691 Däreb Däräsä, 'Selä märét shegesheg', 7 Hedar 1996.

D9693 Käbädä*, Interview, 8–9 Hedar 1996.

D9695 Magegnät Sheshegu, 'Interview', 10 Hedar 1996.

Ege: Interviews and diaries from Wäyra Amba, North Shäwa

D11001 Interview about land inheritance case, 3 Nähasé 2005 (confidential).

D11057 Ege, 'Diary November 2014'.

D10988 Däbäbä Bétä, 'Yä-märét wers-ena gech'etoch', 11 Säné 2005.

D11138 'Note on land tax in Yezaba qäbälé', 23 March 2015.

BOOKS, ARTICLES AND OFFICIAL PUBLICATIONS

(Ethiopian authors are listed by their first name)

Ahmed Hassan. 2002. 'Close Yet Far: Northern Shewa under the Derg', *Remapping Ethiopia: Socialism and After*, ed. Wendy James *et al.* (Oxford, Athens and Addis Ababa: James Currey, Ohio University Press and Addis Ababa University Press), pp. 74–89.

Aklilu Kidanu and Tadesse Alemu. 1994. 'Rapid Population Growth and Access to Farmland: Coping Strategies in Two Peasant Associations in North Shoa', *Land Tenure and Land Policy in Ethiopia After the Derg: Proceedings of the Second Workshop of the Land Tenure Project*, ed. Dessalegn Rahmato (Trondheim: University of Trondheim, Centre of Environment and Development), Working Papers on Ethiopian Development, No. 8, pp. 35–55.

Alemayehu Lirenso. 1989. 'Villagization and Agricultural Production in Ethiopia' (Addis Ababa: Addis Ababa University), Institute of Development Research, Research Report No. 37.

Amhara Regional Government. 2002 E.C. [2010 G.C.]. 'Yä-gät'är märét astädadär-ena at'äqaqäm awaj, dänb-ena mämäriya' (Bahir Dar: Amhara Regional Government, Akababi t'ebäqa, märét astädadär-ena at'äqaqäm biro).

Askebir Gebru Kasa. 2012. *The 1997 Amhara Land Redistribution Program and Its Socio-Economic Impacts: A Case Study in Libo-Kemkem Woreda, South-Gondar, Ethiopia* (Saarbrücken: LAP LAMBERT Academic Publishing).

Asmelash Woldemariam. 2006. *The Effects of Land Reform on Peasant Social Organisation: A Study of Village-level Dynamics in Central Tigray, 1974–1994* (Addis Ababa: Addis Ababa University), Department of Sociology and Social Anthropology: Social Anthropology Dissertation Series, No. 7.

Asnake Ali. 1988. 'A Historical Survey of Social and Economic Conditions in Wallo, 1872–1917', *Proceedings of the 8th International Conference of Ethiopian Studies*, Vol. 1 (Addis Ababa), pp. 263–76.

Aspen, Harald. 1993. *Competition and Co-operation: North Ethiopian Peasant Households and Their Resource Base* (Trondheim: University of Trondheim, Centre for Environment and Development).

—1995. The *1995 National and Regional Elections in Ethiopia: Local Perspectives* (Trondheim: University of Trondheim, Centre for Environment and Development).

—2002. 'Models of Democracy – Perceptions of Power', *Ethiopia: The Challenge of Democracy from Below*, ed. Bahru Zewde and Siegfried Pausewang (Addis Ababa: Forum for Social Studies and Uppsala: Nordiska Afrikainstitutet), pp. 61–70.

—2007. 'Houses of the Amhara', *Encyclopaedia Aethiopica,* Vol. 3, ed. Siegbert Uhlig (Wiesbaden: Harrassowitz Verlag), pp. 76–8.

—2009. 'Peasant Entrepreneurs in Emergent Towns in Mäqét *wäräda*, North Wälo', paper presented at the *17th International Conference of*

Ethiopian Studies, Addis Ababa, 1–5 November 2009 (unpublished).
—2011. 'Sicurezza alimentare e livelihood dei contadini nel Wälo/Food Security and Peasant Livelihoods in Wälo', *Afriche e Orienti*, Special Issue 1, 2011: Sviluppo rurale e riduzione della povertà in Etiopia/ Rural Development and Poverty Reduction in Ethiopia (in Italian and English) a cura di Mario Zamponi, pp. 105–40.
Aspen, Harald and Svein Ege. 2010. *Peasant Livelihoods in North Wälo, Ethiopia: A Survey of Key Indicators in Tiweha, Dänkäna and Debeko qäbälé, Mäqét wäräda* (Trondheim: Norwegian University of Science and Technology, Department of Social Anthropology).
Aster Akalu. 1982. *The Process of Land Nationalization in Ethiopia: Land Nationalization and the Peasants* (Lund: CWK Gleerup), Acta Regiae Societas Humanorium Litterarum Lundensis No. 76.
Atakilte Beyene. 2003. 'Soil Conservation, Land Use and Property Rights in Northern Ethiopia: Understanding Environmental Change in Smallholder Farming Systems' (Uppsala: Swedish University of Agricultural Sciences), *Acta Universitatis Agriculturae Sueciae, Agraria* 395, Ph.D. thesis.
—2018. *Agricultural Transformation in Ethiopia: State Policy and Smallholder Farming* (London and New York: Zed Books).
Ayele Tariku. 2012. *A History of Hulät Iju Inäsé Wäräda, (East Gojjam: Ethiopia), 1941–1991* (Saarbrücken: LAP Lambert Academic Publishing).
Baker, Jonathan. 1994. 'Rural Towns Study in Ethiopia: Report Prepared for the Infrastructure Division, SIDA, October, 1994' (Uppsala: Nordiska Afrikainstitutet).
Barrows, Richard and Michael Roth. 1990. 'Land Tenure and Investment in African Agriculture: Theory and Evidence', *Journal of Modern African Studies*, Vol. 28(2), pp. 265–97.
Bassett, Thomas J. 1993. 'Introduction: The Land Question and Agricultural Transformation in Sub-Saharan Africa', *Land in African Agrarian Systems*, ed. Thomas J. Bassett and Donald E. Crummey (Madison: The University of Wisconsin Press), pp. 3–31.
Bassett, Thomas J. and Donald E. Crummey (eds.). 1993. *Land in African Agrarian Systems* (Madison: The University of Wisconsin Press).
Bauer, Dan Franz. 1973. 'Land, Leadership and Legitimacy among the Inderta Tigray of Ethiopia'. The University of Rochester, Ph.D. thesis.
—1975. 'For Want of an Ox...: Land, Capital, and Social Stratification in Tigre', *Proceedings of the First United States Conference on Ethiopian Studies, 1973* (East Lansing: African Studies Center), Occasional Papers Series, Monograph No. 3, pp. 235–48.
—1985. *Household and Society in Ethiopia*, 2nd edn (1st edn 1977) (East Lansing: Michigan State University), African Studies Center: Monograph No. 6.
Bekalu Molla. 1994. 'Traditional Agricultural Practices and Resource Management among the Agaw of Gojjam'. Addis Ababa University, M.A. thesis.
Bekele Shiferaw. 1998. 'Peasant Agriculture and Sustainable Land Use

in Ethiopia: Economic Analyses of Constraints and Incentives for Soil Conservation' (Ås: Agricultural University of Norway), Department of Economics and Social Sciences, Dissertation No. 1998:1.

Benin, Samuel. 2006. 'Policies and Programs Affecting Land Management Practices, Input Use, and Productivity in the Highlands of Amhara Region, Ethiopia', *Strategies for Sustainable Land Management in the East African Highlands*, ed. John Pender, Frank Place, and Simeon Ehui (Washington D.C.: International Food Policy Research Institute), pp. 217–56.

Benin, Samuel and John Pender. 2009. 'Land Rental Markets and Land Management in the Highlands of Ethiopia', *The Emergence of Land Markets in Africa: Assessing the Impacts on Poverty, Equity and Efficiency*, ed. Stein Holden, Keijiro Otsuka and Frank M. Place (Washington D.C.: Resources for the Future Press), pp. 213–37.

Bereket Kebede. 2008. 'Land Reform, Distribution of Land and Institutions in Rural Ethiopia: Analysis of Inequality with Dirty Data', *Journal of African Economies*, Vol. 17(4), pp. 550–77.

Berhanu Abegaz. 2004. 'Escaping Ethiopia's Poverty Trap: The Case for a Second Agrarian Reform', *Journal of Modern African Studies*, Vol. 42(3), pp. 313–42.

Berhanu Gebremedhin. 1998. 'The Economics of Soil Conservation Investments in the Tigray Region of Ethiopia', Michigan State University, Ph.D. thesis.

Berhanu Gebremedhin, John Pender and Simeon Ehui. 2003. 'Land Tenure and Land Management in the Highlands of Northern Ethiopia', paper presented at the International Conference on Development Studies, Ethiopia, 11–12 July 2003 (accessed 13 December 2013, available from: http://scholarworks.wmich.edu/africancenter_icad_archive/74/).

Berhanu Nega, B. Adenew and S. Gebre Sellasie. 2003. 'Current Land Policy Issues in Ethiopia', *Land Reform: Land Settlement and Cooperatives (FAO)*, Special Issue No. 3, pp. 103–24.

Berihun M. Mekonnen and Harald Aspen. 2010. 'Early Marriage and the Campaign against It in Ethiopia', *Research in Ethiopian Studies: Selected Papers of the 16th International Conference of Ethiopia Studies, Trondheim July 2007*, ed. Harald Aspen *et al.* (Wiesbaden: Harrassowitz Verlag: Aethiopistische Forschungen), Vol. 72, pp. 432–43.

Birhanu Megersa and Mamo Hebo. 2010. *Exploring the Dynamic Linkages: Land Tenure Systems, Agricultural Investment and Food Security among Smallholder Farmers in Sululta, Oromia Regional State* (Saarbrücken: VDM Verlag Dr Müller).

Bruce, John W. 1989. 'The Variety of Reform: A Review of Recent Experience with Land Reform and the Reform of Land Tenure, with Particular Reference to the African Experience', pp. 13–56.

—1993. 'Do Indigenous Tenure Systems Constrain Agricultural Development?', *Land in African Agrarian Systems*, ed. Thomas J. Bassett and Donald E. Crummey (Madison: The University of Wisconsin Press), pp. 35–56.

Bruce, John W., Allan Hoben and Dessalegn Rahmato. 1994, 'After the Derg: An Assessment of Rural Land Tenure Issues in Ethiopia', University of Wisconsin-Madison, Land Tenure Center.
Chayanov, Alexander V. 1986. *The Theory of Peasant Economy* (Madison: University of Wisconsin Press).
Chiari, Gian Paolo. 2003. 'Land Tenure and Livelihood Security in Tigray, Ethiopia', University of Sussex, Ph.D. thesis.
Clapham, Christopher. 1988. *Transformation and Continuity in Revolutionary Ethiopia* (Cambridge: Cambridge University Press), African Studies Series No. 61.
Cohen, John M. and Dov Weintraub. 1975. *Land and Peasants in Imperial Ethiopia: The Social Background to a Revolution* (Assen: Van Gorcum & Co.).
Cotula, Lorenzo, Camilla Toulmin and Ced Hesse. 2004. *Land Tenure and Administration in Africa: Lessons of Experience and Emerging Issues* (London: International Institute for Environment and Development).
Cox, Terry. 1979. 'Awkward Class or Awkward Classes? Class Relations in the Russian Peasantry before Collectivisation', *Journal of Peasant Studies*, Vol. 7(1), pp. 70–85.
Crummey, Donald. 2000. *Land and Society in the Christian Kingdom of Ethiopia* (Addis Ababa: Addis Ababa University Press/Champaign, IL: University of Illinois Press/Oxford: James Currey).
CSA. 2000. 'Agricultural Sample Survey 2000/2001 (1993 E.C.) (September 2000–February 2001)', Vol. 1 (Addis Ababa: Central Statistical Authority).
—2007. 'The 2007 Population and Housing Census of Ethiopia: Statistical Report for Amhara Region' (Addis Ababa: Central Statistical Authority).
—2012. 'Agriculture Statistics Abstracts 2012' (accessed 5 November 2013, available from: http://www.csa.gov.et/index.php/2013-02-20-13-43-35/national-statistics-abstract).
Daniel Kassahun. 2006. 'Towards the Development of Differential Land Taxation in Ethiopia', *Land and the Challenge of Sustainable Development in Ethiopia. Conference Proceedings*, ed. Dessalegn Rahmato and Taye Assefa (Addis Ababa: Forum for Social Studies), pp. 103–28.
Darkwah, R. H. Kofi. 1975. *Shewa, Menilek and the Ethiopian Empire 1813–1889* (London: Heinemann).
Degefa Tolossa. 2003. 'Issues of Land Tenure and Food Security Situations: The Case of Three Communities of Munessa *wereda*, South-Central Ethiopia', *Norwegian Journal of Geography*, Vol. 57, pp. 9–19.
—2005. 'Rural Livelihoods, Poverty and Food Insecurity in Ethiopia: A Case Study of Erenssa and Garbi Communities in Oromiya Zone, Amhara National Regional State' (Trondheim: Norwegian University of Science and Technology), Ph.D. thesis at NTNU, No. 106.
Deininger, Klaus. 2008. 'Implementing Low-Cost Rural Land Certification: The Case of Ethiopia' (Washington D.C.: The World Bank).
Deininger, Klaus and Gershon Feder, 2009. 'Land Registration, Governance, and Development: Evidence and Implications for Policy', *The*

World Bank Research Observed, Vol. 24(2), pp. 233–66.

Deininger, Klaus, G. Feder, G. Gordillo de Anda and P. Munro-Faure. 2003a. 'Land Policy to Facilitate Growth and Poverty Reduction', *Land Reform: Land Settlement and Cooperatives (FAO)*, Special Issue No.3, pp. 5–17.

Deininger, Klaus, Songqing Jin, Berhanu Adenew, Samuel Gebre-Selassie, Berhanu Nega. 2003b. 'Tenure Security and Land-related Investment: Evidence from Ethiopia' (Washington D.C.: The World Bank), Policy Research Working Paper No. 2991.

Deininger, Klaus, Daniel Ayalew Ali, Stein Holden, and Jaap Zevenbergen. 2007. 'Rural Land Certification in Ethiopia: Process, Initial Impact, and Implications for Other African Countries' (Washington D.C.: The World Bank), Policy Research Working Paper No. 4218.

Deininger, Klaus, Daniel Ayalew Ali and Tekie Alemu. 2008. 'Assessing the Functioning of Land Rental Markets in Ethiopia', *Economic Development and Cultural Change*, Vol. 57(1), pp. 67–100.

Deininger, Klaus, Daniel Ayalew Ali and Tekie Alemu. 2009. 'Land Rental Markets: Transaction Costs and Tenure Insecurity in Rural Ethiopia', *The Emergence of Land Markets in Africa: Assessing the Impacts on Poverty, Equity and Efficiency*, ed. Stein Holden, Keijiro Otsuka and Frank M. Place (Washington D.C.: Resources for the Future Press), pp. 57–73.

Deininger, Klaus, Daniel Ayalew Ali and Tekie Alemu. 2011a. 'Impacts of Land Certification on Tenure Security: Investment, and Land Market Participation: Evidence from Ethiopia', *Land Economics*, Vol. 87, pp. 312–34.

Deininger, Klaus, Daniel Ayalew Ali and Tekie Alemu. 2011b. 'Productivity Effects of Land Rental Markets in Ethiopia: Evidence from a Matched Tenant-Landlord Sample' (Washington D.C.: The World Bank), Policy Research Working Papers, WPS5727.

Dercon, Stefan and Daniel Ayalew. 2007. 'Land Rights, Power and Trees in Rural Ethiopia' (Oxford: Centre for the Study of African Economies), WPS2007-07.

Dessalegn Rahmato. 1984. *Agrarian Reform in Ethiopia* (Uppsala: Scandinavian Institute of African Studies).

—1986. 'Moral Crusaders and Incipient Capitalists: Mechanized Agriculture and its Critics in Ethiopia', *Proceedings of the Third Annual Seminar of the Department of History* (Addis Ababa: Addis Ababa University), pp. 69–90.

—(ed.). 1994a. *Land Tenure and Land Policy in Ethiopia After the Derg: Proceedings of the Second Workshop of the Land Tenure Project* (Trondheim, University of Trondheim), Centre of Environment and Development: Working Papers on Ethiopian Development, No. 8.

—1994b. 'Land Policy in Ethiopia at the Crossroads', *Land Tenure and Land Policy in Ethiopia After the Derg: Proceedings of the Second Workshop of the Land Tenure Project*, ed. Dessalegn Rahmato (Trondheim: University of Trondheim, Centre of Environment and Development), Working Papers on Ethiopian Development, No. 8, pp. 1–20.

—1997. 'Manufacturing Poverty: Rural Policy and Micro-agriculture', paper presented at the Workshop on Access to Land and Resource Management, Institute of Development Research, 28–29 November 1997.

—2006. 'From Heterogeneity to Homogeneity: Agrarian Class Structure in Ethiopia since the 1950s', *Land and the Challenge of Sustainable Development in Ethiopia. Conference Proceedings*, ed. Dessalegn Rahmato and Taye Assefa (Addis Ababa: Forum for Social Studies), pp. 3–18.

—2008. *The Peasant and the State: Studies in Agrarian Change in Ethiopia 1950s–2000s* (Custom Books Publishing).

—2009. 'Peasants and Agrarian Reforms: The Unfinished Quest for Secure Land Rights in Ethiopia', *Legalising Land Rights: Local Practices, State Responses and Tenure Security in Africa, Asia and Latin America*, ed. Janine M. Ubink *et al.* (Leiden: Leiden University Press).

Dessalegn Rahmato and Taye Assefa (eds.). 2006. *Land and the Challenge of Sustainable Development in Ethiopia. Conference Proceedings* (Addis Ababa: Forum for Social Studies).

Devereux, Stephen, Amdissa Teshome and Rachel Sabates-Wheeler. 2005. 'Too Much Inequality or Too Little? Inequality and Stagnation in Ethiopian Agriculture'. *IDS Bulletin*, Vol. 36(2), pp. 121–6.

Djurfeldt, Göran, Hans Holmén, Magnus Jirström *et al.* (eds.). 2005. *The African Food Crisis: Lessons from the Asian Green Revolution* (Wallingford: CABI).

Dwyer, P. D. and M. Minnegal. 2010. 'Theorizing Social Change', *Journal of the Royal Anthropological Institute*, Vol. 16, pp. 629–45.

EEA. 2002. *Land Tenure and Agricultural Development in Ethiopia* (Addis Ababa: Ethiopian Economic Association and Ethiopian Economic Policy Research Institute).

EFAP. 1991. Ethiopian Forestry Action Programme (EFAP). 'Main Reports of Task Forces', Vol. 1 (Addis Ababa).

Ege, Svein. 1990. 'Changing Patterns of Land Tenure in Ayné, Mafud *wäräda*', *Ethiopia: Problems of Sustainable Development. A Conference Report*, ed. Svein Ege (Trondheim: University of Trondheim), Centre for Development Studies, pp. 225–36.

—1994a. 'Land Sales and Similar Practices: Yefat 1974–1993', *New Trends in Ethiopian Studies: Papers of the 12th International Conference of Ethiopian Studies*, Vol. 2, ed. Harold G. Marcus (Lawrenceville: Red Sea Press), pp. 285–310.

—1994b. 'Land Tenancy in Northern Shäwa', *Land Tenure and Land Policy in Ethiopia After the Derg: Proceedings of the Second Workshop of the Land Tenure Project*, ed. Dessalegn Rahmato (Trondheim: University of Trondheim, Centre of Environment and Development), Working Papers on Ethiopian Development, No. 8, pp. 163–89.

—1996. *Class, State and Power in Africa: A Case Study of the Kingdom of Shäwa (Ethiopia) about 1840* (Wiesbaden: Harrassowitz Verlag), Aethiopistische Forschungen Vol. 46.

—1997a. 'Land, Law and Tactics: A Case Study from Ayné, Northern

Shäwa', *Ethiopia in Broader Perspective: Papers of 13th International Conference of Ethiopian Studies*, Vol. 1, ed. Katsuyoshi Fukui *et al.* (Kyoto: Shokado Book Sellers), pp. 35–56.

—1997b. *The Promised Land: The Amhara Land Redistribution of 1997* (Trondheim: Norwegian University of Science and Technology, Centre for Environment and Development).

—1999. 'Oxen as Indicators of Wealth in Ethiopian Peasant Agriculture: Some Methodological Problems', *Poverty and Resources: Ethiopian Rural Realities*, ed. Harald Aspen and Abdulhamid Bedri Kello (Trondheim: Norwegian University of Science and Technology, Centre for Environment and Development), pp. 41–63.

—2000. 'Land Tenure under the Därg: A Reinterpretation. A Sketch Submitted for Discussion by the PPDE Project, 13.01.00', unpublished paper.

—2002a. *Livestock Systems: Patterns of Livestock Distribution in North Wälo and Selected Districts of South Wälo and North Shäwa* (Trondheim: Norwegian University of Science and Technology, Department of Social Anthropology).

—2002b. *North Wälo 1:100,000: Topographic and Administrative Map of North Wälo Zone, Amhara Region, Ethiopia* (Trondheim: Norwegian University of Science and Technology, Department of Social Anthropology).

—2002c. 'Peasant Participation in Land Reform', *Ethiopia: The Challenge of Democracy from Below*, ed. Bahru Zewde and Siegfried Pausewang (Uppsala and Addis Ababa: Nordiska Afrikainstitutet and Forum for Social Studies), pp. 71–86.

—2002d. 'Rural Class Formation in Ethiopia: The State of the Art', *Ethiopian Studies at the End of the Second Millennium: Proceedings of the XIVth International Conference of Ethiopian Studies*, Vol. 3, ed. Baye Yimam *et al.* (Addis Ababa: Institute of Ethiopian Studies), pp. 1437–55.

—2006. 'The Role of Oxen in Peasant Agriculture: *Ch'enät* Rentals in Ch'orisa, South Wälo', *Proceedings of the XVth International Conference of Ethiopian Studies, Hamburg* 2003, ed. Siegbert Uhlig (Wiesbaden: Harrassowitz Verlag), pp. 1034–41.

—2011. 'Land Tenure in Ayné', unpublished draft paper.

—2015. 'The New Economy: Agricultural Transformation in North Shäwa, Ethiopia', paper presented at the 19th International Conference of Ethiopian Studies, 24–28 August 2015.

—2017. 'Land Tenure Insecurity in Post-certification Amhara, Ethiopia', *Land Use Policy*, Vol. 64, pp. 56–63.

Ege, Svein and Harald Aspen. 2003. *On the Brink of Famine: Ch'orisa, Qalu 2002* (Trondheim: Norwegian University of Science and Technology, Department of Social Anthropology).

Ege, Svein and Yigremew Adal. 2002. *Farming Assets in North Wälo: Statistics, Maps and Impressions from a Travel to North Wälo, October 2000* (Trondheim: Norwegian University of Science and Technology, Department of Social Anthropology).

Eleni Z. Gabre-Madhin. 1999. *Of Markets and Middlemen: The Role of Brokers in Ethiopia* (Washington, D.C.: International Food Policy Research Institute), MSSD Discussion Paper No. 39.

Ellison, James. 2006. '"Everyone Can Do As He Wants": Economic Liberalization and Emergent Forms of Antipathy in Southern Ethiopia', *American Ethnologist*, Vol. 33(4), pp. 665–86.

Ethiopian Government. 1975. 'A Proclamation to Provide for the Public Ownership of Rural Lands', Proclamation No. 31 of 1975, *Negarit Gazeta*, 29 April 1975.

—1995. *The Constitution of the Federal Republic of Ethiopia* (Addis Ababa: Federal Negarit Gazeta of the Federal Democratic Republic of Ethiopia), Year 1, No. 1.

—2011. 'Urban Land Lease Holding Proclamation No. 721/2011', *Federal Negarit Gazeta.*

FAO. 2012. *Statistical Yearbook 2012. Africa Food and Agriculture* (Accra: Food and Agriculture Organization of the United Nations Regional Office for Africa).

—2017. *Defining Small Scale Food Producers to Monitor Target 2.3 of the 2030 Agenda for Sustainable Development* (Rome: FAO Statistics Division), Working Paper Series ESS/17-12.

Ferguson, James. 1999. *Expectations of Modernity: Myths and Meanings of Urban Life in the Zambian Copperbelt* (Berkeley: University of California Press).

Fortes, Meyer. 1969 [1958]. 'Introduction', *The Developmental Cycle in Domestic Groups*, ed. Jack Goody (Cambridge: Cambridge University Press).

Frehiwot Tesfaye. 1998. 'Food Security and Peasants' Survival Strategy: A Study of a Village in Northern Shewa, Ethiopia'. University of Toronto, Ph.D. thesis.

Gascon, Alian. 2010. 'Roads', *Encyclopedia Aethiopica,* Vol. 4, ed. Siegbert Uhlig (Wiesbaden: Harrassowitz Verlag), pp. 394–95.

Gebrehaweria Gebregziabher and Stein T. Holden. 2011. 'Distress Rentals and the Land Rental Market as a Safety Net: Contract Choice Evidence from Tigray, Ethiopia', *Agricultural Economics*, Vol. 42, Supplement, pp. 45–60.

Getie Gelaye. 1999. 'Peasant Poetics and State Discourse in Ethiopia: Amharic Oral Poetry as a Response to the 1996–97 Land Redistribution Policy', *Northeast African Studies*, Vol. 6(1–2), pp. 171–206.

Gill, Peter. 2010. *Famine and Foreigners: Ethiopia since Live Aid* (Oxford: Oxford University Press).

Gollin, Douglas. 2014. 'Smallholder Agriculture in Africa: An Overview of Implications for Policy' (London: International Institute for Environment and Development), Working Paper, October 2014.

Gryseels, Guido and Frank M. Anderson. 1983. *Research on Farm and Livestock Productivity in the Central Ethiopian Highlands: Initial Results, 1977–1980*, (Addis Ababa: International Livestock Centre for Africa), ILCA Research Report No. 4.

Haugerud, Angelica. 1989. 'Land Tenure and Agrarian Change in

Kenya', *Africa*, Vol. 59(1), pp. 61–90.

Hendrie, Barbara. 1999. '"Now the People are Like a Lord" – Local Effects of Revolutionary Reform in A Tigray Village, Northern Ethiopia', University College London, Ph.D. thesis.

Hoben, Allan. 1973. *Land Tenure among the Amhara of Ethiopia: The Dynamics of Cognatic Descent* (Chicago and London: The University of Chicago Press).

—1997. 'The Cultural Construction of Environmental Policy: Paradigms and Politics in Ethiopia', *Ecologist*, Vol. 27(2), pp. 55–63.

Holden, Stein. 2008. 'From Being Property of Men to Becoming Equal Owners? Early Impacts of Land Registration and Certification on Women in Southern Ethiopia', final research report prepared for UNHABITAT, Shelter Branch, Land Tenure and Property Administration Section, 1 December 2007 (revised 2 January 2008).

Holden, Stein and Hailu Yohannes. 2001. 'Land Redistribution, Tenure Insecurity, and Intensity of Production: A Study of Farm Households in Southern Ethiopia' (Washington D.C.: IFPRI), CAPRI Working Paper No. 21.

Holden, Stein, Klaus Deininger and Hosa'ena Ghebru. 2007. 'Impact of Land Certification on Land Rental Market Participation in Tigray Region, Northern Ethiopia', MPRA Paper No. 5211 (accessed 1 December 2011, available from: http://mpra.ub.uni-muenchen.de/5211/).

Holden, Stein, Keijiro Otsuka and Frank M. Place (eds.). 2009a. *The Emergence of Land Markets in Africa: Assessing the Impacts on Poverty, Equity and Efficiency* (Washington D.C.: Resources for the Future Press).

Holden, Stein, Keijiro Otsuka and Frank M. Place. 2009b. 'Land Markets and Development in Africa', *The Emergence of Land Markets in Africa: Assessing the Impacts on Poverty, Equity and Efficiency*, ed. Stein Holden, Keijiro Otsuka and Frank M. Place (Washington D.C.: Resources for the Future Press), pp. 3–17.

Holden, Stein, Keijiro Otsuka and Frank M. Place. 2009c. 'Land Markets and Poverty in Perspective', *The Emergence of Land Markets in Africa: Assessing the Impacts on Poverty, Equity and Efficiency*, ed. Stein Holden, Keijiro Otsuka and Frank M. Place (Washington D.C.: Resources for the Future Press), pp. 273–96.

Holden, Stein, Keijiro Otsuka and Frank M. Place. 2009d. 'Understanding Land Markets: Questions and Hypotheses', *The Emergence of Land Markets in Africa: Assessing the Impacts on Poverty, Equity and Efficiency*, ed. Stein Holden, Keijiro Otsuka and Frank M. Place (Washington D.C.: Resources for the Future Press), pp. 18–54.

Holden, Stein T., Klaus Deininger and Hosaena Ghebru. 2011. 'Tenure Insecurity, Gender, Low-cost Land Certification and Land Rental Market Participation in Ethiopia', *Journal of Development Studies*, 47 (1), pp. 31–47.

Holden, Stein T., Keijiro Otsuka and Klaus Deininger (eds.). 2013. *Land Tenure Reform in Asia and Africa: Assessing Impacts on Poverty and*

Natural Resource Management (Basingstoke: Palgrave Macmillan).

Hosaena Ghebru and Stein T. Holden. 2009. 'Factor Market Imperfections and Rural Land Rental Markets in Northern Ethiopian Highlands', *The Emergence of Land Markets in Africa: Assessing the Impacts on Poverty, Equity and Efficiency*, ed. Stein Holden, Keijiro Otsuka and Frank M. Place (Washington D.C.: Resources for the Future Press), pp. 74–92.

Jayne, T.S., David Mather and Elliot Mghenyi. 2010. 'Principal Challenges Confronting Smallholder Agriculture in Sub-Saharan Africa', *World Development*, Vol. 38(10), pp. 1384–98.

Jåstad, Trine. 2014. 'Enslige kvinner i Kozeba qabale – Aktører i søken etter et levebrød', Trondheim: Norwegian University of Science and Technology, M.A. thesis.

Leach, Edmund R. 1967. 'An Anthropologist's Reflection on Social Survey', *Anthropologists in the Field*, ed. Deuwe G. Jongmans and Peter C.W. Gutkind (Assen: Van Gorcum).

Lefort, René. 2010. 'Powers – *mengist* – and Peasants in Rural Ethiopia: The Post-2005 Interlude', *Journal of Modern African Studies*, Vol. 48, pp. 435–60.

—2012. 'Free Market Economy, "Developmental State" and Party-State Hegemony in Ethiopia: The Case of the 'Model Farmers', *Journal of Modern African Studies*, Vol. 50, pp. 681–706.

Leslau, Wolf. 1976. *Concise Amharic Dictionary* (Wiesbaden: Harrassowitz), pp. xiii–xiv.

Li, Tania. 2007. *Will to Improve: Governmentality, Development, and the Practice of Politics* (Durham: Duke University Press).

Mains, Daniel. 2012. 'Blackouts and Progress: Privatization, Infrastructure, and a Developmentalist State in Jimma, Ethiopia', *Cultural Anthropology*, Vol. 27(1), pp. 3–27.

Makonen Getu. 1987. *Socialism, Participation, and Agricultural Development in Post-revolutionary Ethiopia: A Study of Constraints* (Stockholm: Almqvist & Wiksell International), Stockholm Studies in Economic History, No. 11., University of Stockholm, Department of Economic History, Ph.D. thesis.

Markakis, John. 1974. *Ethiopia: Anatomy of a Traditional Polity* (Oxford: Clarendon Press).

Markos Ezra. 1997. 'Demographic Responses to Ecological Degradation and Food Insecurity: Drought Prone Areas in Northern Ethiopia', Amsterdam, Netherlands Graduate School of Research in Demography, Ph.D. thesis.

Matondi, Prosper B., Kjell Havnevik and Atakilte Beyene (eds.). 2011. *Biofuels, Land Grabbing and Food Security in Africa* (London and New York: Zed Books).

McCann, James C. 1987a. *From Poverty to Famine in Northeast Ethiopia: A Rural History 1900–1935* (Philadelphia: University of Pennsylvania Press).

—1987b. 'The Social Impact of Drought in Ethiopia: Oxen, Households, and Some Implications for Rehabilitation', *Drought and Hunger in*

Africa: Denying Famine a Future, ed. Michael H. Glanzt (Cambridge: Cambridge University Press), pp. 245–67.

—1995. *People of the Plow: An Agricultural History of Ethiopia, 1800–1990* (Madison: University of Wisconsin Press).

Mekonnen Lulie, 1999. 'Land Reform and Its Impact on the Environment: The Case of Gidan Woreda', *Food Security through Sustainable Land Use*, ed. Taye Assefa (Addis Ababa: NOVIB Partners Forum on Sustainable Land Use), pp. 175–201.

Melasuo, Tuomo and Amare Worku. 1990. *Peasant Association Study in Wollo, Ethiopia* (Tampere: Tampere Peace Research Institute), Occasional Papers No. 42.

Menale Kassie and Stein T. Holden. 2009. 'Kinship, Tenure Insecurity, Input Use and Land Productivity: The Case of Sharecropping in Ethiopia', *The Emergence of Land Markets in Africa: Assessing the Impacts on Poverty, Equity and Efficiency*, ed. Stein Holden, Keijiro Otsuka and Frank M. Place (Washington D.C.: Resources for the Future Press), pp. 197–209.

Mengistu Woube. 1986. *Problems of Land Reform Implementation in Rural Ethiopia* (Uppsala: Kulturgeografiska Institutionen vid Uppsala Universitet), Geografiska regionstudier No. 16.

Migot-Adholla, Shem, *et al.* 1991. 'Indigenous Land Rights Systems in Sub-Saharan Africa: A Constraint on Productivity?', *The World Bank Economic Review*, Vol. 5(1), pp. 155–75.

Mirgissa Kaba. 1994. 'Land Tenure and Resource Management in a West Shewa Oromo Community', *Land Tenure and Land Policy in Ethiopia After the Derg: Proceedings of the Second Workshop of the Land Tenure Project*, ed. Dessalegn Rahmato (Trondheim: University of Trondheim, Centre of Environment and Development), Working Papers on Ethiopian Development, No. 8, pp. 117–27.

Mitiku Haile, Wray Witten, Kinfe Abraha, Sintayo Fissha, Adane Kebede, Getahun Kassa and Getachew Reda. 2005. *Land Registration in Tigray, Northern Ethiopia* (London: International Institute for Environment and Development), Research Report No. 2.

MoA. 1989. 'Selä märét shegesheg-ena shenshena yä-qäräbä riport' (Addis Ababa: Ministry of Agriculture).

Morell, Mats. 1997. 'New Estimates on Agricultural Productivity and Yields of Developed Countries, 1800–1990', *Economic Development and Agricultural Productivity*, ed. Amit Bhaduri and Rune Skarstein (Cheltenham: Edward Elgar Publisher).

Nässén, Kristina. 2009. 'Mark är som barn: Genus, fattigdom och försörjning i Södra Wollo, Etiopien', University of Göteborg, Institutionen för globala studier, Ph.D. thesis.

nazret.com. 2008. 'Ethiopia 4th Fastest Growing Economy in the World in 09 – Economist' (accessed 2 May 2015, available from: http://nazret.com/blog/index.php/2008/12/26/economist_magazine_predicts_ethiopia_as__09).

Pankhurst, Helen. 1992. *Gender, Development and Identity* (London and New Jersey: Zed Books).

Pausewang, Siegfried. 1990. 'Meret le arrashu', *Ethiopia: Rural Development Options*, ed. Siegfried Pausewang, Fantu Cheru, Stefan Brüne and Eshetu Chole (London: Zed Books), pp. 38–48.

—2004. 'The Need for a Third Alternative: The Amputated Debate on Land Tenure in Ethiopia', paper presented at the 11th World Congress of Rural Sociology, Trondheim, Norway, 25–30 July 2004.

Pausewang, Siegfried, Fantu Cheru, Stefan Brüne and Eshetu Chole (eds.). 1990. *Ethiopia: Rural Development Options* (London: Zed Books).

Peters, Pauline E. 2009. 'Challenges in Land Tenure and Land Reform in Africa: Anthropological Contributions', *World Development*, Vol. 37(8), pp. 1317–25.

Platteau, Jean-Philippe. 1996. 'The Evolutionary Theory of Land Rights as Applied to Sub-Saharan Africa: A Critical Assessment', *Development and Change*, Vol. 27(1), pp. 29–86.

Poluha, Eva. 1989. *Central Planning and Local Reality: The Case of a Producers Cooperative in Ethiopia* (Stockholm: Stockholm Studies in Social Anthropology), No. 23.

Ranger, Terence. 1993. 'The Communal Areas of Zimbabwe', *Land in African Agrarian Systems*, ed. Thomas J. Bassett and Donald E. Crummey (Madison: The University of Wisconsin Press), pp. 354–85.

Ribot, Jesse C. and Nancy Lee Peluso. 2003. 'A Theory of Access', *Rural Sociology*, Vol. 68(2), pp. 153–81.

Scott, James C. 1998. *Seeing Like a State: How Certain Schemes to Improve the Human Condition Have Failed* (New Haven and London: Yale University Press).

Shifa, Muna, Murray Leibbrandt and Martin Wittenberg. 2015. *Does Tenure Insecurity Explain the Variations in Land-related Investment Decisions in Rural Ethiopia?* (Cape Town: SALDRU), Working Paper No. 150.

Sjaastad, Espen and Ben Cousins. 2008. 'Formalisation of Land Rights in the South: An Overview', *Land Use Policy*, Vol. 26, pp. 1–9.

Ståhl, Michael. 1974. *Ethiopia: Political Contradictions in Agricultural Development* (Stockholm: Rabén & Sjögren).

—1990. 'Environmental Degradation and Political Constraints in Ethiopia' *Disasters*, Vol. 14(2), pp. 140–50.

—(ed.). 2015. *Looking Back, Looking Ahead: Land, Agriculture and Society in East Africa* (Uppsala: The Nordic Africa Institute).

Teferi Abate. 1994. 'Land Scarcity and Landlessness in North Shewa: A Case Study from Wayu and Anget Mewgiya PA', *Land Tenure and Land Policy in Ethiopia After the Derg: Proceedings of the Second Workshop of the Land Tenure Project*, ed. Dessalegn Rahmato (Trondheim: University of Trondheim, Centre of Environment and Development), Working Papers on Ethiopian Development, No. 8, pp. 163–89.

—1997. 'Struggle over Policy Loose-ends: Idioms of Livelihood and the Many Ways of Obtaining and Loosing Land in South Wollo, Amhara', paper presented at the Workshop on Access to Land and Resource Management, Institute of Development Research, 28–29 November 1997.

—1998. *Land, Capital and Labour in the Social Organization of Farmers: A Study of Household Dynamics in Southwestern Wollo, 1974–1993* (Addis Ababa: Addis Ababa University, Department of Sociology and Social Administration).
—2000. 'Government Intervention and Socioeconomic Change in a Northeast Ethiopian Community: An Anthropological Study', Boston University, Ph.D. thesis.
Tesfaye Tafesse. 1995. *Villagization in Northern Shewa, Ethiopia: Impact Assessment* (Münster: Lit).
Tronvoll, Kjetil. 1998. *Mai Weini: A Highland Village in Eritrea: A Study of the People, Their Livelihood, and Land Tenure during Times of Turbulence* (Lawrenceville: Red Sea Press).
Yared Amare. 1995a. 'Household Economic Status, Seasonality & Food Strategies in Ethiopia: The Case of Wogda, Northern Shewa', Boston University, Ph.D. thesis.
—1995b. 'Land Redistribution and its Implications for Peasant Differentiation in Wogda, Northern Shewa', *Ethiopian Journal of Development Research*, Vol. 17(1), pp. 1–22.
Yeraswork Admassie. 2000. *Twenty Years to Nowhere: Property Rights, Land Management & Conservation in Ethiopia* (Lawrenceville: Red Sea Press).
Yigremew Adal. 1997. 'Rural Land Holding Readjustment in West Gojjam, Amhara Region', *Ethiopian Journal of Development Research*, Vol. 19(2), pp. 57–89.
—2000a. 'Land Tenure and Soil Conservation in Two Communities in Ankober, Ethiopia', paper presented at the First International Policy Research Workshop of the Regional and Local Development Studies, Addis Ababa, April.
—2000b. 'Preliminary Assessment of the Impacts of the Post-Derg Land Policy on Agricultural Production. A Case Study of Land Redistribution in Two Communities in North-West Ethiopia', *Proceedings of the Fourth Annual Conference of the Agricultural Economics Society of Ethiopia*, Addis Ababa, pp. 173–90.
—2001. *Land Redistribution and Female-Headed Households: A Study of Two Rural Communities in Northwest Ethiopia* (Addis Ababa: Forum for Social Studies), FSS Discussion Paper No. 5.
Young, John. 1997. *Peasant Revolution in Ethiopia: The Tigray People's Liberation Front, 1975–1991* (Cambridge: Cambridge University Press).
Zeray Yihdego, Alistair Rieu-Clarke and Ana Elisa Cascão (eds.). 2018. *The Grand Ethiopian Renaissance Dam and the Nile Basin: Implications for Transboundary Water Cooperation* (Abingdon and New York: Routledge).

Index

EASTERN AFRICAN STUDIES

These titles published in the United States and Canada by Ohio University Press

Revealing Prophets
Edited by DAVID M. ANDERSON & DOUGLAS H. JOHNSON

East African Expressions of Christianity
Edited by THOMAS SPEAR & ISARIA N. KIMAMBO

The Poor Are Not Us
Edited by DAVID M. ANDERSON & VIGDIS BROCH-DUE

Potent Brews
JUSTIN WILLIS

Swahili Origins
JAMES DE VERE ALLEN

Being Maasai
Edited by THOMAS SPEAR & RICHARD WALLER

Jua Kali Kenya
KENNETH KING

Control & Crisis in Colonial Kenya
BRUCE BERMAN

Unhappy Valley
Book One: State & Class
Book Two: Violence & Ethnicity
BRUCE BERMAN & JOHN LONSDALE

Mau Mau from Below
GREET KERSHAW

The Mau Mau War in Perspective
FRANK FUREDI

Squatters & the Roots of Mau Mau 1905-63
TABITHA KANOGO

Economic & Social Origins of Mau Mau 1945-53
DAVID W. THROUP

Multi-Party Politics in Kenya
DAVID W. THROUP & CHARLES HORNSBY

Empire State-Building
JOANNA LEWIS

Decolonization & Independence in Kenya 1940-93
Edited by B.A. OGOT & WILLIAM R. OCHIENG'

Eroding the Commons
DAVID ANDERSON

Penetration & Protest in Tanzania
ISARIA N. KIMAMBO

Custodians of the Land
Edited by GREGORY MADDOX, JAMES L. GIBLIN & ISARIA N. KIMAMBO

Education in the Development of Tanzania 1919-1990
LENE BUCHERT

The Second Economy in Tanzania
T.L. MALIYAMKONO & M.S.D. BAGACHWA

Ecology Control & Economic Development in East African History
HELGE KJEKSHUS

Siaya
DAVID WILLIAM COHEN & E.S. ATIENO ODHIAMBO

Uganda Now • Changing Uganda Developing Uganda • From Chaos to Order • Religion & Politics in East Africa
Edited by HOLGER BERNT HANSEN & MICHAEL TWADDLE

Kakungulu & the Creation of Uganda 1868-1928
MICHAEL TWADDLE

Controlling Anger
SUZETTE HEALD

Kampala Women Getting By
SANDRA WALLMAN

Political Power in Pre-Colonial Buganda
RICHARD J. REID

Alice Lakwena & the Holy Spirits
HEIKE BEHREND

Slaves, Spices & Ivory in Zanzibar
ABDUL SHERIFF

Zanzibar Under Colonial Rule
Edited by ABDUL SHERIFF & ED FERGUSON

The History & Conservation of Zanzibar Stone Town
Edited by ABDUL SHERIFF

Pastimes & Politics
LAURA FAIR

Ethnicity & Conflict in the Horn of Africa
Edited by KATSUYOSHI FUKUI & JOHN MARKAKIS

Conflict, Age & Power in North East Africa
Edited by EISEI KURIMOTO & SIMON SIMONSE

Property Rights & Political Development in Ethiopia & Eritrea
SANDRA FULLERTON JOIREMAN

Revolution & Religion in Ethiopia
ØYVIND M. EIDE

Brothers at War
TEKESTE NEGASH & KJETIL TRONVOLL

From Guerrillas to Government
DAVID POOL

Mau Mau & Nationhood
Edited by E.S. ATIENO ODHIAMBO & JOHN LONSDALE

A History of Modern Ethiopia, 1855-1991(2nd edn)
BAHRU ZEWDE

Pioneers of Change in Ethiopia
BAHRU ZEWDE

Remapping Ethiopia
Edited by W. JAMES, D. DONHAM, E. KURIMOTO & A. TRIULZI

Southern Marches of Imperial Ethiopia
Edited by DONALD L. DONHAM & WENDY JAMES

A Modern History of the Somali (4th edn)
I.M. LEWIS

Islands of Intensive Agriculture in East Africa
Edited by MATS WIDGREN & JOHN E.G. SUTTON

Leaf of Allah
EZEKIEL GEBISSA

Dhows & the Colonial Economy of Zanzibar 1860-1970
ERIK GILBERT

African Womanhood in Colonial Kenya
TABITHA KANOGO

African Underclass
ANDREW BURTON

In Search of a Nation
Edited by GREGORY H. MADDOX & JAMES L. GIBLIN

A History of the Excluded
JAMES L. GIBLIN

Black Poachers, White Hunters
EDWARD I. STEINHART

Ethnic Federalism
DAVID TURTON

Crisis & Decline in Bunyoro
SHANE DOYLE

Emancipation without Abolition in German East Africa
JAN-GEORG DEUTSCH

Women, Work & Domestic Virtue in Uganda 1900-2003
GRACE BANTEBYA KYOMUHENDO & MARJORIE KENISTON McINTOSH

Cultivating Success in Uganda
GRACE CARSWELL

War in Pre-Colonial Eastern Africa
RICHARD REID

Slavery in the Great Lakes Region of East Africa
Edited by HENRI MÉDARD & SHANE DOYLE

The Benefits of Famine
DAVID KEEN